She Was Murdered!

I suspected this when I first heard the report of her death in 1962.

But the official cover-up was already in place—a slipshod job, but good enough and powerful enough to eliminate any thorough investigation for 30 years.

Twice, in 1982 and again in 1985, we tried to get a grand jury investigation going in Los Angeles...both times we were derailed by the forces behind the scenes.

Now, in 1992, we have finally amassed enough evidence, public support and media cooperation to push this case to a legal conclusion.

This was not an accident.

This was not probable suicide, either.

Several key witnesses were lying.

The police bungled the investigation.

The coroner's investigation was not complete.

The district attorney was part of the cover-up.

Marilyn didn't have a chance. Neither did justice.

The Marilyn Files is a complete documentation of this case, and a total refutation of the "official story." We know exactly who was involved the day Marilyn died, what they did, why they did it...and where that very last piece of evidence is...."

—*Robert F. Slatzer*

To Marilyn . . .

I've told it,
not the way they think it was,
or the way they heard it was,
or the way they wish it was,
but the way it really was . . .
the only way you'd want it told.

—RFS

THE MARILYN FILES

Robert F. Slatzer

S.P.i.
BOOKS

A division of Shapolsky Publishers, Inc.

The Marilyn Files

S.P.I. BOOKS

A division of Shapolsky Publishers, Inc.

For any additional information, contact:
S.P.I. BOOKS/Shapolsky Publishers, Inc.
136 West 22nd Street
New York, NY 10011
(212) 633-2022
FAX (212) 633-2123

All photographs property of the author.

ISBN: 1-56171-147-0

10 9 8 7 6 5 4 3 2 1

Printed and bound in the United States of America

Table of Contents

Acknowledgments

I would like to thank the numerous people who have helped to make this possible:

Andrew Ettinger, who again guided me conceptually and editorially, and somehow kept all the people, pieces and pages together.

Stanley J. Corwin, for his enthusiasm and publishing expertise.

Mel Bergman and William Speckin of Producers Video, Inc., of Los Angeles, for their support and encouragement, and for making the video and television version of *The Marilyn Files* happen.

S.P.I. Books' Publisher, Ian Shapolsky, who believed in this project from the very beginning. Also to Nolan Bennett, Don Hayes, Tom Dougherty and others from ICD/Hearst for their enthusiasm in promoting the sales of this book.

Many thanks to Jean Stine for his editorial assistance; and to Aidan Kelly and Janrae Frank, too.

My special gratitude to Deborah Thompson, my lovely assistant, who helped me with all the research, interviewing, and general production of this book.

Special appreciation to the Editor in charge of this project, JoAnna Cimino, for her outstanding editorial skills at every level in the process, and to the S.P.I. staff: Sherrel Farnsworth, Managing Editor, Julian Serer, Production Staff, Ann Cassouto, Director of Sales/Associate Editor, Annie Cohen, Director of Marketing, Stacey Wike, Publicity Director, Dana Millman and Pamela Medley.

A special thanks also to Antoinette Giancana.

I would also like to thank, in random order, the following people for their invaluable contribution over the years: Frank A. Capell, Florabel Muir, Jeane Carmen, Dr. J. DeWitt Fox, M.D., John Miner, Moton B. Holt, Pete

Noyes, Terry Moore, Pat Wilkes Battle, Sanford Firestone, M.D., James Hal, Hon. Sam Yorty, Jack Clemmons, Alex D'Arcy, Sidney Weinberg, M.D., Eleanor "Bebe" Goddard, Walter Schaefer, Patricia Newcomb, Lionel Grandison, Eunice Murray, Inez Melson, Hazel Washington, Peter Harry Brown, Patte B. Barham, Pamela Twedell Brown, Alan "Whitey" Snyder, Marge Plecher, Bernard Spindel, Fred Otash, Peter Lawford, Milo Speriglio, Natalie Jacobs, E. Forrest Chapman, M.D., Murray Leib, Robert Byron, Walter Winchell, Susan Zanuck, Joseph Miller, Ralph Roberts, Nunnally Johnson, Rupert Allen, Evelyn Moriarity, Jane Ellen Wayne, Frank Neill, John Campbell, John Danoff, Vincent Barbi, Eddie Jaffee, Paula Strasberg, Susan Strasberg, Thad Brown, Finis Brown, Lee Remick, Dorothy Kilgallen, Tommy Noonan, Glory Hernandez, Michelle Hernandez, Doug Dobransky, Betty Pollard, Abe Landau, William F. Roemer, Buddy Greco, Richard Lewis, George Cukor, Agnes Flanagan, Roman Hryniszak, and Franz Planer.

Also the following organizations:

Academy of Motion Picture Arts and Sciences; Federal Bureau of Investigation; Los Angeles City News Service; Los Angeles County Coroner's Ofice; Los Angeles County Medical Library; Los Angeles County Sheriff's Department; Los Angeles County Superior Court; Los Angeles County Hall of Records; *Los Angeles Herald Examiner; The Los Angeles Times; New York Post; New York Journal-American; The New York Times;* Nick Harris Detective Agency; Twentieth Century–Fox Studios; University of Southern California Medical Library and Pathology Department; Westwood Memorial Park and Village Mortuary; Schaefer Ambulance Company; Santa Monica Hospital; Cal-Neva Lodge; The Beverly Hills Hotel; The Beverly Hilton Hotel; Vincente Pharmacy; Abbott Laboratories; Coroner's Office of Suffolk County; N.Y.; the Los Angeles County Board of Supervisors; Hollygrove Orpanage; and the United States Department of Justice.

Editor's Preface

Marilyn Monroe, the legendary film goddess, died 30 years ago. Since that tragic night of August 4, 1962, one man has led a relentless investigation into her mysterious and controversial death.

His name is Robert F. Slatzer. He was her friend and confidant—for a brief time he was her husband—and he still carries the torch of her memory.

The incredible popularity of Marilyn Monroe has grown to mythic proportions over the last three decades. Along with Elvis, she has commanded the world's fascination with her life of triumph and tragedy. She will always be the quintessential, unforgettable Hollywood sex symbol. But there is more to her than the ever-growing legend. There is also the truth.

A seemingly endless number of books, articles, photographs and other revelations keep surfacing about Marilyn. But none have surpassed the depth, scope and authenticity of Bob Slatzer's 1974 bestseller, *The Life and Curious Death of Marilyn Monroe*. It was the first major investigative effort to uncover the facts of her alleged "probable suicide."

Even then, Bob Slatzer knew that he was battling a massive cover-up that involved the White House, The US Justice Department, the FBI, the CIA, the Mafia, the County of Los Angeles, the LAPD, and an unholy cast of doctors, lawyers, psychiatrists, publicists, politicians, journalists, coroners, friends, celebrities and others who were lying to or otherwise misleading the media and the public.

His ground-breaking book and his continuing detective work has served to motivate dozens of authors and books, television shows and news stories. His research has been credited universally. . .There is no question that he is *the* pre-eminent authority on this subject.

Now, in *The Marilyn Files*, the book and its video and television counterparts, the results of Bob Slatzer's dedicated sleuthing have created a clear analysis of those last days in the life of Marilyn Monroe; when powerful forces triggered circumstances that ended a fabulous life and robbed the world of a singularly special personality.

Sadly, it all could have been avoided; it was almost prevented. But the momentum was irreversible. Even a last-minute miracle was snuffed out. And she died. She knew too much. She was alone and defenseless.

Some of the most important people in Marilyn's life were with her on that last day. They all had a chance to do something, but didn't, or couldn't. They either did nothing, or did the unspeakable.

August 4, 1962 was a day of decision. . .for Marilyn, and for some individuals who would soon become part of one of the biggest crime cover-ups in our nation's history. The day became a night of lies and deception. It is now revealed as a sordid picture of guilt, greed, fear. . .and murder.

The Marilyn Files will dare to present all the facts, name the names, recreate the crime, describe all the possible scenarios, and tell the truth about what has been a despicable conspiracy.

At least 12 people knew it was murder. Five of them are now dead. Six of them have never been forced to testify under oath. Not yet, that is.

Robert Slatzer is the twelfth person. He knows it was murder. . .and now he will prove it.

— A. E.

Introduction

In 1962 Hollywood's famous star-system was nearly abolished. Many luminaries like Jimmy Stewart, John Wayne, Jane Fonda, Elizabeth Taylor, and others were suddenly without home studios, and were freelancing in the industry. They set their own deals, many of which afforded returns more lucrative than those previously provided by their studio contracts. In some cases, a piece of the action added a few more digits to their salary.

One victim of the old rules was Marilyn Monroe who, in 1962, was at the peak of her illustrious career. She was beginning her last film for Twentieth Century-Fox Studio, *Something's Got To Give*. Her compensation was based upon the old contract she had signed in the mid-fifties and was only $100,000 per picture. Compared to Elizabeth Taylor's compensation for her role in Cleopatra— $1,000,000 plus plenty of overtime...on a film that was running millions and millions of dollars over-budget—it is no wonder the disintegration of the studio system encouraged great talents to independently strike more profitable deals with other studios and leading independent producers. In fact, when speaking with Robert Taylor about his long-term contract with MGM—and he stayed there to the very end—he remarked that he and Marilyn Monroe were the two lowest paid stars in Hollywood.

When Marilyn was filming *Something's Got to Give,* she was certainly making much less money per film than any of her contemporaries. After her termination by Fox, her actual worth was substantiated by the numerous high-priced offers she received. Although she was never materialistic, and lived her life modestly, she nevertheless expected equal pay to that of other actors and actresses. In that era, by the time she paid high taxes, agents and manager's fees, plus monies to her acting coaches (Paula and Lee Strasberg), few funds remained. However, in spite of her firing—and her eventual reinstatement to finish the film—her outlook on her career prospects was optimistic and her confidence in her ability to handle the future, greatly improved.

Never before had Marilyn realized her talents were so appreciated and so much in demand. She had purchased a secluded, Mexican-style hacienda home in the exclusive Brentwood area, and recognized, in each increasingly more responsible action she undertook, a stabilizing and more positive image of herself developing.

I recall her telling me, "I'm getting my life in order, taking the bull by the horns, and starting to make my own decisions." And she was doing just that!

Unfortunately, she was still surrounded by those who were shamelessly using and manipulating her; of these individuals, Bobby Kennedy, trying to rival the playboy status and exploits of his famous older brother, was the most prominently offensive. There was also a doctor, a housekeeper-companion, drama coaches and a few others on her payroll that she planned to fire before resuming work on her film in October. Her plans to do all of this—in addition to calling her own press conference the following Monday morning to expose the brothers Kennedy and announce her future plans—were cut short by her untimely and mysterious demise.

I had met Marilyn in the summer of 1946, back when her name was Norma Jeane Baker. She was a hard-working model with high hopes of making a lifetime ambition of becoming a famous actress come true. Both of us were struggling in our respective careers. We were friends, lovers, confidants to each other and, for a brief period in 1952, man and wife—a short-lived liaison that was broken up by her studio. However, that severance brought us even closer together in the ensuing years, especially in that last spring and summer of her life in 1962. Whenever Marilyn was teased about the marriage she would say it lasted longer than most Broadway plays.

When I first heard the tragic news that Sunday morning from our mutual friend, Dr. Sanford Firestone, and later by Walter Winchell, I was stunned. No words could explain that hollow feeling. When a reporter called me for a comment, all I could think of saying was: "I lost the best drinking buddy I ever had."

At Marilyn's house with Inez Melson before the burial services, I again saw the places she loved so much and realized that now all those high hopes had died, too. But then I saw something that was the key to this whole thing—the window that Dr. Greenson had allegedly broken to gain entry to her bedroom. It had been repaired the night of her death, but what startled me was the broken glass still on the ground. One would think that if a window had been broken from the outside, the bulk of the glass would be inside. Not in this instance. It was scattered below on the ground which made me suspicious.

Further conversation with a couple of policemen about the alleged phone in her hand, the locked door, and the story Mrs. Murray had told the police, made me have serious doubts as to how she really died. Although I didn't want to believe the suicide verdict, I was more determined than ever to look into this case a little deeper; to see what else I could find.

Like Pandora's box, it was now open and pieces began to fit together; things got curiouser and curiouser. That's when I became convinced that Marilyn did not commit suicide. There were just too many inconsistencies.

Well, that was thirty years ago, and today we have more answers. But there are a few key people who were involved that night who still refuse to talk about what really happened. At the funeral, everybody who was either in show business or politics was banned—thanks to Joe DiMaggio's selfish decision. He callously kept out most of the people who knew and loved Marilyn.

I then decided to devote a great part of my time to investigating this case—and I have done just that over the past thirty years. There were solid tips, mysterious tips, crazy tips—even crazy people who came to me—I had to listen to them all. But I continued my own investigation, putting aside a lot of good assignments that would have strengthened my pocketbook, and set out on what seemingly was a journey into nowhere.

However, it eventually paid off—not monetarily—but with the satisfaction that comes when all the pieces fit together like a puzzle, and things began to make sense.

Yes, I might be able to help Marilyn escape from the false accusations of suicide. Asked once by a police officer, who helped me with some clues, why I was so persistent in pursuing this when I could have been away hunting and fishing, I merely replied, "When your best friend is murdered, all one wants to do is find out who did it!"

I now feel I have come closer than anyone else. I do not regret those wild goose chases, those clandestine meetings in the middle of the night, my telephone ringing off the hook with tips, anonymous letters, and even a death threat.

As it turned out, a great many members of the media shared my convictions. Now, after thirty years, we still may not have all the answers, but we do know a lot more about what really happened that fateful Saturday night of August 4, 1962...as you'll now learn in this book. The spirit of Marilyn Monroe still lives—gloriously so—and I'm sure wherever she is, she's been watching this whole string of events with great interest.

Robert F. Slatzer
Hollywood, California
June 1, 1992

FILE #1

One Cop's Story

August 5, 1962. 4:25 in the morning. Sergeant Jack Clemmons of the Los Angeles Police Department, acting watch commander, western division, answered the station house phone. Unknown to Clemmons at the time, that early morning call would involve him in a mystery which has remained, until now, unresolved for thirty years. It is a mystery that involves the cold-blooded murder of a motion picture superstar, the amorous escapades of the president of the United States, the romantic involvement of the attorney general of the United States, the sinister machinations of the Mafia, and a web of lies, duplicities and deliberate cover-ups that stretch from Hollywood to Washington. And at its tragic center is the nude, dead body of Marilyn Monroe.

The memory of this telephone call was still vivid for Clemmons when he described it in an exclusive interview for this book. What follows is his own account of the fateful event's next three hours.

"It was a very dead night, absolutely dead. I don't think even the station house cockroaches were alive. The radio hadn't let out a peep for at least two hours. I was having trouble staying awake, so I decided to go out and talk to the desk officer. He was having trouble staying awake, too. I figured we'd help each other stay awake."

As the two officers conversed drowsily, Clemmons had no way of knowing that the night's stillness and silence were about to be shattered by a call that would change his life, and the lives of many others, forever.

"One of the phones rang. It was right by my elbow, so I grabbed it automatically and identified myself. 'Sergeant Clemmons, West LA Police Station, can I help you?' A man's voice on the other end said, 'This is Dr. Greenson. Marilyn Monroe is dead. She's committed suicide.' "

"That woke me up right away. I was so stunned I couldn't believe my ears, and I blurted out: 'What did you say?' "

"He repeated himself: 'I told you that Marilyn Monroe has taken an overdose of barbiturates, and she's dead.' "

Clemmons took down the address, phone number, and time. Although in routine cases of suicide, the watch commander does not leave the station house, Clemmons realized he had a unique situation on his hands. Marilyn Monroe was a world-famous movie star. If the call was genuine, and word of her death got out — and considering her status, it would get out fast — the media would descend on the scene in droves.

The police often receive false death reports about the famous and near-famous. Clemmons wanted to spare the LAPD the embarrassment which would surely follow if, after notifying city officials and the media, the whole incident was nothing more than a college prank. He decided to verify the call himself.

As he drove his squad car through the dark, deserted streets of nighttime Brentwood, Clemmons radioed for a back-up unit to help him control the crowds that were certain to gather if the report proved true. Like most men who have seen Marilyn on the screen or off, he had been attracted to her unique combination of vulnerability and beauty. He couldn't help wondering why someone who was so successful, who apparently had everything to live for, had committed suicide. It would be many years before he would begin to suspect the sinister answer.

A few minutes later, Clemmons arrived at the address Greenson had given: 12305 Fifth Helena Drive. It was an unpretentious house that bore no resemblance to the Hollywood mansion Marilyn Monroe's movie star status had led him to expect. Clemmons was greeted at the front door by a dark-haired, bespectacled woman in late middle age who introduced herself as Mrs. Eunice Murray, "Marilyn's housekeeper." Mrs. Murray responded to Clemmons' first question by confirming that the call had indeed been genuine — Marilyn Monroe was dead. Clemmons knew that he and many of his fellow officers in the LAPD were in for a long night.

THE MISSING FOUR HOURS

As they entered the house, Sergeant Clemmons asked the housekeeper who else was present on the premises. Mrs. Murray responded: "Only Dr. Greenson and Dr. Engelberg." Next, Clemmons asked how long the doctors had been at the death scene.

He was surprised to learn that they had arrived shortly after midnight. "They were both professional men. They knew that they were required to call us immediately. It's a matter of law." This was only the first of many baffling questions that were to trouble this seasoned investigator before the night was over.

Inside, Mrs. Murray introduced Clemmons to the two doctors. The taller, who had a dark drooping mustache, thinning gray hair, and dark-ringed eyes, she identified as Dr. Ralph Greenson, the psychiatrist who had reported Marilyn Monroe's death. The other, a slender, gray-haired man who looked to be in his early fifties, she introduced as Dr. Hyman Engelberg, the star's personal physician.

"I asked who discovered the body," Clemmons recalls. "Mrs. Murray said, 'I did.' I asked her to tell me about it, and this is Mrs. Murray's story to me:

"'About ten o'clock, I went to bed, and the light was on under Marilyn's door. I just assumed Marilyn was sleeping or talking on the telephone with a friend so I went to bed. I woke up at midnight, and had to go to the bathroom. The light was still on underneath Marilyn's door.' "

At this point, Mrs. Murray said she became concerned. She tried the door and found it was locked from the inside. She rapped on the door in an attempt to arouse the star. Failing to receive any response, her concern increased, and she called Marilyn's psychiatrist.

"She told me that Greenson, who only lived a short distance away, came over quickly. Greenson also failed to get a response when he tried knocking on Marilyn's door so he went outside and looked through her bedroom window. Inside, he saw her lying motionless, face down on the bed. He smashed the window and gained entry into the bedroom. Finding Marilyn dead, he called Dr. Engelberg, Marilyn's regular physician, who also lived in the immediate neighborhood. Dr. Engelberg arrived and also pronounced the actress dead."

Several aspects of Mrs. Murray's story troubled Clemmons. If her story was true, these events must have occurred shortly after midnight. Yet Dr. Greenson had not called the station house to report the death until 4:25 A.M. Three people had spent four hours alone in the house with a dead body before calling the police.

Clemmons asked why they hadn't notified the police sooner.

"No one wanted to answer. They tried to ignore me, but I thought it was important, so I asked them again, 'Why didn't you let us know sooner?' Finally, Dr. Greenson spoke. 'We had to get permission from the publicity department of her studio before we could notify anybody.' That's not an answer."

THE DEATH SCENE

Next, Sergeant Clemmons asked to see the body. Mrs. Murray and the doctors conducted him to Marilyn's room. Clemmons walked over to the bed. "Marilyn was lying face down on the bed; a sheet was pulled up over her body, and a wisp of blond hair was sticking out. I didn't want to touch anything while I was there. I didn't even pull the sheet back. I could see she was dead."

The star's face was buried in a pillow, hands by her sides, her legs completely parallel. Clemmons, who knew that death from drug overdose usually causes convulsions, felt that the body must have been deliberately posed in that position.

Clemmons could also see the typical bluish coloring that indicates postmortem lividity has set in. This confirmed the doctors' story that Marilyn had been dead for several hours by the time the police were notified.

Clemmons asked Dr. Greenson if anyone had moved the body. The physician replied that no one had touched the body beyond ascertaining that the actress was dead. This explanation struck a sour note. Because of the position of the body, Clemmons was convinced it must have been rearranged. Both men were doctors and had the legal right to move the body. If they had moved Marilyn's body, there seemed to be no reason for them to lie about it — unless they were hiding something.

Sergeant Clemmons also saw other signs that the death scene had been rearranged and cleaned up before his arrival. "The whole place was very neat. The whole part of the house I saw had been picked up. That's not characteristic, because when there's been a suicide, things are usually left lying around the room. Almost nobody is very neat when they are going to commit suicide."

Of course, much of the room's condition could be attributed to the housekeeper. Curiously, throughout the course of the night, whenever she was not being directly questioned, Mrs. Murray had been cleaning the house. From appearances, Clemmons judged that she had been at work for some time. The laundry equipment was going; he could hear her vacuuming, and saw her picking up.

"I didn't think too much of it at the time," Clemmons said. "I assumed they knew that a lot of people would be in and out of the house before the day was over. Marilyn Monroe was a big star, and it made sense that they would be concerned with appearances."

Although he understood Mrs. Murray's concern for appearances, Clemmons worried that the housekeeper might have inadvertently destroyed evidence that could shed further light on the star's suicide. More significant, it is against the law to alter or tamper with the scene of a death. The housekeeper might not have been aware of this law, but Sergeant Clemmons knew that both Dr. Greenson and Dr. Engelberg were; yet, neither of them had asked Mrs. Murray to stop.

Puzzling as these matters were, "nothing actually alerted me at that point to the fact that there was a possible crime here." It was only later that the more sinister implications of this cleanup occurred to him: how thoroughly it would have erased damning clues that might have told an entirely different story about Marilyn Monroe's death.

THE MISSING GLASS OF WATER
AND OTHER INCONSISTENCIES

During the next ninety minutes, Clemmons was to face even more of the puzzling inconsistencies he encountered throughout his preliminary investigation into the death of Marilyn Monroe.

The first, and perhaps most significant, of these involved a simple glass of water. "I asked how she had killed herself," Clemmons recalls. "Dr. Greenson pointed out about eight bottles that had contained various kinds of prescription drugs, mostly sleeping pills. I can still see the man as he stood there. His eyes settled on one bottle closest to Marilyn's bed. He made a grand gesture toward it and said, 'She must have taken all the pills in that bottle.' "

In Clemmons' experience, when someone commits suicide by swallowing a large number of pills, there is usually an empty, or partially empty, glass of either water or some other liquid nearby. Clemmons conducted a thorough search for such a glass. No glass was found in either Marilyn's bedroom or in the small private bathroom adjoining it. In fact, there was no container of any sort she could have used to hold the liquid needed to swallow the fatal pills.

Dr. Greenson's attitude also seemed "out of place" to Clemmons. "He was sarcastic with me. One thing a policeman always notices is attitude. If someone's attitude doesn't fit a scene, he begins to ask himself 'Why?' Under the circumstances, his attitude just didn't make any sense. And he had the strangest look on his face, a sort of leer. I kept thinking, 'What's the matter with this guy? What is it with him?' "

Once Clemmons' attention had been drawn to Dr. Greenson's antagonistic attitude, he noticed that the attitudes of the other two witnesses were also "very much out of place." There was something he didn't like about "the way they were acting." None of the three ever volunteered any information. Every answer he got out of them was in response to a specific question. When he did manage to get an answer, it usually came through Dr. Greenson, who "did most of the talking." To Clemmons' trained eye, the three were "obviously not being aboveboard about everything."

Another link in the chain of curious inconsistencies was forged when Clemmons asked if anyone had found a suicide note. He knew that many people who commit suicide leave a note to justify their action, or to blame those they believe drove them to it. But Dr. Greenson said, "No one found any note."

In spite of all these puzzling contradictions, nothing at that point aroused Clemmons' suspicions that Marilyn Monroe's death was anything other than a suicide. He knew that people rarely act normal around death scenes. He was surprised, however, that the two doctors, who must have had extensive prior exposure to death scenes, had acted so strangely, even unprofessionally. He supposed their behavior might be explained by the great pressure of their position — a psychiatrist and physician find one of their most celebrated patients dead by her own hand. Clemmons would later discover that every word he had heard was a deliberately rehearsed falsehood contrived to obfuscate Marilyn's murder. He would come to recognize their words as the first misguided step in a miscarriage of justice.

UNANSWERED QUESTIONS

As Clemmons pondered the puzzling contradictions uncovered by his preliminary investigation, he was interrupted by the arrival of his relief, Sergeant Marvin Iannone. Clemmons instructed Iannone to just "guard the scene," since the detective who would take official charge of the suicide investigation was on his way to the site. Sergeant Iannone was simply to handle the traffic outside when investigators and the media began to gather.

Moments later, Clemmons' relief, Sergeant Robert Byron, who would take charge of the official investigation, arrived. Free to leave, Clemmons climbed into his own car and headed back to the station. He had driven to the scene of Marilyn Monroe's death through silent, shadowed, nighttime streets. Now, three hours later, Clemmons was surprised to find himself in bright daylight, the streets busy with cars and pedestrians. Inside he had been suspended in a timeless moment, caught in the circumstances and tragedy of a great star's death. It had seemed to him as if the world must have stopped, but the world had hardly heeded it at all.

As he drove, the inconsistencies in the three witnesses' stories, and the questions his own investigation of the scene had left unanswered, kept running through his mind. He asked himself what Marilyn's housekeeper and doctors had been doing during the four hours before they reported the star's death to the police. He also wondered how anyone could possibly have taken as many pills as Dr. Greenson indicated Marilyn Monroe had swallowed, with neither water nor some other liquid to help get them down. And why had they lied about moving the body when he could clearly see that it had been carefully arranged on the bed?

Although his questions disturbed him, Clemmons returned to the station to write his report. He knew that two officers, a detective and an area inspector, both of whom had extensive experience in investigating death scenes, were about to arrive. Furthermore, the efforts of the coroner, the district attorney's office, and possibly, a grand jury, would soon be added to theirs. Clemmons felt assured that a thorough and extensive investigation would be made. The actual circumstances surrounding Marilyn Monroe's death, and answers to the previous night's unanswered questions would be brought to light.

But Sergeant Jack Clemmons had no way of knowing that, for the next three decades, he and the world would vainly seek answers to those unanswered questions. He did not know that when the answers came, they would not point to Marilyn Monroe's suicide, but, inescapably, to her murder.

He could not have guessed that investigators would unveil one of the most successful and complex government cover-ups in history, a cover-up deliberately designed to conceal the identity and position of her killer.

FILE #2

Marilyn, the Legend

Marilyn Monroe is an American screen legend. She burst upon the public in the early 1950s in a series of box office successes that captured the hearts of millions. Through all of her motion picture roles, the shapely platinum-blonde Marilyn managed to combine sexuality, innocence, vulnerability, and a self-deprecating sense of humor into a unique and alluring persona fascinating audiences for four decades.

Marilyn's best films, *How to Marry a Millionaire*, *Bus Stop*, *Gentlemen Prefer Blondes*, *The Misfits*, *The Seven Year Itch*, are more popular than ever. The better-known among them can be seen more than fifty times a year on cable television.

These films have not only kept Marilyn's legend alive but have, every year since her death, won her new fans and audiences. Interest in the actress's life, public and private, has only grown stronger. More than one hundred books, movies, and television specials have paid tribute to her unique appeal. In 1992, the thirtieth anniversary of her death, another dozen were added to that list.

There is another side to the legend of Marilyn Monroe — a darker side. Her tragic death of a barbiturate overdose at the age of thirty-six cut short one of the screen's most promising careers. The police and coroner ruled her death "suicide" her friends and a few investigators call it murder.

In the wake of Marilyn's death, a whole new legend arose — the legend of her death. In one legend, the coroner was right: her death was suicide. In another legend, it was an accident, the result of an unintentional overdose. In yet other legends, she was murdered by the Mafia . . . murdered to conceal government secrets . . . murdered for personal gain . . . murdered for love. The truth, when it finally emerged three decades later, made mere legend seem pale by comparison.

SEX SYMBOL

Love Goddess. Blond Bombshell. Marilyn Monroe's public legend had many faces. One, however, was celebrated above all the rest: Marilyn was the greatest sex symbol the motion picture industry ever produced. Contemporaries dubbed her, without exaggeration, "the reigning Sex Goddess of the silver screen."

Men were her biggest fans, though millions of women adored and imitated her, too. Everything about Marilyn exuded sexuality — her sinuous walk, her sultry voice, her sensuous face, her spectacular figure. She possessed a unique sexual magnetism unequaled by any actress before or since.

Men everywhere became entranced by her radiant sexuality. Marilyn became America's pin-up girl. Her picture was pasted into lockers at schools, factories, military barracks, and athletic playing fields. It adorned the walls of gas stations, police stations, barber shops, and basement workrooms. Pasted on the wall or ceiling above their beds, Marilyn's image was the last thing millions of single men saw before they fell asleep at night.

The camera was kind to Marilyn. It captured and magnified her sultry sensuality one hundredfold. Blown-up larger than life on the theater screen, radiating sexuality, Marilyn's persona loomed over audiences like a blond Aphrodite rising from the sea. She seemed the goddess of love incarnate.

"She lit up the screen," says actress Terry Moore, one of Marilyn Monroe's friends. "Marilyn was remarkable. She was bigger than life, the ultimate in glamour. Yet she had that little-girl vulnerability. Two words I would use for her, even more than Rita Hayworth, are the Love Goddess."

Alex D'Arcy, Marilyn's co-star in *How to Marry a Millionaire*, is another who attributes her unique appeal to her sexuality. "Marilyn was great. There's no question. She was a sex symbol."

One male friend recalled Marilyn's potent magnetism and the effect it had on the men around her. "She seemed to have a certain radiance when she walked into a room — which very few people have — that could hold you spellbound. It wasn't just the exotic shape and the way she moved, the way she looked. There was a special sexual magnetism that drew one to her."

Much has been written and said about Marilyn Monroe's extraordinary sex appeal, but few people have ever identified its sources. Jeanne Carmen, one of Marilyn's closest friends, has her own explanation. "Marilyn was flawless. She was the most beautiful person in everything about her."

Bebe Goddard, whose parents became Marilyn's guardians when she was nine, attributes the star's unique appeal to a different source. "Her great beauty was a projection of the beautiful person she was inside. The goodness, the innocence, the vulnerability were so intense that people in the audience, especially men, wanted to reach out to protect, and love, and help her."

But for Terry Moore, the source of Marilyn's timeless appeal will always defy analysis. "When the camera went on Marilyn, it became just total magic. No one had any idea that that was going to happen."

MARILYN THE COMEDIENNE

There was another and far different side to Marilyn Monroe's public legend, one that lent piquant appeal to her almost overpowering sexuality. Marilyn also possessed a unique comedic talent that propelled her through a series of blockbuster musical-comedies like *The Prince and the Showgirl, How to Marry a Millionaire, Let's Make Love,* and *Monkey Business.* The essence of her comedic gifts lay in Marilyn's lack of pretense and her willing ability to kid her own image as a sex goddess. In a series of memorable roles, she won the hearts of audiences everywhere with tongue-in-cheek performances that spoofed the "dumb blond" stereotype and those who believed in it. "When she was willing to make fun of her self and play the dumb blond, she was fantastic," remembers Alex D'Arcy.

Marilyn and Hollywood discovered this talent at the same moment. The young actress had won a dramatic role in the film, *Niagara*, as a sexually restless young wife stalked by her jealous, psychopathic husband. Audience reaction made the aspiring actress's career prospects look dim, according to Terry Moore. "At the beginning, everyone thought she was going to be a great failure, because when she did *Niagara*, her breathy way of talking made everyone at the preview audience laugh at her. But one of Marilyn's best friends, Elia Kazan, the director, told her, 'Marilyn, you're a wonderful comedienne. You can make people laugh.' When she realized that, she went on to do *How to Marry a Millionaire, Seven Year Itch*, and all those big hits. Kazan made her realize that she was funny, and that people were laughing with her and not at her. That's when Marilyn became a star."

THE HEDONIST

Gossip magazines and supermarket tabloids have created a legend of Marilyn as promiscuous and hedonistic. Some have even labeled her a "nymphomaniac" who actively sought out innumerable encounters. The reputed list of the actress's liaisons and supposed amours was extensive. Many of these rumors were manufactured by the tabloid press to boost sales; others were created, mostly after her death, by men who wished to enhance their own reputations at her expense.

Marilyn's stunning beauty and high-voltage sex appeal did make her the object of men's desires. The superstar was at one time or another linked romantically with many famous, and not so famous, men. Her amours were said to have included such luminaries as: cover photographer Andre de Dienes; José Bolanos, the Mexican scriptwriter; superstar Marlon Brando; filmscore composer Fred Karger; Greek actor/producer Nico Minardos; Yves Montand, the celebrated French entertainer; Hal Schaefer, the brilliant composer and voice coach; studio head Joe Schenck; Frank Sinatra; and the ill-fated Kennedy brothers: Jack, the president of the United States, and his younger brother Bobby, the attorney general.

Marilyn's, however, friends paint a far different picture. "Promiscuous? No. Never," says childhood companion Bebe Goddard. "My mother was a nymphomaniac, so I knew what that was. There was nothing like that in Marilyn's personality. Of course, she liked men, liked to express her gratitude. When somebody was very nice to her and she really liked them a lot, she thought that it was a gift. But Marilyn wasn't looking for a rich man to marry or anything like that. She wouldn't marry anyone or go with them unless she felt at that time that she was in love with them."

I was briefly married to Marilyn Monroe during the early 1950s and was close to her ever since. . . . I don't think she was promiscuous. I think she was very selective. Many writers have commented on the fact that she dated a lot of men. Most of those dates were arranged by the studios who often sent their aspiring male and female stars to premiers together for publicity purposes. But when it came to anything more, Marilyn drew the line. In fact, when it came to affairs, Marilyn was very selective. Of course, by her own admission, she made some bad choices. But haven't most of us at one time or another?

The oft-wed actress's four marriages in 36 short years — which included two men as different as baseball Hall of Famer Joe DiMaggio and Pulitzer Prize winning playwright Arthur Miller — are frequently cited as proof of her promiscuity. But those who knew her best, attribute Marilyn's marital troubles to a different source: her search for a father figure whose love could replace that of the real father who had deserted her before birth.

Marilyn's four husbands were all men whom the actress perceived as being more mature and more powerful than herself, Terry Moore tells us. "Marilyn, in her relationships, needed a father mentor. With all the men that she talked to me about — Arthur Miller, Bob — she didn't go for looks so much as she did someone who was really intelligent, a mentor. She always wanted someone that she could look up to — that could be her father. She was always looking for the man that she wished her father was."

Bebe Goddard, Marilyn's childhood friend, believes Moore is right. "Marilyn really admired intelligence. She also needed someone who could be sympathetic to her needs and emotional problems . . . which were caused by exhaustion from working hard and trying so hard. When she met Arthur Miller, she just was overwhelmed with admiration."

Superstar. Sex symbol. Comedienne. Hedonist. The Marilyn Monroe of legend was many things to the public. But there was more to Marilyn Monroe. Much more. Few guessed that behind her bubbly, vivacious exterior, Marilyn Monroe, superstar, lived a haunted private life which was to lead to a tragic end on August 4, 1962.

FILE #3

Marilyn, the Person

The legend of Marilyn Monroe, the glamorous, sexy, tempestuous actress whose life came early to a sudden and tragic close, is known to millions. But there was another face, a private face known only to her closest friends. Those friends say that face represented the real Marilyn Monroe. If so, then Marilyn's private face was that of Norma Jeane Mortensen, a wholesome, straightforward, all-American girl-next-door who liked to flop around the house in a bathrobe with cream on her face, run barefoot down beaches, chat with friends on the phone, and eat hamburgers with ketchup and fries.

THE GIRL NEXT DOOR

According to confidante Terry Moore, who was under contract at RKO when Marilyn was under contract at Columbia Studios, the differences between Marilyn's public and private faces were so extreme that she literally changed appearance off stage. Strangers didn't even recognize the private Marilyn when they saw her on the streets. "Where Michael Jackson and other stars have to go to all this trouble to put on major disguises, all Marilyn had to do was leave her makeup off and put Vaseline on her face, and nobody recognized her. She was still lovely and beautiful, but in a very sweet way that would go unnoticed. But when she started putting the makeup back on again, her whole countenance changed, her whole posture. She glowed. She became the Marilyn Monroe that we knew. It was such a total transformation that it was unbelievable."

Marilyn's friend and neighbor, actress Jeanne Carmen, also observed a sharp distinction between the public legend and the private person. "When you look at her photographs, you see her as a happy person. But she was happy from the doorway out. From the doorway back inside, a lot of the happiness folded, because her insecurities came out. When she was Norma Jeane, she was insecure. When she was Marilyn Monroe, the world was hers."

Underneath the makeup, behind the public legend, was a private persona, a real human being not much different from any other girl her age. As Jeanne Carmen describes it: "When she walked out the door and faced the public, she was zany, crazy, wild Marilyn Monroe. But once the doors closed, she was Norma Jeane, just a normal girl. She was just a normal kid that wore dirty bathrobes and no makeup. Just a fun girl."

Terry Moore echoes this view of the real Marilyn as girl-next-door: "People nowadays make Marilyn out to be a very complicated person. She wasn't complicated. She was a very simple girl. And I mean that in the nicest sense. People complicated her life — situations, studios. But she always remained little Norma Jeane."

Alex D'Arcy, who appeared with her in *How to Marry a Millionaire*, also saw the private Marilyn as a normal, uncomplicated young woman. "When she was relaxed, she was very nice. Nice and sweet."

What was the private Marilyn Monroe really like? Though her public persona was bright, bubbly, extroverted, unselfconscious and full of fun, those who knew her best describe Marilyn as painfully shy, insecure, almost frightened.

Terry Moore remembers the private Marilyn as being extraordinarily sensitive: "She was very sweet and vulnerable. Marilyn was one of the most sensitive girls in the whole world and took everything you told her to heart. And she was so afraid of being laughed at."

This is the Marilyn childhood roommate Bebe Goddard knew as well. "She was a tremendously shy, insecure person." Who was the woman known to Marilyn Monroe's closest friends as Norma Jeane? And how did she become the screen legend her public knew? The answers lie in what have been called Marilyn Monroe's tragic beginnings, beginnings that bore the seeds of her tragic end and helped set the stage for her murder only thirty-six short years later.

TRAGIC BEGINNINGS

Born Norma Jeane Mortensen (Monroe was her mother's maiden name) to Gladys Mortensen, a filmcutter who was separated and soon to be divorced from an absent husband, at Los Angeles General Hospital in 1926, Marilyn Monroe's first years were destined to be unhappy ones. Soon after the birth, Gladys, a reluctant mother at best, returned to work, depositing her baby in a series of foster homes made up of relatives or friends. Always the sore thumb and outsider in any of the succession of families she was foisted upon, Norma Jeane soon developed an almost painful insecurity along with a desperate need for approval.

Things began to look brighter for the young Norma Jeane when, at the age of seven, she moved back in with her mother for what looked like a permanent stay. Then, in the first of the tragedies that were to haunt and ultimately end the legendary screen goddess's private life, Gladys had a severe nervous breakdown and was institutionalized in a mental hospital. Ironically, this had been Gladys Mortensen's greatest dread; her mother, Norma Jeane's grandmother, Della Monroe, had also been institutionalized.

Some close friends believe that her grandmother and mother's mental breakdowns created a lifelong fear in Norma Jeane that she too might one day go crazy and be locked up in an institution for life. Bebe Goddard, whose own mother suffered mental illness, is one who shares this view: "That was another thing we had in common. My mother was really not a sane person. And my grandmother had died in an institution. So we did worry about whether we would inherit these same traits."

Others who knew Norma Jeane equally well disagree. "We discussed the emotional problems of her family over a period of time," one close friend said. "Of course her mother's illness embarrassed her. She also indicated that her grandmother and grandfather on the maternal side had mental problems. I believe both passed away in institutions. But I don't think Marilyn was concerned too much about going insane."

HER YOUNG WOMANHOOD

As a result of her mother's breakdown and confinement, the young Norma Jeane was once again uprooted and thrust into a new home as an outsider. But soon the home was that of Grace McKee, one of Gladys's closest friends, who had been appointed the future actress's legal guardian and under whose roof Norma Jeane was to find a haven of stability at last. Bebe Goddard, McKee's stepdaughter, was almost the same age as Norma Jeane, and the two girls soon became close friends.

Bebe still recalls the bond they formed with warm affection.

"My stepmother was Norma Jeane's guardian. There was only six months and seventeen days difference in our ages. We occupied this very tiny bedroom. There was only one bed, so we occupied the same bed. We became instant friends. We called ourselves stepsisters."

For the next five years Norma Jeane was to know the longest period of stability she was ever to enjoy in life, and the first feeling of belonging to a family she had ever known. At some period during her school days, Norma Jeane may have been teased or ostracized by students over either her mother's mental illness or her family's lack of money. This is indicated by the fact that during this period, even though she studied hard and was very popular with boys, the shyness and insecurity which haunted her up through the final tragic days of her life began to intensify.

"We both went to Van Nuys High School. Norma Jeane was a very vivacious, fun person with really darling mannerisms and a good sense of humor. Boys followed her around in droves, and she received many compliments on her looks. But at the same time, she was a very shy, insecure, and self-conscious person — not at all sure about her beauty. Norma Jeane really did not believe she was that beautiful. But she was. Nothing needed changing, even then."

These were the days Marilyn Monroe remembered with the most fondness in later years. But in 1942, Norma Jeane's idyll came to an end. Work called the Goddards back east, and the young Norma Jeane had to grow up fast. Unable to take her with them, and unwilling to abandon her in California, the Goddards persuaded her to marry twenty-one-year-old James Dougherty, a war worker who was considered unusually mature for his age. The Goddards thought Norma Jeane was a bit flighty and hoped the more sedate Dougherty would help settle her down.

In June, only a few days after her sixteenth birthday, Norma

Jeane Mortensen was wed to James Edward Dougherty. The marriage between the future actress and the more mature factory worker was doomed from the start. Because of her disjointed upbringing, Norma Jeane Dougherty was still little more than a child. Like most girls her age, she enjoyed dancing and socializing. Her new husband was fond of home life and did not like the activities his wife enjoyed; he resented the dent they put in his meager earnings.

Although the difficulties of the marriage to Dougherty were apparent right from the start, Norma Jeane attempted to "make a go of it," according to Bebe Goddard who attended the wedding. "She really devoted herself to being the best wife she could possibly be. She worked very hard. Being married was a different lifestyle for her. It was a little strange."

Two years later, it was obvious to both that their marriage was a failure; they were just incompatible. James Dougherty, knowing he was likely to be drafted soon, and thinking of the many benefits the dependents of married servicemen receive, enlisted in the Merchant Marines. He may have hoped a cooling off period would help them both become more mature, and to adjust successfully to the stress of married life.

Now seventeen, her voluptuous curves outlined in tight sweaters a size too small — hand-me-downs from relatives — Norma Jeane had begun to attract the eyes of men everywhere she went. This attention incensed her husband, and his jealousy was a source of increasing tension between them. Although Norma Jeane was at first unaware of the overwhelming effect of her newly developed curves and skin-tight sweaters on neighborhood men, she grew to recognizer its power. She later admitted that once she realized what was happening, she continued to wear her tight-fitting tops partly to needle her husband.

More significantly, Norma Jeane encouraged the looks

brought by her tight sweaters simply for the attention. "Men were looking at me for the first time," she told me once. "It made me feel important. And I liked it."

Like so many other war wives whose men were away from home, Norma Jeane took a job in a war plant and moved in with her husband's parents during his absence. It looked as if her life would follow the pattern of so many other lower-middle-class women — marriage, family, years of struggle to make ends meet — a life that would grind down her youth and beauty and doom her to an early old age. But life was about to take a dramatic turn for Norma Jeane Dougherty.

A STAR IS BORN

In a scenario that reads like something out of a Hollywood movie, the event that transformed Norma Jeane Dougherty into Marilyn Monroe occurred in the most prosaic of places — an airplane factory. According to Bebe Goddard: "Norma Jeane went to work at the war plant. One day David Conover, a photographer for the Army publication, *Stars and Stripes*, went to the factory to take pictures of its beautiful war workers as part of a morale-boosting campaign — and he discovered Norma Jeane. He suggested that she should be in modeling and took those marvelous pictures. Then he introduced her to the head of the Bluebook Modeling Agency. Once she did start modeling, she was in demand everywhere. She was one of the busiest models her agency had ever had."

Norma Jeane's voluptuous curves and unforgettable face — with its unique blend of the sensual and the innocent — soon made her a much sought after figure model. When Norma Jeane's theatrical agent, Helen Ainsworth, received a phone call from a representative of multimillionaire Howard Hughes, then a Hollywood mogul and owner of RKO Studios, Ainsworth astutely parlayed the situation into an even better deal with Twentieth Century–Fox. At Fox, she was soon renamed from then on, for the public, she would always be known by the far sultrier name of Marilyn Monroe. Norma Jeane Dougherty, whose background and future had seemed to hold so little promise only a short time ago, was now a contract player for a major motion picture studio, and on her way to becoming a legendary superstar.

More important, Norma Jeane was on her way to fulfilling a childhood ambition. Like many young girls, Norma Jeane had fantasized about becoming a wealthy, glamorous movie star. For her, the dream had greater urgency than most. It promised an escape from a bleak and lonely life, where even the skin-tight sweaters that made her the pin-up girl of millions of men around the globe were hand-me-downs.

Marilyn said that acting was a childhood ambition. She used to walk down to Grauman's Chinese Theatre and put her tiny feet into the cement imprints of Hollywood's leading actresses of the time. Marilyn's success on the screen was a childhood dream she made come true.

THE HARD-WORKING ACTRESS

If the public movie star fulfilled a dream by becoming a motion-picture phenomenon, it was because the private Norma Jeane was a hard-working, dedicated actress who constantly, obsessively, sought to improve her performance and develop her talents.

Although she might have traded — as many actresses did — simply on her looks and sex appeal, from the very beginning of her career Marilyn Monroe sought out and trained with a succession of the most demanding and highly regarded acting coaches in the world, including mentor Natasha Lytess and the husband-and-wife team of Paula and Lee Strasberg.

Even as a young girl, Marilyn possessed a fierce drive not only to succeed, but to go beyond success to excellence. According to Bebe Goddard, during the period when they were growing up together, "Whatever Marilyn did, she wanted to do the best possible job. She was always trying to improve her mind when we were going to school."

Terry Moore still maintains vivid memories of this aspect of the private Marilyn. "Marilyn had tremendous drive. She was there every day studying, singing, doing scenes, improving herself. She was always studying makeup. No one did a better makeup job than she did."

Alex D'Arcy, whose work with her certainly qualifies him as a judge, also describes Marilyn as an ambitious, dedicated actress always reaching for that little bit extra in her attempt to improve her work. "She was ambitious. She was worried all the time about her performance. Is it good enough? She was only satisfied if she thought she was the best."

In spite of her success and her efforts to improve herself as an actress, the career of the private Marilyn Monroe contained a secret tragedy. Although her films earned millions of dollars and were acclaimed around the world, she never received the same recognition or financial rewards as her peers in the entertainment industry. Instead, Marilyn was often ridiculed and her acting abilities criticized. Her pay scale was a fraction of that enjoyed by other stars with equal box off ice attraction.

Terry Moore remembers the lack of respect that much of Hollywood felt toward Marilyn in those days: "Harry Cohn, head of Columbia, who was the first studio head to hire her after Fox dropped her contract, said, 'She's never going to be a star.' Darryl Zanuck, president of Twentieth Century–Fox, even though she became a big star, and made him and the studio millions with *Gentlemen Prefer Blondes* and all those other hits — he didn't believe it. The people, the big people in the industry, never took her seriously. The public did . . . the world has . . . they all loved her and accepted her. But it was so unreal to see that Hollywood wouldn't."

Insecure, embarrassed by her background, ever doubting herself and her professional abilities, unable to achieve either recognition from those in her profession or sustain a lasting marital relationship, the private Marilyn Monroe became an increasingly haunted woman isolated from the world; her isolation in part, caused by the shadow of her own legend.

As haunted as her past and present were, her future was destined to be even more haunted. The encounter that would lead to her murder had already taken place. Soon a series of events were to occur that would lead Norma Jeane Mortensen step-by-step to an ending even more tragic than her beginnings.

FILE #4

Marilyn and JFK

If Marilyn Monroe was the reigning female movie star of the silver screen, John Fitzgerald Kennedy, the man who would be president, was her counterpart in the political world. As leading lights of their own respective worlds, the two were destined to meet when those worlds overlapped.

In 1954, a short time after the actress had wed baseball superslugger Joe DiMaggio, Marilyn met the handsome, charismatic senator from Massachusetts at a reception given for JFK and his wife, Jacqueline Bouvier Kennedy, by Marilyn's agent, Charles Feldman. JFK, who had a notorious eye for the ladies, reportedly asked mutual acquaintance Peter Lawford, the British-born matine idol, for an introduction.

Marilyn was aware of JFK's interest in her. She told friends he couldn't keep his eyes off her at the party. Lawford's introduction resulted in Jack asking Marilyn for her phone number. Two figures of unique magnetism, Marilyn and JFK were drawn to each other as passionately as others were draw to them.

Marilyn was used to being approached by actors, producers, and others in the entertainment industry. A United States senator with an Ivy League education and a distinguished lineage was a new experience. Flattered by JFK's interest, touched by what she described later as the "shy" way he asked if he could have her number, and almost swept off her feet by his legendary charm and enthusiasm, Marilyn wrote the number of her private line down for him.

Marilyn's headline-making marriage to DiMaggio reached its headline-making end after a short nine months. She was already seeing JFK before her relationship to the Yankee Slugger was over. Soon what began as a casual acquaintance turned into a raging love affair.

After her marriage to DiMaggio failed, Marilyn was determined to leave Los Angeles and start over fresh in New York. It was here, while studying acting seriously with the famed acting coach Lee Strasberg, that the actress entered into her mismatched relationship with Arthur Miller, one of the East Coast's leading intellectuals and playwrights. Deeply attracted to intelligent men, Marilyn soon agreed to marry the tall, bespectacled playwright.

But Marilyn's affair with the senator from Massachusetts was too hot for the rather cerebral Miller to cool down. Recently disclosed FBI reports place the actress in JFK's plush suite at the Carlyle Hotel during his frequent visits to Manhattan.

Oddly, Marilyn's liaison with JFK was to prove one of the most enduring in her life. It continued through two marriages and eventually spanned most of a decade, ending only when JFK's ascension to the presidency turned the relationship into a political liability of the first magnitude.

Back in California — her New York sojourn ended with her divorce from Arthur Miller — Marilyn and JFK's affair continued to grow hotter. JFK was making frequent trips to the West Coast, ostensibly for political and business reasons. To protect his career and family, their relationship was kept secret with the help of Jack Kennedy's brother-in-law, screen star Peter Lawford at whose Santa Monica beachside hideaway they first met.

Marilyn's friend, Jeanne Carmen, was present at many a rendezvous JFK kept with the star. "It didn't seem difficult. In Hollywood, people don't pay that much attention — especially out at someone's beach house. Marilyn attended a lot of parties at Peter Lawford's house. They were very close friends. Sometimes Kennedy flew in by helicopter or just drove up there. They just came in at different times, from different directions."

Major public figures, the senator and the actress attended the same functions and moved in the midst of a continual entourage of public relations experts, aides-de-camp, managers, and hangers-on of every sort. This, coupled with their inability to remain apart when guests at the same events, rendered their romantic relationship readily visible to the upper echelon of the political and entertainment worlds — although unknown to the general public.

Former Los Angeles Mayor Sam Yorty was one government official who heard of their notorious alliance. "It was pretty well-known. I don't think it was very hush hush. Rumors were all over the place." Actor Alex D'Arcy acknowledges the affair was common knowledge in filmland circles: "Kennedy? It was no secret. It was public knowledge. Everybody knew about it."

Jeanne Carmen agrees that JFK's romance with Marilyn was no secret in Hollywood. "It was known in the industry.

I don't think it ever got out to the public. I don't think the public would believe it if they heard it. They would close their minds to it. The public doesn't want to hear stuff like that. I wonder if they believe it even now. But the industry knew. I mean, they were very brazen. I'm amazed it didn't get out."

Marilyn was conspicuously on JFK's arm during receptions at the Beverly Hilton Hotel and Bing Crosby's home — where they spent weekends as guests. Further, her frequent late-night entrances to the Hilton's Presidential Suite while JFK was in residence have been confirmed by former hotel employees.

JFK's Charisma

The future president's affair with Marilyn Monroe was not the first time the handsome young Kennedy heir had strayed from the marital bed of his beautiful and cultured wife, Jacqueline Bouvier Kennedy. JFK's amours were notorious among those in the know. His much celebrated Irish good looks and devil-may-care vitality made him almost irresistibly attractive to women, while his roving Irish eye made beautiful women almost irresistibly attractive to him.

Actress Terry Moore, who met JFK on numerous occasions, attests to his sexual magnetism. "Jack Kennedy in person had such charisma, even more than in his photographs. He was certainly everything that any woman could visualize. He'd been a war hero. He was as exciting as Elvis Presley or any of our heroes." Jeanne Carmen, one of the hundreds of women whom history says were recipients of JFK's attentions, recalls his interest in the opposite sex vividly. "I kind of think Jack wanted to make sure that he hit on every woman that was around, that he wanted. He hated to think that he might miss one."

Just as she was not the first woman to receive JFK's attentions, Marilyn was not the first actress to receive them. JFK, who had asked Lawford for an introduction to Marilyn, asked other Hollywood friends for introductions to actresses who caught his eye.

Sam Yorty recalls one celebrated tryst that took place during his own tenure as mayor of the City of Angels: "There was another actress that Jack was supposed to meet down in Palm Springs, and they went and closed the door, and the FBI would guard the place. I don't remember her name. But she's a very well-known actress." (Mayor Yorty was speaking of Angie Dickinson, of "Police Woman" fame. Later, as president, JFK's affair with yet another actress, twenty-six-year-old Judith Campbell, became a national security matter when it was discovered that the sometime partygirl was simultaneously carrying on an affair with Mafia head Sam Giancana.)

MARILYN'S VULNERABILITY

Chronic insecurity may have made Marilyn Monroe even more vulnerable than most women to the future president's charms. The scars of Marilyn's childhood ran deep — the outsider's need for approval, the hunger of the fatherless for a father image, the yearning of the underprivileged for privilege. These scars had made the superstar vulnerable to men before. This time they would lead, indirectly, to her death.

Terry Moore recalls the devastating effect that the insecurities of her childhood had on the adult Marilyn. "She was always insecure about things like her looks, about being in orphanages, and about whether people would accept her because she wasn't born into a fancy family. She had a strong side. But she was just a little girl underneath it all, and quite insecure. She was the most vulnerable person I ever met."

To a young woman from the wrong side of the tracks desperately seeking approval and acceptance, the attention of the handsome, powerful senator with his silver-spoon aura and prestigious family was irresistible.

JFK's position and background proved a powerful aphrodisiac for the star, as Jeanne Carmen remembers it. "Marilyn wanted to be part of that life and be accepted. It was exciting being with the president of the United States, and having all this hoopla going on."

Terry Moore also shares this view: "When Marilyn fell in love with Jack Kennedy, she felt that she could finally be taken seriously. Not only was he a handsome, attractive man but he was the number one, most powerful man in the whole world. She dreamed she might become the First Lady of her country — not just Norma Jeane to Marilyn Monroe. And I think so much of it was just to be taken seriously."

With a man who possessed the unique power and prestige of JFK paying court to her, Marilyn no longer felt insecure about being accepted. According to Alex D'Arcy, "She was captivated by that life. She felt she was in another world. Her insecurity was being held in check by knowing these people and thinking they appreciated her."

There was another and simpler reason, however, that Marilyn Monroe was attracted to Jack Kennedy. As Terry Moore puts it: "Marilyn loved intellectual men. Intelligent men. And Jack was very intelligent."

The longevity of Marilyn and JFK's relationship suggests that more than mere passion was involved. But however deep their feelings for each other might have run, the liaison had been doomed from its beginning by the ambitions of the man who had initiated it. As a senator, the young JFK had dreamed of great political achievement — of winning the presidency — and those dreams were about to be fulfilled.

THE BIRTHDAY BASH

JFK's successful bid for the presidency of the United States forced him to distance himself more and more from his relationship with Marilyn. As a senator, he and the movie star had been able, with the cooperation of the press, to keep the affair from the public. The increased public scrutiny that accompanied the presidency, however, meant that an increasing number of people would become aware of the relationship.

According to insiders, Jacqueline Bouvier Kennedy didn't approve of her husband's womanizing, but was willing to look the other way for the sake of their children, the family, and his political ambitions. Previous affairs had been short-term; none had involved the woman that most men considered "the most beautiful woman in the world." The affair with Marilyn was more serious and more threatening. Jackie decided to deliver an ultimatum to her husband.

Marilyn had sensed the growing distance between her and the president. He had been less attentive, returned her calls less often, and had made trips to see her less frequently since his election to the presidency. Peter Lawford's suggestion that Marilyn fly out to New York and sing in a gala birthday tribute had seemed like a heaven-sent opportunity to be alone once more with the president of the United States.

JFK's spring 1962 birthday gala at Madison Square Garden was really a fundraiser for the Democratic Party. Because of Jackie Kennedy's ultimatum to her husband, it was also to mark the end of Marilyn Monroe's eight-year love affair with its honoree.

Later Marilyn confided to friends that Jackie had refused

to attend the evening's festivities after learning of Lawford's plan. Jackie told the president, "If that slut shows up, I'm not coming." The arrangements for Marilyn's appearance had already been made; to change them at such a late date would involve public humiliation. The president begged for an opportunity to break off the relationship. Jackie agreed. To the amazement of society columnists, Jacqueline Bouvier Kennedy was conspicuous by her absence the night of her husband's birthday gala. She had gone fox hunting instead.

This account of events is substantiated by political insiders as well. According to Sam Yorty, "Marilyn went back and sang at Jack's birthday, and Jack's wife didn't show up for it. There was obviously some jealousy there."

Later that night, at a reception after the fundraiser, JFK and his younger brother Bobby, the attorney general of the United States, took Marilyn aside. Unless JFK broke off their affair, Jackie had threatened to divorce the president and humiliate him publicly, the two brothers told her. Presidential marital scandals had remained hidden from the public before. Divorce would have meant complete disgrace for JFK, the end of his hopes of re-election, and of all future political or public service.

It is not clear whether JFK told Marilyn the relationship had to end that night or simply suggested they be more discreet in the future. But the president did ask Marilyn never to call him through the switchboard at the White House again. Although she didn't understand at the time, Marilyn Monroe, the glamorous love goddess, was being dumped by the president of the United States.

Marilyn was bewildered at first. Her letters went unanswered, and JFK never called her again after that night. Finally, the actress realized her worst childhood fears had come true. The poor girl from the wrong side of the tracks had given her love to the rich society boy, only to be dropped cold when she became an embarrassment.

Marilyn felt hurt, betrayed — and angry. Her anger quickly became known to Kennedy intimate, Peter Lawford, and through Lawford to the president. Afraid of exposure, JFK appointed his brother Bobby to put out the fire between him and the actress.

The attorney general flew to L.A. intending only to speak with Marilyn and calm her down. Face to face with the star, Bobby, too, felt himself responding to her magnetic sexuality.

Boyish, fun-loving Bobby touched a responsive chord in Marilyn that his serious, reserved older brother never had. Although the heat was taken off JFK, Bobby Kennedy, in his turn, became involved with Marilyn. As Jeanne Carmen describes it: "Bobby was sent by Jack to cut off that relationship and got involved by accident. He got in deeper than he realized and deeper than he could handle."

As with her romance with his more-celebrated brother, Marilyn Monroe's affair with Bobby Kennedy was doomed to run through the same course of passion, intimacy, and then betrayal — only this time the results were to be fatal. Although no one guessed it at the time, her involvement with Bobby had unwittingly provided a motive for murder.

FILE #5

Marilyn and Bobby

Marilyn Monroe's intense sexual magnetism made most men fall in love with her instantly, on and off the screen. Jack Kennedy, Frank Sinatra, Yves Montand, Joe DiMaggio, Marlon Brando, Arthur Miller, and her audiences all lost their hearts to this supreme sex goddess of the screen. Bobby Kennedy was to prove no exception.

Surprisingly, the feeling was mutual. Whereas Marilyn had been infatuated with JFK because of his image, his power, his family, and his charisma, she fell head over heels in love with his brother Bobby. Things heated up rapidly between Marilyn and the attorney general. The actress began the affair on the rebound, but her feelings for RFK soon blazed into one of the most important and most ill-fated love affairs of her life.

The depth of Marilyn Monroe's feelings for Robert Kennedy was apparent to all her friends. "Marilyn really loved Bobby," Terry Moore told me. "Much more than Jack. She admired Jack Kennedy, but she never really believed he would leave Jackie and marry her."

Once again, loyal Kennedy in-law Peter Lawford helped

cover Marilyn's affair with Bobby as he had with JFK. Lawford hosted dinner parties at which the attorney general and the actress were often coincidentally among the attendees. Afterward, Bobby and Marilyn would take long romantic walks along the Santa Monica shore together, hand-in-hand.

By summer, the affair had become so serious that Bobby was making regular flights to Los Angeles just to bed Marilyn. He had even given the actress his private telephone number at the Justice Department, so they could remain in constant touch when he was in Washington. Marilyn's anger with JFK was forgotten in the glow of her new found love for his younger brother.

Bobby's excuse for making so many trips to the West Coast was that a major movie studio, Twentieth Century-Fox, had optioned his book, *The Enemy Within*, his election-year exposé of the Mafia's secret operations in America. The hard-hitting book took particular aim at puppet organizations such as the Teamsters Union. Headed by the Mafia's hand-picked president, Jimmy Hoffa, the Teamster's Union was of especial interest because of its enormous influence. Its strangle-hold on the nation's transportation industry provided the Mob with a clever "cash cow," concealed by a virtually unassailabe legal facade, and financed at the expense of every American consumer. The Teamsters extortionate labor charges artificially inflated the cost of almost every item purchased in the United States.

Marilyn read *The Enemy Within* soon after their affair began. The attorney general's crusading zeal deepened her admiration for him. His book, in fact, was tantamount to a formal declaration of war against the Mob — a war Bobby had already begun to fight in his first years as a senator. Neither Marilyn nor Bobby guessed that the hostile political climate surrounding this battle would eventually invade and dominate their personal lives.

While the summer was young, the two lovers felt young. Although Marilyn was thirty-six and Bobby in his forties, something in their relationship had brought back the magic and innocence of youth for both of them. Those who saw them together said they acted more like a couple of college kids than one of the screen's leading actresses and the attorney general of the United States. Certainly Mrs. Murray, Marilyn's housekeeper witnessed this collegiate side of their relationship.

Bobby often called for Marilyn in a sweater, jeans, and sneakers. He would pull up into the driveway of her Brentwood home in a convertible with the top down. Marilyn would tie a scarf over her hair, don dark glasses, and run out to meet him. She would join him in the car, and leave for the day.

THE NEW FIRST LADY

For Marilyn Monroe, her relationship with Bobby Kennedy was no casual affair. Some believe he was the one true love of her life. Even those not in the know at the time were aware that something special was going on in her life.

Friend and fellow actress Terry Moore guessed that someone had replaced JFK in Marilyn's affections from the way she acted. "She did not discuss the Kennedys with me then. But I knew there was something going on, because Marilyn looked like a bubble that was about to burst. She looked so excited and elated."

Marilyn's newfound happiness was based on Bobby Kennedy's assurances that he loved her and wanted to marry her. A staunch Roman Catholic with a wife, many children, and his own dream of the presidency, the attorney general would seem to have been an unlikely candidate for divorce. But Marilyn believed him.

"Bobby told her he would marry her someday," Jeanne Carmen confirms. Marilyn bought it all the way. She was naive enough to believe that he really cared and that it would work. She thought he was going to marry her and leave the family."

Terry Moore learned of the actress's affair with the attorney general late in its course, when Marilyn confessed that Bobby had talked of divorcing his wife and marrying her. "With Bobby, she believed he loved her," Moore remembers. "She thought that he would be president, and that she would be First Lady."

Throughout that summer Marilyn confided to various members of her circle that "Bobby Kennedy promised to marry me." Then she would ask, seeking reassurance that this dream could be true: "What do you think?" Marilyn's friends warned her that no divorced man could hope to win the presidency, and that Bobby was too ambitious to sacrifice his political future for her. But the actress didn't believe them. The attorney general's lovemaking had been too convincing. Marilyn believed every word Bobby Kennedy said.

A more politically sophisticated woman would have known better. But Marilyn Monroe knew almost nothing about politics. Growing up poor, passed from family to family, politics had not been a big concern of hers. Later, her meteoric rise in the movies had left little time for anything but work and study. Friends doubt that she even knew the difference between Republicans and Democrats.

For Marilyn Monroe, who had spent more than a decade among the beguiling fantasies of the motion picture world — where happy endings are routine, and dreams always come true just before the fade out — a future in which she might be both a Kennedy wife and First Lady seemed very real.

THREE OMINOUS EVENTS

In the early summer of 1962, Marilyn Monroe believed her future was bright and full of promise. But ominous clouds gathering on the horizon were already beginning to cast their shadow across her romance with Bobby Kennedy. These clouds took the form of three events that would be harbingers of the storm to come.

The first of these clouds was Marilyn's growing suspicion that she was under surveillance. She became afraid to discuss anything important on her own telephone. The actress told friends she was convinced her phone conversations were being tapped. Marilyn no longer called confidantes like Jeanne Carmen from her house. "Marilyn was going outside to make a lot of her calls. She thought her phone was bugged. Most of her phone calls to me were made from phone booths."

And, in fact, a government agency was watching Marilyn, JFK, and Bobby Kennedy. Declassified FBI reports reveal that J. Edgar Hoover, then head of the FBI, maintained surveillance on many federal and local officials, including the president and attorney general. The name of Marilyn Monroe appears prominently in several of these reports.

The FBI wasn't the only government agency keeping tabs on the superstar. The CIA was also eavesdropping on Marilyn. At the time, the U.S. spy agency was involved in two major clandestine operations: the ill-fated Bay of Pigs invasion of Cuba, and an equally unsuccessful plot to assassinate Cuba's president, Fidel Castro. Fearful the attorney general might disclose these operations, both blatant violations of international law, during his more intimate moments with Marilyn, CIA agents had begun their own surveillance program. (Although Marilyn's suspicions were not confirmed prior to her death, Milo Speriglio, CEO of the Nick Harris Detective Agency, and I discovered that her phones and rooms were tapped by the CIA.)

Considering this surveillance, the second event to cast its shadow over Marilyn's life that summer assumes an even more ominous form.

At the time of her liaison with Bobby, Marilyn was keeping a diary. In this red-covered book, she recorded details of their affair, including unguarded conversations with Bobby about government figures, activities, and secrets. Late in their relationship, the two lovers are said to have quarreled violently over this diary.

Jeanne Carmen is one friend who can attest that Marilyn's diary is no myth. "Yes. Marilyn kept a diary." I saw it with my own eyes. She had written down things Bobby Kennedy had said.

Lionel Grandison, deputy coroner's aide for Los Angeles County, actually held the diary in his hands on the day following her death. Grandison was charged with locating Marilyn's next of kin so that burial arrangements could be made. In examining her personal effects for the names of family members, he discovered the star's diary.

Grandison supports Jeanne Carmen's account of its contents. "I found this little red diary that hopefully would lead us to a next of kin. In this capacity, I began to look through this red book. The book didn't have references to any next of kin, but it had a very interesting series of stories, assessments, and evaluations about things that were apparently going on in her life. She made reference to John Kennedy, Robert Kennedy, the Mafia, and the CIA. Her references to the Mafia and CIA stood out especially because those were terms you didn't hear very often in 1962."

Considering its sizzling hot contents, those few friends who knew of Marilyn's diary warned her about keeping it. The diary was a walking time bomb. By keeping it and letting others see it, she was playing with fire. I advised her to at least keep her diary away from other people. At that time, she told me that two or three other persons had already seen it, including Bobby Kennedy.

At first, Marilyn had quietly kept the diary to herself. When Bobby finally learned of it, he blew up. Marilyn showed it to him herself. Politically naive, she had no idea how violent his reaction would be. . . . She quickly learned.

Jeanne Carmen was present the day Bobby saw the actress's diary and witnessed his explosive reaction. "Bobby got very angry. He said, 'Marilyn, what is this?' And she just said, 'I've just been keeping some notes so that I could know what to talk about with you.' He threw it on the coffee table, and said, 'Get rid of this; get rid of this, immediately.' I don't think Bobby thought that she was trying to harm him. I think that he felt maybe she was not as bright as he had thought, and maybe just by accident, might let something get out. It worried him. He told Marilyn, 'Even Miss Carmen shouldn't be seeing this diary.' And that's when their relationship started going down the tubes."

Although I can't pinpoint the exact date of that encounter witnessed by Jeanne Carmen, it wasn't too far removed from June 14. Doctor's records for this date show a circumspect Marilyn keeping an appointment with prominent Beverly Hills plastic surgeon, Dr. Michael Gurdin. According to Peter Harry Brown, in research for his book, *Marilyn, The Last Take*, Dr. Ralph Greenson brought a heavily disguised Marilyn to Gurdin's office because of his concern "for an injury to her nose." Dr. Gurdin had done some minor plastic surgery on Marilyn previously. She trusted him.

Dr. Greenson said that Marilyn's injury was caused by a

fall in the shower, and hitting the tiling around the tub. An odd story, I thought, because she rarely took showers, preferring baths instead. In my opinion she had been beaten by someone . . . and my guess was Bobby Kennedy, in anger over the diary and other notes Marilyn had been keeping.

Dr. Greenson was very concerned about the injury and requested that X-rays be taken. Fortunately they showed no fracture. Marilyn left quickly for home, to care for the bruises and discoloration. Within a week or so, she was busily doing interviews and posing for publicity photos.

The third and final shadow across Marilyn's love affair with Bobby took the form of threatening phone calls she received just before her death.

These calls explain why the breakup of her relationship with RFK was so abrupt. Jackie Kennedy may not have been the only Kennedy wife to threaten her husband with divorce unless he broke off his relationship with Marilyn immediately.

On two occasions Marilyn answered her unlisted number to someone unfamilar to her. The woman's voice on the other end screamed hysterically, "I want you to keep away from my husband!" — and then slammed the phone down. On the second occasion, the caller screamed, "Leave Bobby alone, you tramp!" Friends suggested that Ethel Kennedy might have been responsible.

THE BUBBLE BURSTS

What had started as an infatuation with Jack Kennedy had, for Marilyn Monroe, become a passionate love affair with Bobby. At first the insecure actress had been living out a dream, now the dream was quickly evolving into a nightmare.

Aware that Bobby Kennedy's political ambitions precluded divorce, Marilyn's friends became increasingly disturbed about the depth of her emotional involvement with him. According to Terry Moore, "I was very concerned about her, because both Kennedys were married men. They were both men that couldn't afford to have their relationship with her known."

Jeanne Carmen shared this concern. "Bobby Kennedy was a very ambitious man. He wanted to be president someday. Maybe if he hadn't been ambitious, he couldn't have fallen for her. But I really doubt that he ever meant to marry her. With Bobby, you couldn't tell. He was like a little boy, actually. He was just as adventurous as Marilyn."

Soon the star's supporters discovered their greatest fears were coming true. Shortly after the incident with the diary, Bobby Kennedy brutally broke off his affair with Marilyn without explanation or fanfare. Suddenly, his private number at the Justice Department was disconnected. Like his brother, Bobby failed to take or return Marilyn's calls.

Marilyn became frantic. She tried reaching him through the switchboard of the Justice Department. Representatives told her the attorney general was not in, or was in a meeting and couldn't be interrupted. The star was devastated and angry.

In the midst of Marilyn's inability to reach Bobby and the turmoil on the set of *Something's Got to Give*, another heavily emotional issue was plaguing Marilyn's life — she had just become aware she was pregnant. Only a few very intimate friends knew of her predicament. No one knew whether the father was JFK or Bobby, and Marilyn wasn't saying. Based on what little she told me after the fact, I'd guess it was Bobby ... if only for the timing aspects. She seemed to be about 4-6 weeks along when she finally decided to have an abortion. I believe that Peter Lawford helped her during this situation, and arranged for a specialist to meet her in Mexico.

More than anything else during this time, Bobby's rejection and the abortion are what really triggered Marilyn's bouts of anger and despondency. She knew that she could handle Fox, and the nastiness of Cukor, even the rumors of the press . . . but the loss of her great dream to have a child, coupled with the swift and cold rejection by the man she loved were extremely painful. Marilyn was heartbroken over her failed attempts to bear a child. With every abortion, she knew that she was hurting her chances of being able to successfully bear children . . . and in addition to the reawakening of this old sorrow she couldn't even get Bobby on the phone. A lot of promises and dreams were crashing down on her again . . . and many of those dreams involved Bobby Kennedy.

Jeanne Carmen also attributes Bobby's rejection as a major cause of Marilyn's anger. She explains, "The way Bobby cut off the relationship was very bad. I don't think he knew how to cut it off. All of a sudden, she couldn't get through to him. He had disconnected his telephone. She had no idea what happened, why she couldn't get through. That's why it really hit the fan in the end. Had he sat down and explained it to her, possibly she wouldn't have had that feeling. She was a scorned woman. She was extremely angry, and she wasn't going to take no for an answer. For the first time in her life, she decided to fight back against someone who had used her."

THE LAST PRESS CONFERENCE

By Friday, August 3, 1962, Marilyn Monroe had become frustrated at being used and then dumped by the Kennedy brothers. She told her closest friends that the Kennedy brothers had made her many promises, only to betray her trust and break those promises. She had decided to hold a press conference and expose them both for what they were. The two men were idolized by the media and the public as champions of justice and fair play. Yet in their private lives, they proved to be exploitive, hypocritical, and cowardly. Marilyn felt it was time the public learned the truth.

One of the first people to whom she confided her decision was Jeanne Carmen. "Marilyn was definitely going to go public about the affair with Bobby because she was angry about the way he cut it off. She said, 'That's it. I'm going to talk. I'm gonna tell the press everything.' And she would have."

Terry Moore received a similar impression from her own conversations with Marilyn. "Marilyn did want it known at this time, especially when she felt that she was being passed around from one brother to the other."

Marilyn prepared to expose her romances with the Kennedys. Before doing so, however, she decided to reach Bobby one last time. If this attempt failed, she planned to hold the press conference the following Monday, August 6.

The few friends to whom the actress confided her plans, aware of the power and influence of the presidency and the Kennedy millions, advised her not to hold the press conference. Jeanne Carmen was one of those friends. "I warned her against doing anything, and she wouldn't listen. Marilyn said, 'Carmen, this is my affair. I love you dearly, but I have to do this my way. I'm the one that got hurt, not you.' And I said, 'Well, if you have to go for it, you have to go for it.' "

I also warned her against proceeding with the press conference, and advised that she be more discreet in revealing her plans to others. She said, 'Well, I've told a couple of people already.' It didn't seem to matter to her. She seemed to be pretty careless in her attitude. I urged her to keep quiet about the press conference, and wait and see what happens over the weekend. Unfortunately, she didn't listen."

Marilyn was fated never to hold the press conference. Just one day later, Saturday, August 4 — thirty-six hours before the conference was to have taken place — Marilyn Monroe lay dead in her Brentwood home. To me, this shows much more than coincidence; it shows cause and effect.

The coroner called her death suicide. I call it murder.

Although her relationships with the Kennedys gave them and those associated with them an obvious motive for murder, Bobby's crusade against organized crime may have given someone else an equally strong motive for wanting Marilyn dead. No investigation into the possibilities of her murder would be complete without an extensive examination into her connection with the Mob and the Mob's potential interest in seeing her dead.

Marilyn had read admiringly of Bobby's successful campaign against organized crime in his book, *The Enemy Within*. Some of those familiar with the circumstances surrounding her death believe that in RFK's book she unknowingly, read the name of the man who would be instrumental in her murder.

FILE #6

Marilyn and The Mafia

Marilyn may have understood the personal dangers she faced through involvements with such prominent political figures as the Kennedys. It is doubtful, however, she realized the existence of a far more portentous threat: her exposure to organized crime. By the summer of 1962, Marilyn had unknowingly become a target of the Mafia.

Marilyn suspected that her phone was bugged. She believed it was by the Kennedys or someone working for the Kennedys. In fact, her house had become a veritable network of wire taps from various sources. Government files now prove that both the CIA and FBI were involved in tapping Marilyn's phones.

The man responsible for most of the tapping was not a Kennedy friend; he was RFK's sworn enemy, Jimmy Hoffa, head of the powerful, mob-controlled Teamsters Union. Hoffa had reportedly ordered the execution of several men. His obsession with destroying Bobby Kennedy is seen by some people as a possible motive for the murder of Marilyn.

MARILYN AND THE TEAMSTER PRESIDENT

First as a fledgling senator, and then as attorney general under his brother's presidency, Robert Kennedy engaged in an all-out war with organized crime and their captive tool, the Teamsters Union. This was a new experience for the Mafia, and one they did not enjoy.

For more than half a century, the Mob had operated with complete freedom in the U.S., protected from interference by a widespread network of bribes and blackmail. Suddenly, Mafia dons and their henchmen found their identities and activities exposed to the world. Bobby Kennedy grilled them mercilessly before the television cameras in a succession of Senate and Justice Department investigations.

Over the course of this conflict, the Teamster president and the attorney general came to hate each other. Hoffa disparaged Bobby as "a man who had no principles."

The union leaders arrogant demeanor infuriated the attorney general. He saw it as nothing less than the criminal underworld's contempt for a legal system rendered impotent by men as powerful and influential as Jimmy Hoffa. Over the nation's airwaves Bobby personalized the attack, branding Hoffa and the Teamsters "a conspiracy of evil."

Hoffa decided to fight back. The Union president had been keeping tabs on both Kennedys, whose reputation for womanizing had come to his attention. Hoping to amass evidence of the Kennedys' infidelities — blackmail material for his and other mob bosses' future use — Hoffa enlisted the services of electronic surveillance wizard, private detective Bernard Spindel.

Upon Hoffa's request, Spindel bugged Peter Lawford's home. Through the Lawford bug, Hoffa learned of the Kennedys' affair with Marilyn. Soon he had Marilyn's house and phone bugged as well.

Milo Speriglio can verify Hoffa's personal involvement in the bugging of Marilyn's Brentwood home.

"Marilyn's phones and rooms were being tapped by Jimmy Hoffa," Speriglio states without hesitation.

MARILYN AND THE CHICAGO MAFIA

James Hoffa wasn't the only organized crime figure whose shadow had fallen over Marilyn Monroe's final days. Sam Giancana, notorious godfather of the Chicago Mafia, had taken offense at Bobby's personal crusade against organized crime, and decided to keep tabs on his activities. Giancana was bolder. He tapped the attorney general's own telephone lines at the Justice Department in Washington, D.C.

Whether Giancana was also bugging Lawford's beachside home or Marilyn's house is not known. It is known that Giancana and Hoffa pooled information of vital importance to Mob interests. However, Sam Giancana may have had an even more diabolical method of keeping tabs on Bobby Kennedy's affair with Marilyn Monroe — the actress's friendship with Johnny Roselli.

Roselli was one of Giancana's right-hand men. Roselli had long represented the Mafia in their West Coast operations. Early on, organized crime had gained control of key Hollywood unions. Using the threat of labor trouble, the Mafia extorted millions of dollars in protection money from the motion-picture industry. Roselli would eventually serve time in jail for his part in this mob-led shakedown of the major motion picture studios.

The darkly handsome Roselli's purported job as a labor negotiator allowed him to move freely in Hollywood's upper echelon. Unaware of the true nature of Roselli's background, Marilyn dated him briefly.

Marilyn's friend, Jeanne Carmen, saw the actress and the mobster together on more than one occasion. "I met Roselli with Marilyn a couple of times. We had lunch together. They were being charming. That's all I know."

There is good reason to believe that Marilyn knew Giancana. One of Marilyn's acquaintances, songstress Phyllis McGuire of the McGuire Sisters, was the Mafia don's constant traveling companion. It would have been difficult for Marilyn to have seen McGuire without having encountered Giancana.

Giancana's shadow fell over Marilyn through yet a third Hollywood connection, Frank Sinatra. Marilyn and Sinatra had dated often during the late 50s and enjoyed a torrid rematch in 1960. Giancana and McGuire had frequently been guests at Sinatra's Lake Tahoe casino. The Chicago mobster even owned an interest in the casino for a time.

Because of Sinatra's involvement, the Cal-Neva was a popular watering hole with the Hollywood crowd. Many celebrities made it their stop over of choice when making a getaway to Tahoe for gambling and relaxation. One of these visitors was Marilyn Monroe. Her last visit to Cal-Neva — the week before her death — was rumored to have been horrific.

The story is sordid. According to witnesses, Giancana also had designs on the blond love goddess. The Chicago godfather is said to have taken advantage of Marilyn while she was drunk forcing her to have sex with him. The next day, repulsed and disgusted, the actress is rumored to have made an attempt on her own life.

Giancana was reported to be furious over Marilyn's reaction. He had ordered men killed for less.

THE PLOT TO KILL CASTRO

Since the focus of Mafia surveillance was Bobby Kennedy, Marilyn Monroe would not have appeared to be in danger from the Mob. However, there is reason to believe that the actress may have learned a deadly secret from Bobby during one of their more intimate moments. This secret concerned a combined Mafia-CIA plot to kill Cuba's staunchly anti-American leader, Fidel Castro.

With the round-the-clock bugging of her home, Marilyn's possession of this secret would have quickly become known to Hoffa, Giancana, and the other organized crime chiefs — as well as their cohorts in the CIA. If so, the movie star would have been viewed as a danger by the two organizations accused by Warren Report critics of conspiring to assassinate her former lover, Jack Kennedy, fifteen months later.

Recently declassified government records show that there was such a plot. Castro's overthrow of pro-American Cuban strongman Fulgencio Batista, had embarrassed the U.S. government. Within months, various branches of the CIA were generating plans for Castro's overthrow.

Although Castro's successful Communist takeover of Cuba embarrassed American government officials, it had a much more devastating effect on the Mafia. Cuba, not far off the U.S. mainland, was the nation's top playground. Gambling was legal; prostitution winked at. Under Batista, organized crime had enjoyed a virtual monopoly on the island's casinos and bordellos. The mob had raked in millions of dollars from their Cuban operations every week.

Aware of the mob's financial losses resulting from Castro's crackdown on their Cuban empire, the CIA approached the Mafia with a highly unconventional proposal. Through Robert A. Maheu, a former CIA operative, and private investigator for secretive multimillionaire Howard Hughes, Col. Sheffield Edwards, the head of the CIA's Office of Security, contacted Sam Giancana. If the Mafia would provide hitmen to take out Castro, the U.S. government would guarantee the return of Mafia casinos and cat houses.

It was an agreement that would benefit both parties. If the hitmen were caught, they would know only that their orders came from high up in the mob. They could never be connected with the U.S. government or the CIA in any way. If the hitmen were successful, Castro's death would stop organized crime's multi-million-dollar losses.

There was a chilling downside to the arrangement. The Mafia was now in possession of a proposal allowing them to blackmail not just individual politicians but the entire U.S. government. Significantly, four years later, when a crusading member of the attorney general's staff, Edward V. Hanrahan, jailed Giancana for refusal to testify before a federal grand jury, Giancana was set free in a few months. Hanrahan's superiors in the Justice Department had decided, in effect, to drop all charges. High-ranking Justice Department officials have since charged that the Mafia boss was set free because of pressure from the CIA, who feared that Giancana might reveal the federal government's complicity in a blatantly illegal plot to assassinate the head of another government.

To the individual who knew of this agreement, the knowledge was both powerful and dangerous. Two of the nation's most secretive and influential organizations stood to come under close public scrutiny if their involvement with each other was ever revealed. Neither organization had stopped at murder to gain their ends before.

For an outsider like Marilyn Monroe, possession of such a secret might have been deadly. Significantly, not long before she died, Marilyn showed me her personal diary, whose most recent entries chronicled her involvement with Bobby. One began: "Bobby told me he was going to have Castro murdered by some mobsters." Marilyn's knowledge of the Castro plot, her rejection of Sam Giancana's sexual advances, Jimmy Hoffa's obsession with ruining Robert Kennedy, and the Mafia's surveillance of the superstar may have been motives for Marilyn's murder.

But there are some who believe the motives for Marilyn's murder to be much less exotic than Mafia-CIA assassination plots , sexual jealousy and consuming obsessions. Some who have studied her death believe the motives behind her demise lay much closer to home in the motion picture industry.

FILE #7

Marilyn and "Friends"

Thousands of loyal fans mobbed Marilyn Monroe's every public appearance. Millions of men dreamed only of spending a single night in her arms. People everywhere wanted to be introduced to her, to get to know her, to be her friend.

Yet, paradoxically, Marilyn Monroe was a very lonely woman. In the summer of 1962, the glamorous love goddess was often depressed because she had no date for the weekend. Surrounded constantly by people who wanted to exploit her and her position, she had very few close friends she could trust.

Marilyn's confidante, Terry Moore, knows firsthand how quickly the phony and greedy move in on an actor or actress who becomes a success. "It's really hard to know who's your friend when you become a big star. Everybody wants to be. Most of them are all-around bloodsuckers. It's really difficult."

Abused and betrayed by the men in her life, many of whom she had met and worked with at the studios, Marilyn had increasingly withdrawn into a solitary existence. Hidden behind dark glasses, with a pale, listless face that have associated with her vivacious screen image, the star rarely left her secluded Brentwood home. During the last critical weeks of Marilyn's life, her personal contacts were limited to only half a dozen people.

This group is important, because Marilyn saw each of them almost every day. They were a dominant influence during the events that preceded her death. Whatever the star's mental state at the time of her death, every participant in Marilyn's intimate inner circle had directly affected it in some way. There are journalists who believe that the members of this select group harbored several potential motives for murder.

Two traits in common were held by everyone in this group. First, they all depended on Marilyn for some — or all — of their livelihood. She, in turn, depended on each of them to take care of her personal and professional needs. Marilyn may have felt these people trustworthy because they had a vested interest in her continued welfare.

Second, several of them came into Marilyn's life only during the last few months of her life. Curiously, they had all known each other since the late 1940s. This smaller component consisted of four members: Milton "Mickey" Rudin, Marilyn's attorney; Dr. Ralph Greenson, her psychiatrist; Eunice Murray, her housekeeper, and Norman Jeffries II, her handyman.

The Byzantine relationship shared by the group's members rivaled the contrived plot of a bad spy novel. Attorney Rudin was married to Dr. Greenson's sister, Elizabeth. Greenson purchased his house from Mrs. Murray, who was periodically in his employ for more than a decade. Jeffries, ostensibly a handyman, was Mrs. Murray's son-in-law.

The Rudin/Greenson Connection

Rudin may have been the key figure in this group, though he would be the actress's attorney for only two brief months before her death. The influence he exerted on Marilyn's life was far greater than that warranted by his brief associaton with her.

Marilyn first consulted Rudin in late 1961. Not long before, when Twentieth Century–Fox, her longtime studio, initiated a sequence of events that would see her fired off the set of what would have been her last film, *Something's Got to Give*, Marilyn phoned Frank Sinatra for advice. The singer recommended Rudin, his personal attorney. Marilyn called Sinatra because she had heard him brag about his wily attorney and hoped Rudin could help her.

Rudin is a curiously overlooked figure for someone who played such a leading role during Marilyn's final days. The attorney is mentioned only fleetingly by biographers, and rarely approached by television news journalists.

Those who have investigated Marilyn's death have questioned Sinatra's recommendation of an attorney rather than a power-broker agent, or manager, with plenty of Hollywood savvy and muscle. For those who have questioned the recommendation, the answers add a whole new dimension to our understanding of the life — and death — of Marilyn Monroe.

A somewhat mysterious figure, Rudin seems to have deliberately maintained a low profile. Like his client Frank Sinatra, Rudin has sued journalists whose work he felt cast him in a negative light. If such a litigious attitude reflects a deliberate strategy — and some think it does — the strategy seems to work; Rudin's name has rarely appeared in print.

Rudin is a far more powerful figure than most people suspect. His heavyweight political acquaintances have included Senator John Tunney, Vice President Spiro Agnew,

President John Fitzgerald Kennedy, Vice President Hubert Humphrey, President Ronald Reagan, and a host of others. For some time, Rudin and Sinatra rented a townhouse on Embassy Row in Washington, D.C. The duo's frequent bashes drew a host of the city's most glittering political figures, and added to their own circle of influential contacts.

Rudin's roster of entertainment industry contacts was equally extensive: Jack Warner, Jimmy Van Heusen, Tommy Sands, Henry Rogers, Warren Cowen, Alan King, Mia Farrow, Richard Conte, Dean Martin, and dozens more.

His list of high-powered acquaintances also included a few that were not so savory. According to Sinatra biographer Kitty Kelley, Rudin openly admitted to one congressional committee that Sinatra knew "Gaetano Luchese, Sam Giancana, and Joe Fischetti," among others. Presumably, Rudin also knew those whom his client knew. A transcript in FBI files has mobster Gregory DePalma mentioning Rudin by name in connection with an illegal transaction. Rudin also knew and worked with Vegas attorney Harry Claiborne who later became the first federal judge to be convicted of tax evasion.

Rudin's former wife, Elizabeth, has attributed his involvement with organized crime figures to Sinatra. "I don't know if Frank is Mafia or not," she told one journalist, "but I do know that he was involved with some very unethical people. Mickey always left the house to find a pay phone to talk to Frank about some things."

Interestingly, Los Angeles legal insiders say Rudin's contact with underworld figures began prior to his relationship to Sinatra. As a rising young attorney, Rudin's abilities are said to have earned him referrals from one of the region's most influential law firms, whose clients included an intriguing mix of high-profile celebrities and others, some involved in criminal cases.

Rudin's own name has been linked with illegal kickbacks

and profit-skimming in connection with the bankruptcy of a theater that grossed over five million dollars in its first and only year of operation. In April, 1980, Assistant U.S. Attorney Nathaniel Akerman filed papers charging that "evidence . . . clearly provided several avenues of investigation . . . including the involvement of Frank Sinatra, Mickey Rudin, and Jilly Rizzo in skimming of receipts." The U.S. Attorney's office further alleged that "there was tape-recorded evidence that Mickey Rudin, Sinatra's manager and lawyer, also received five thousand dollars."

Then the case took a curious turn. The key witness against Rudin and Sinatra, Louis Pacella, a man listed in the FBI files as a known member of the Mafia, refused to testify under oath even when granted immunity. Pacella chose to spend eighteen months in jail for contempt of court rather than reveal what he knew. Unable to proceed without Pacella's testimony, the Justice Department was forced to forego prosecution.

Rudin knew how to use his wide-ranging network of acquaintances. When the House Select Committee on Organized Crime subpoenaed Sinatra, Rudin flew to New York and pulled strings. Within a week, the committee withdrew the subpoena, which would have required the singer to testify under oath, and extended to him an "invitation" instead. When Sinatra had to unload his famed Cal/Neva Lodge in Lake Tahoe or face public disgrace, Rudin called Jack Warner, president of Warner Brothers, the giant motion picture studio. In just days, Rudin negotiated a complex deal that saved his client financially and publicly: Warner traded its own stock for Sinatra's Cal/Neva stock, received the exclusive right to Sinatra's motion picture services, and granted him a vicepresidency in the Warner Brothers corporation.

All of the preceding may explain why Rudin was the man Frank Sinatra advised Marilyn to contact. Sinatra's advice seems to have been sound; by the time Rudin had finished with Fox, not only had Marilyn been reinstated, she had a two-picture, one million dollar contract — a healthy increase from her former salary of $100,000.

With Sinatra, Rudin's versatile talents seem to have controlled significantly more territory than the usual attorney-client relationship. Over the years, Rudin came to act as Sinatra's agent, personal manager, business manager, investment counselor, and even business partner. When the Italian crooner bought stock or purchased a business, Rudin was usually a partner with him.

Rudin's intricate financial association with his client seems to have paid dividends. On one 1976 transaction, the two men purchased and then sold stock in the Del Webb Corp., which owned several Nevada casinos. Rudin is said to have realized $1,200,000 profit on a $300,000 investment, and he probably also received a commission on Sinatra's end of the transaction. For simply handling the sale of Sinatra's Warner Brothers stock to the Kenney Co. for $22,000,000, the astute attorney reaped a fee of $1,500,000.

This is the man who became Marilyn's attorney. By July, 1962, Rudin was negotiating numerous show business projects for Marilyn. His successful negotiation with Fox was apparently only the beginning.

Those who have studied Rudin's actions during the last days of Marilyn's life have an important question. Did Rudin envision playing as central a role in Marilyn's artistic and financial life as he did in Frank Sinatra's? Rudin refuses to discuss his relationship with Marilyn.

Although he has remained silent, there is reason to think Rudin may have indirectly given us the answer to these queries. Shortly before her death, Marilyn decided to change her will. Rudin told one journalist he deliberately kept postponing the appointment because, in his opinion, the star was too emotionally unstable to make competent decisions about her own life.

"I avoided the subject . . . After all, was she of sound mind?" Rudin also described her as "obviously deeply ill."

Yet on the day of the actress's death, Rudin told reporters, "She appeared to be happy; she was in perfect physical condition, was feeling great." An internal Fox memorandum of meetings between studio representatives and Rudin, dated June 8, reveals that less than two months earlier the attorney had assured the Fox representatives that "She was ready, willing, and able to go to work."

There is a large discrepancy here. Rudin postponed Marilyn's new will because of his concerns about her emotional stability, yet he obviously sold her stability and enthusiasm to the studio and the media. Outside of his interest as a lawyer to attain the most desirable contract for his client and present her in the most flattering manner, was he setting the stage for manipulating the star's finances? Was he coldly trying to push a vulnerable, but talented, woman into emotionally draining obligations in order to maintain her dependence on his negotiating ability . . . with an eye to controlling her future which, obviously, represented his long-term financial interests? Or, if he believed his upbeat remarks to Fox that "she was ready and willing to work," was he deliberately postponing her new will with false pretenses of concern because of another approach he thought more advisable?

Far more disturbing, there were other reasons Mickey Rudin may not have been a disinterested party. The circles in which he operated provided him with access to two different camps — the Kennedys and the Mafia — whose intentions toward the superstar were far from benign.

DR. RALPH GREENSON

Dr. Ralph Greenson, Ph.D., M.D., Marilyn's psychoanalyst, had more in common with his brother-in-law Mickey Rudin than most people suspect. Both were high-powered professionals of internationally recognized repute. Greenson, a respected psychiatrist, and a UCLA professor trained in Vienna at the institute founded by Sigmund Freud, had been Chief of the Combat Fatigue Section of the Army Air Corps during World War II.

Both men had met Marilyn the same way: through Frank Sinatra. Just as Sinatra had recommended Rudin to help Marilyn untangle her legal problems with Fox over the film *Something's Got to Give*, he recommended Greenson to help the star through her emotional difficulties with the film *Let's Make Love*. Clearly, both men must have made an impression on Sinatra.

Marilyn began seeing Greenson in the early months of 1960 during one of her many collapses while making the film. Whatever his psychiatric approach, Greenson was somehow able to help Marilyn pull it together and successfully complete the film. The psychiatrist apparently had similar luck when called clandestinely to the set to help her through similar problems during the filming of *The Misfits*.

In late 1961, permanently back in L. A. after her marriage to Arthur Miller had failed, Marilyn began to consult Greenson regularly. Apparently New York experiences had precipitated a turn for the worse in her mental state. Before she had needed Greenson to help prop up her insecurities only while she was making movies. Soon Marilyn's need for him would become a twice-daily addiction.

Greenson has been much criticized by both the press and his own colleagues for the way he handled Marilyn's case. At the beginning, his efforts were successful, enabling the actress to complete two difficult films. As time progressed, her condition seemed to deteriorate. What went wrong?

The answer is that after Marilyn returned to L.A., Greenson changed his course of treatment. His new way of working with the actress extended well beyond the limits of the normal patient-doctor relationship.

Greenson decided that Marilyn did not need psychoanalysis, the typical treatment of the time, but "supportive therapy."

What constituted Greenson's "supportive therapy"? Greenson removed all limits on his time for Marilyn. He was available to see the star whenever she needed, for as long as she needed. Sessions were held at either his or Marilyn's home in order to protect Marilyn's privacy.

Greenson defended his unorthodox therapeutic procedure in the *Medical Tribune* of October 24, 1973, saying, "It is controversial, I know that. Nevertheless, I have practiced for some thirty-five years, and I did what I thought was best, particularly after other methods of treatment apparently hadn't touched her one iota."

But there was another aspect of Greenson's relationship with the sex goddess that seemed to violate several of the most sacred rules of his profession. He took Marilyn into his own home and made her a surrogate member of his family. The actress spent afternoons, evenings, even whole days with the Greenson household.

Greenson disputed this interpretation. "She was only permitted to come into my home essentially as a friend of my wife or daughter." But critics of Greenson's treatment feel this defense avoids the real issue. Greenson's wife and daughter had met Marilyn through him; she was certainly there with his approval. The distinction seems minor at best.

Even Greenson had second thoughts about the approach he took with Marilyn. "I let her come into my house. . . .

I did it for a purpose," he told the *Medical Tribune*. "My particular method of treatment for this particular woman was, I thought, essential at that time. But it failed. She died."

By loosening the traditional doctor-patient restraints, Greenson made Marilyn feel that she was free to call him at any hour of the day or night. Soon, she did. "Marilyn," Greenson told one friend, "felt at times she was unimportant and insignificant. As she becomes more anxious, she begins to act like an orphan, a waif."

Greenson would "try to help her not to be so lonely and therefore escape into drugs or get involved with destructive people." Within a short time, the psychiatrist found that keeping Marilyn from feeling lonely meant spending a large portion of every day, and some nights, talking her through her problems. "I had become a prisoner of a form of treatment that I thought was correct for her, but almost impossible for me," Greenson wrote. "At times I felt I couldn't go on with this."

Instead of helping the star, however, Greenson's method of treatment seemed to backfire. In the first four months of 1962, her condition worsened visibly. Marilyn became as completely dependent on her psychiatrist as she was on sleeping pills.

Jeanne Carmen, Marilyn's actress friend, noticed Marilyn's deterioration under Greenson's care. "I never liked what was going on with him. I didn't think he was helping her. I thought he was making Marilyn worse. After she started going to Dr. Greenson, she kept getting more despondent and more depressed."

Another who agrees is Terry Moore: "I think Marilyn needed friends much more than a psychiatrist. I think that between the psychiatrist and the drugs, she started trusting people less and less — which is a shame — because there were people around her who cared about her."

Soon Greenson was the only person who could pull Marilyn together for public appearances and motion picture work. She began taking his advice about everything. By the summer of 1962, Greenson would be negotiating with Twentieth Century–Fox on Marilyn's behalf, much as his brother-in-law Mickey Rudin had done for Sinatra.

At the time of his negotiations with Fox, Greenson's influence over Marilyn had grown so strong that he told the studio executives, who were concerned over her chronic lateness and failures to appear for filming, he could personally guarantee Marilyn's appearance and performance. According to a memorandum generated from one such meeting, Greenson said he stood ready to "indemnify with his professional reputation that she could be at work every day . . . for normal shooting, even if he had to lead her to the studio." Studio representatives stated: "Dr. Greenson claimed he had done this in the case of *The Misfits*. . . Dr. Greenson advised us that he would be able to get his patient to go along with any reasonable request."

Greenson's guarantee announced an unshakable confidence in the extent of his influence over Marilyn. His "supportive therapy" was dominating her emotional life.

Some have criticized his degree of involvement in Marilyn's life. Psychiatrists do not normally undertake such aggressively interventionistic roles in a client's life. Rarely are statements guaranteeing a patient's behavior made, unless under extraordinary circumstances.

Even Greenson realized that appearances were against him. In the same Fox memo quoted above, Greenson defends himself to studio representatives. The writer of the memo said: "He did not want us to deem his relationship as a Svengali one." "But in the next breath," the writer continued, "the psychiatrist admitted that . . . 'he, in fact, could persuade her to do anything he wanted.' "

Curiously, the memo writer adds, "I said that it appeared that he would have to be the one to determine . . . what scenes she would or wouldn't do, what rushes were favorable or unfavorable, and all the other creative decisions that had to be made. . . . Dr. Greenson seemed ready to assume responsibility in all creative areas." Apparently Greenson, like Rudin, was willing to go that extra mile for his client.

Greenson was willing to be of assistance to his patient in other areas as well. Feeling that Marilyn needed someone with a background as a psychiatric nurse to keep an eye on her during her more despondent moments, he recommended that she hire Eunice Murray (whom Mickey Rudin also knew) as a housekeeper-factotum.

Not all of Marilyn's friends took a positive view of the way that members of Greenson's circle were beginning to take up daily roles in her life. Jeanne Carmen says: "I don't know why he was putting all his key people in there. I think a lot of stuff goes back to Dr. Greenson. I was told that he sent a bill after her death for visits like every day or three or four times a day. This is lunacy. I thought he was just taking her money and having a good time on it."

Greenson's own statement, filed with the probate court shortly after her death, shows that in the last few months of her life, he was devoting four and five hour sessions to Marilyn almost every day. On the morning of the star's death, Greenson would reportedly be the first one to reach her lifeless body. He would also be the one to tell Jack Clemmons an account of that night's events — an account that, with some variations, became the "official" story of Marilyn's demise.

Some of those who have studied Marilyn's last months believe they can explain the unusual degree of Greenson's involvement in Marilyn's life: they feel that the psychiatrist had fallen in love with his patient. Every other warm-blooded male who met the screen goddess had, except for Lawrence Olivier. It woud be remarkable if Ralph Greenson hadn't.

After Marilyn's death, Greenson retreated behind the barrier of client confidentiality and refused all public interviews about his relationship with her. The psychiatrist broke this silence only once, in an interview he gave writer Maurice Zolotow. But Greenson regretted the decision, and in the *Medical Tribune* article accused Zolotow of inventing portions of the printed interview.

Dr. Ralph Greenson died in 1979. Recently, some shocking allegations have come to light. They suggest that the psychiatrist may have played a more important, perhaps central, role in the death of Marilyn Monroe. One of these accusations would be made by James Hall, an ambulance driver who claimed to have been summoned to the death scene. The other was made in *The Strange Death of Marilyn Monroe*, by Frank A. Capell.

EUNICE MURRAY

To most people, Eunice Murray was simply Marilyn's housekeeper. But Murray had been brought in at the request of Ralph Greenson to keep watch over the increasingly depressed star. The sixty-year-old Murray, who ironically would outlive her employer by more than thirty years, had worked for Dr. Greenson in other households.

Greenson had known Eunice Murray for more than fifteen years. The psychiatrist had even bought her Santa Monica home when she and her husband divorced in the late forties. The two had formed a close bond over the years.

Although Marilyn paid Murray's salary, the older woman's loyalties were to Greenson. Murray later made little secret of the fact that she reported back to Greenson about the actress's activities.

At the time, Jeanne Carmen sensed that Murray wasn't the simple housekeeper-companion she pretended to be. "I wasn't crazy about Mrs. Murray. I don't know what I didn't like about her, but I just thought she was rather sneaky. When she was there, I tried to avoid going around. And Marilyn was getting very suspicious of her. She just started saying, 'Mrs. Murray is acting very weird,' and 'I wonder what's going on?' " Marilyn does not appear to have known about Murray's background, and Dr. Greenson's motives for placing the woman in her household is hard to discern. The star told one friend she felt as if she was being "spied on" in her own home.

The housekeeper-nurse's influence over Marilyn grew almost as rapidly as Dr. Greenson's had. When, at the psychiatrist's suggestion, Marilyn decided to buy a house, Murray was the one who helped pick it out. The house, not far from Greenson's, was just like his, Spanish style.

Mrs. Murray was there with Marilyn during the critical hours surrounding her death. The housekeeper-nurse could have answered many important questions about the events of that night. But her loyalty to Dr. Greenson prevented her from speaking for almost thirty years. Murray's revelations, when she finally spoke, turned the case on its head.

On the Friday before her death, Marilyn had told friends that she was going to take charge of her own life, and get rid of several people whose presence she no longer considered beneficial. One of these was Eunice Murray. Whether the housekeeper-nurse was aware that the actress was preparing to fire her is not known. But within twenty-four hours, Marilyn would be dead.

Private investigator Milo Speriglio has since learned that

a few days later, Eunice Murray left the U.S. on a six-month trip to Europe, and was totally unavailable to the media for comment.

NORMAN JEFFRIES II

When Marilyn needed a handyman to help with the remodeling and landscaping of her new house, Murray suggested her son-in-law, a young man with the unlikely moniker of Norman Jeffries II. Norman had also known Dr. Greenson for some time. Greenson added his recommendation, and Norman soon was around almost every day, working at one chore or another. On the morning of Marilyn's death, Jeffries replaced the pane of glass in her bedroom that Greenson said he had broken in order to gain access to the star's dead body.

Norman's duties reputedly included interior decorating, guarding the gate when visitors were expected, and overseeing the workmen. For this relatively untaxing work, he received $180 a week, excellent pay in the early 1960s especially for a young man. Unfortunately for him, this sinecure was about to come to an end. Norman was one of those Marilyn decided to put out of her life only a few days before her untimely death.

PAT NEWCOMB

Marilyn's most complex relationship at the time may have been with her publicist, Patricia Newcomb. By turns the two women seem to have acted out the roles of friends, sisters, rivals, business associates, and — if some rumors are to be believed — lovers. Though their relationship was at times volatile, the two women were very close during the final months of the actress's life. Newcomb even spent the night before Marilyn's death at the star's home, reportedly leaving only in the afternoon a few hours before the death occurred.

Marilyn had met Pat Newcomb on the set of *Bus Stop*. Newcomb worked for public relations whiz Arthur Jacobs whose organization handled a number of responsibilities, including motion picture publicity, for Twentieth Century-Fox.

At first the two women hit it off, but by the end of filming, Marilyn refused to speak with Newcomb. Marilyn later admitted the tiff had been caused by a mistaken case of jealousy. The star thought Newcomb had become a romantic rival for a man in whom Marilyn was interested.

Four years later, Marilyn forgave Newcomb. The two made up, and Newcomb became the actress's personal press representative. Though Newcomb had other clients, her directive from Fox and Jacobs was clear: handle the care and feeding of that oh! so inflammable actress, Marilyn Monroe. Newcomb was an early "spin doctor;" her duty was to keep as many of the mercurial star's indiscretions out of the papers as she could, and to put as positive a spin as possible on the rest.

Though Marilyn insisted Newcomb be assigned to her, the relationship between the two women continued to blow hot and cold. Sometimes, they were the best of friends; at other moments, they engaged in screaming matches with each other. Usually the fights were over men, often provoked by Marilyn's unfounded jealousy of Newcomb.

But there was one jealousy that wasn't unfounded. Pat Newcomb was deeply attracted to Bobby Kennedy. There are several reasons to believe that Bobby may have begun to return that affection toward the end of his relationship with the star.

Could Newcomb, the cool, professional publicist, have fallen just as deeply for Bobby as Marilyn had? Dean

Martin's former wife, Jeanne, told one British reporter that she had: "Pat got too far involved; she was deeply in love with Bobby Kennedy."

As the negative publicity surrounding Marilyn's dismissal from the set of *Something's Got to Give* continued to mount during the early summer of 1962, Newcomb was at Marilyn's house almost every day. The publicist was there partly in her professional capacity, and partly as one more emotional support thought necessary to prop up the unstable superstar. Sometimes Newcomb would spend the night when Eunice Murray could not be there.

Around the end of July or the beginning of August, Marilyn seems to have become convinced she and Newcomb were romantic rivals. On the afternoon before Marilyn's death, the two women are said to have quarreled again. Dr. Ralph Greenson later told a professional group that the actress was "angry and resentful toward her friend Pat that night." Others, including Eunice Murray, confirm this account.

Some people believe the fight was a minor one over Marilyn's resentment of Newcomb's ability to sleep soundly while the anxious actress paced the floors through the night. Others believe the fight began when Newcomb took Bobby Kennedy's side, and tried to dissuade the star from her threatened Monday press conference. Still others believe that the fight was caused by Marilyn's jealousy over Bobby Kennedy.

The two women parted on angry terms. By the next morning, it would be too late to smooth over their quarrel the way they had so many times before. No one knows whether Newcomb's boss, Arthur Jacobs, was aware of this fight. Curiously, on the afternoon of August 5, only hours after Marilyn's death had been reported, Jacobs fired his long-time associate.

After Marilyn's funeral, Newcomb withdrew behind a wall of silence, refusing all public comment, as had numerous others from Marilyn's inner circle.

Many believe that her silence still hides many secrets — and suspect the discreetly silent publicist is in a better position than most to dispel the mystery that surrounds her client's death. Why does Newcomb keep silent? Jeanne Carmen is one of those who would like to know. "I don't know why Pat hasn't come forth. I'm sure she knows more than anyone else, because she was there all the time. I'm sure she could tell a lot."

Several eyewitnesses, including Eunice Murray, would later place Newcomb at Marilyn's house on the night of her death. One piece of television news footage even showed her exiting the house early on the morning after the death. Yet when Sergeant Jack Clemmons first arrived on the scene, Newcomb was nowhere to be seen. To this day, Newcomb denies that she was there.

However, Newcomb's memory does not seem to be very reliable about the presence of another key figure there on that fateful night. Several eyewitnesses and government insiders, including former LAPD Chief Daryl Gates, have placed Bobby Kennedy in Los Angeles on the afternoon before Marilyn's body was discovered. Yet Newcomb and other Kennedy loyalists have denied the possibility that he was in town.

Newcomb's memory also seems to fail her about Bobby's presence at Marilyn's home that night. Marilyn's neighbors and Mrs. Murray have since told journalists that the attorney general did pay a visit to the actress's house on the afternoon of August 4. But Newcomb once insisted that: "Bobby did not talk to Marilyn that night. It never happened. Bobby was not even in the state. . . . I know that as a fact." Asked for her source on this information, Newcomb's reply seemed to undercut her own statement. "I know that from him," she told an astonished journalist.

Milo Speriglio also confirms that, like Eunice Murray, Newcomb left on an "extended European vacation immediately after Marilyn's death and was unavailable for comment." The publicist's first stop was Hyannis, the Kennedy clan's Cape Cod vacation home — but an unusual locale for a departure to the continent.

Shortly after Newcomb's return, she was offered a position in Washington with the United States Information Agency. Her office was adjacent to that of her friend (and some say lover) Robert Kennedy, the attorney general. Many have pointed to this appointment as the way Bobby rewarded someone who put loyalty to the Kennedy interests above loyalty to her client, Marilyn Monroe.

Paula Strasberg

Marilyn's acting coach, Paula Strasberg, had a distinguished reputation in New York theatrical circles. The Strasbergs were a theatrical family. Paula's husband, Lee Strasberg, was a world-renowned acting instructor. Their daughter Susan would become a famous actress.

The Strasbergs had met Marilyn when she moved to New York in 1955. The star sought out Lee Strasberg. Tired of her dumb blond image, insecure about her acting abilities, painfully aware that she had never received any training in her craft, Marilyn hoped that Lee Strasberg could help her find herself as an actress.

Strasberg was the founder of the famed Actors Studio, where he taught a new approach to the craft called "method acting." Previous acting instructors had focused on the externals of acting. They taught their students how to simulate the expressions and movements of anger, joy, grief, surprise or whatever reaction the scene called for. Strasberg taught actors and actresses to focus on the internal aspects of acting: to try to identify with the character so completely that when they are on stage, they actually become that character for the performance. Method actors and actresses are deeply concerned with finding their character's motivations, and then reacting realistically from those motivations.

Lee Strasberg may have considered Marilyn his greatest challenge. Untrained, unskilled, she had gone on to guarrantee the success of three critically acclaimed musical classics: *Gentlemen Prefer Blonds*, *How to Marry a Millionaire*, and *There's No Business Like Show Business*. Marilyn was a star, audiences loved her, but could she really act? Strasberg thought so. The acting teacher was a perceptive man. He appears to have seen more deeply into Marilyn than most.

Strasberg seems to have seen the incandescent talent that, even in its raw, untrained form, had made Marilyn Monroe a star. "I saw that what she looked like was not what she really was, and what was going on inside was not what was going on outside and that always means there may be something there to work with."

Strasberg was right. Several years later he would say: "I have worked with hundreds and hundreds of actors, and there are only two that stand out way above the rest: Marlon Brando and Marilyn Monroe."

Strasberg's Actors Studio was the training ground for aspiring actors during the 1950s and 1960s. During this period, it generated most of the box office stars: Paul Newman, Maureen Stapleton, Marlon Brando, James Dean, Steve McQueen, Anne Jackson, Shelley Winters, and others. At the time she was studying with Strasberg, Marilyn would have had the opportunity to work with most of these actors and actresses. The star was getting the crash course in acting that she felt she needed — and from the best practitioners the country had to offer.

Sensing Marilyn's vulnerability and loneliness, Lee Strasberg took Marilyn into his family. Never having had a real family of her own, the actress eagerly made herself a part of the Strasberg household as completely as she had with the Goddards, and later, with the Greensons. During much of her stay in the Big Apple, Marilyn would practically live at the Strasbergs.

Paula Strasberg, a large, matronly, Jewish woman, took Marilyn under her wing the way a duck does a stray duckling. The star, whose own mother had tried to kill her, felt her heart go out to the older woman. Paula was sympathetic, listened to Marilyn's troubles, offered friendly advice — she was the mother Marilyn had never had. Paula soon became an indispensable part of the insecure star's life.

Marilyn repaid the Strasberg's support many times during their association. She purchased plane tickets, gave their son her car when she returned to Hollywood, bought food, and loaned money. When Lee, who liked to play the stock market, experienced heavy losses — which he often did — Marilyn covered his losses.

After a year under Lee Strasberg's tutelage, Marilyn felt confident enough in her acting abilities to begin her next motion picture, *Bus Stop*. She also decided to end her relationship with her long-term acting coach Natasha Lytess.

Marilyn had met Lytess in 1948, when the older woman was head drama coach at Columbia Studios. Over the years, the two women were thought to have a strange and secretive relationship, giving rise to persistent rumors of a lesbian affair.

Lytess offered the aspiring young actress free acting lessons. The inexperienced Marilyn, desperate for guidance, came to depend heavily on the older acting coach. Soon the divorced Lytess and her three-year-old daughter had moved in with Marilyn.

Many of those who knew Marilyn at the time felt Lytess tried to dominate the younger woman and run her life. They claimed Lytess appeared to be jealous of the men in Marilyn's life, and would quarrel over them bitterly with her pupil. But Marilyn lacked the confidence to cope with the complexities of Hollywood life on her own. Marilyn felt she needed the older woman to help her steer a wise course through the difficult decisions her increasing success as a performer thrust upon her.

By 1956, Marilyn was growing restless under the older woman's constant control. Many of the star's New York friends were also telling her that she had outgrown Lytess. When the opportunity to make a serious picture with acclaimed director Joshua Logan arose, Marilyn knew there was no longer a place in her life for Lytess.

Marilyn was still insecure about her own abilities. *Bus Stop* would be a serious movie, and she would be venturing into a serious role for the first time since studying under Lee Strasberg. She wanted to show herself off to best advantage.

Marilyn begged Lee Strasberg to come with her to L.A., even for a short time, to see her through the beginning of the film. Strasberg's commitments to his studio and students made this impossible. But Paula was available.

Paula Strasberg had experience both as an actress and as an acting coach. She had taught at the Actors Studio. Even more importantly, she had spent years absorbing the craft of acting from one of its chief exponents, Lee Strasberg. Having Paula was almost the same as having Lee.

The Strasbergs' services came high. If Marilyn wanted Paula around for comfort and counsel between films, she had to pay for those services. The Strasbergs' studio in New

York was an artistic success, but not necessarily a commercial one. Lee was often forced to draw money in advance in order to help keep it going.

Paula Strasberg accompanied Marilyn back to Hollywood at a salary that would sometimes reach two thousand dollars a week. By the time the two women reached L.A., they had decided that in addition to being Marilyn's acting coach, Paula Strasberg would also be on the set to help advise the star when she was uncertain about makeup, lighting, camera angles, the reading of a line.

The film's director and producer did not welcome this news with open arms. After some negotiation, Paula agreed to remain in the dressing room and off the set. But Marilyn still sought her advice in everything, and the older woman does not seem to have been reluctant to give it.

Eight years later, by the time Marilyn began filming *Something's Got to Give*, the black-garbed, heavily bejeweled Paula had made her way to the set. The film's director, producer, and staff all made their displeasure known.

Paula, like Natasha Lytess, was becoming more of a liability than an asset. Marilyn and others in her circle seem to have been aware of this. When the star's attorney, Mickey Rudin, tried to placate Twentieth Century–Fox executives after she had been fired off her final picture, the first thing he asked was whether the studio would like to "lay down conditions regarding Mrs. Strasberg."

A few days before her death, the studio would reinstate Marilyn in *Something's Got to Give*. That Friday, the star would tell Paula Strasberg that she no longer needed the services of an acting coach. Paula was to return to New York on a ticket that Marilyn had purchased for her.

Lee and Paula Strasberg were among the major beneficiaries of Marilyn's will. According to her attorney, Mickey Rudin, and several other close friends, the actress had made an appointment to change her will the following Monday. Death would prevent Marilyn from keeping that appointment.

Some journalists have slyly hinted that the Strasbergs might have been implicated in Marilyn's death — that they may have killed her for financial gain. If anyone had wanted to kill Marilyn over the money they were to receive in her will, they were due for a disappointment: ironically, Marilyn Monroe died nearly broke. The expense of maintaining all her doctors, coaches, attorneys, makeup men, hairdressers, household help, and a dozen other hangers-on during the months between films, and after *Something's Got to Give* had shut down production, had drained the star's bank accounts dry.

Marilyn's assets at the time of her death were practically worthless. Many years later, with the advent of cable television and videocassette sales, and an array of lucrative licensing deals, money started pouring into her estate. Paula Strasberg had passed away by then, and Lee did not live long enough to enjoy his wealth. But a young actress, Anna Mizrahi, whom Lee Strasberg married after Paula's death, enjoys, with her two sons, the millions generated annually by Marilyn's estate. Incredibly, Marilyn Monroe's estate earns more money now than Marilyn did when she was alive.

BAD ADVICE

Marilyn's life was full of ironies. But there is one tragic irony that is worse than all the rest. In the final months of her life when Marilyn most needed friends and support, all of those upon whom she relied seemed to have lost sight of her as a person. Instead, they blindly pursued their own agendas and manipulated the actress for their own ends.

Actor Alex D'Arcy had his doubts about this circle of people. "She was surrounded by people who took advantage of her. And she was badly advised. She listened to certain people too much. That's why she got into so much trouble. Her fights with her studio and what she did after that made me believe she was badly advised."

Jealousy, greed, the lust for power were typical traits possessed by this inner circle of "friends" surrounding Marilyn in the last days of July 1962. Although each of these traits could be a motive for crime, it is hard to believe that any of Marilyn's inner circle would have committed murder, or been actively involved in a cover-up. Over the years, however, journalists have implicated all members of this group in either Marilyn's demise or its subsequent cover-up.

FILE #8

Marilyn vs. Fox

For years, those who sought to shore up the official verdict of suicide in the death of Marilyn Monroe have suggested that the making of her ill-fated last film, *Something's Got to Give*, caused her demise. They may be right, but for reasons other than those they think.

The party line — which later became part of the official — story, claims that Marilyn was despondent about her dismissal from the film and her inability to find work as a result of her reputation for lateness. Her death by suicide was the consequence of her depression. Those who knew Marilyn best believe that nothing could be further from the truth. Offers for motion pictures, television appearances, and even her own Las Vegas stage production were rolling in. Twentieth Century–Fox, the studio that had fired her, found out that it couldn't get along without her, and had already agreed to reinstate her in the film.

Some of those who have studied the actress's death believe it is possible the film killed her, but not as a result of depression or despondency. Instead, they claim that the complex financial and legal difficulties that the studio was having at the time supplied a half-dozen motives for murder. Marilyn's death might have materially benefitted a number of people.

THE STUDIO

In 1962, Twentieth Century–Fox, the studio where Marilyn had been a reigning star for more than a decade, was undergoing the worst financial crisis in its history. Many motion picture studios were. The combined blows of the increasingly dominant television networks and the forced divestitures of motion picture theaters under an antitrust ruling were causing devastating declines in the studios' annual revenues.

Added to these factors was the sudden crumbling of the studio system and the rise of the "star" system. A series of California Supreme Court verdicts freed most major motion picture stars from long-term contracts, forcing studios to bid for the services of top-name actors. Salaries rose astronomically. Caught between a rock and a hard place, most studios changed managements and ownerships. Smaller studios (Republic and Monogram) folded their tents and vanished. Fox was hit harder than most studios. Fortunately, however, it still had some assets.

One of these assets was the ground the studio stood on. Fox had been located miles outside the suburbs of Los Angeles, in the middle of farmland, when it first opened up for business. But over the ensuing half-century the city had grown out around it, and now the land the studio occupied was worth many millions of dollars.

A recently elected board of directors voted unanimously to raze most of the studio lot and auction it for development. This entailed the destruction of many priceless stages and sets where historic motion pictures had been made. Throughout the making of *Something's Got to Give*, bulldozers would plow under two-thirds of the studio lot. Marilyn's last picture would be the old Twentieth Century–Fox's final film as well.

Today the gleaming concrete towers of Century City rise where Bette Davis, Dan Daley, Ethel Merman, Mickey Rooney, Claudette Colbert, Ginger Rogers, Zsa Zsa Gabor, Cary Grant, and, of course, Marilyn Monroe, made some of their finest movies.

The studio's financial crisis had been precipitated by a single film, *Cleopatra*, whose mismanagement during a change between boards of directors had lead to the largest cost overruns in motion picture history. Fox's investment in *Cleopatra*, a somewhat incoherent account of love and passion in ancient Egypt, would eventually surpass $40,000,000. At that time, few movies had ever earned enough money to recoup such a gargantuan budget.

The reason for these overruns was the movie's star, Elizabeth Taylor. The Oscar winner's continual lateness, illnesses, and demands — they had to tear down a vast Roman set in England and rebuild it in Italy because Taylor couldn't withstand the raw climate — had escalated the film's cost astronomically.

Ironically, it was also lateness and illness for which Fox fired Marilyn and closed down her movie. Yet the studio had only $2,000,000 invested in *Something's Got to Give* (a figure many dispute and attribute to press agentry — a cost of $500,000 maximum seems more likely). Of the two films, *Something's Got to Give*, a bright frothy comedy staring Marilyn Monroe and Dean Martin, two leading boxoffice draws, on which only $2,000,000 had been spent, would seem a better investment than a pretentious historical drama featuring Elizabeth Taylor and a relatively unknown British actor upon which tens of millions had already been squandered.

However, the film Marilyn was making had an insurance policy that would cover all the expenses it had generated so far if production had to be suspended because of the incapacitation of either star. Fox had a policy on *Cleopatra*, also, but not enough to cover its overruns. Marilyn's inability to work during most of the first six weeks of shooting may have played right into the studio's hands.

Their claim of a $2,000,000 investment in a comedy that was being shot on their own sets and had been filming for less than two months is clearly inflated. Fox management may have hoped to supply desperately needed cash flow by collecting a sum several times larger than the film's actual cost from its insurance company. This is not unlikely. The practice has almost become a matter of policy for many hard-pressed companies.

But the policy on the film wasn't the only insurance policy Fox had on Marilyn. Stars were the studios' biggest assets. A star's death could cost a studio millions of dollars in future earnings. To protect these priceless assets, studios routinely took out large insurance policies on their major stars.

Former Los Angeles Police Sergeant Jack Clemmons confirms that there was such a policy for Marilyn, and that the insurance company paid off in full. "The LAPD did know at the time that the studio collected on a multi-million dollar policy."

Actress Terry Moore told me that she wondered if Marilyn might have been driven to her death by her experience with Fox. "Marilyn was one of the most vulnerable human beings I've ever known. If anyone had wanted her dead, they could have driven her to it. I don't think it would have been very hard. Her heart was broken, she was still upset over this picture, she was on a lot of sleeping pills, a lot of wake-up pills . . ."

Many have found the idea that executives of a major

motion-picture studio could deliberately conspire to hound one of their biggest stars to her death too incredible to believe. But it is no more incredible than the idea that the Mafia would have microphones in her bedroom — a proven fact, according to FBI files. There's another fact: The Lloyd's $3,000,000 life insurance police the studio carried on Marilyn could help defray their runaway expenses on *Cleopatra*. Plus, a $10,000,000 production insurance coverage from Continental Casualty of New York!

THE MOVIE

Something's Got to Give, the film Marilyn never finished, was a remake of a classic 1939 Cary Grant—Irene Dunne farce, *My Favorite Wife*. It told the story of a wife (Marilyn) who returns home, after having been thought lost at sea years earlier, to find her husband (Dean Martin) about to remarry.

The remake was to be a high-budget comedy with lavish sets and high-profile co-stars. In addition to Monroe and Martin, it featured the talents of Cyd Charisse, Phil Silvers, Wally Cox, and Tommy Noonan. The studio apparently had a lot of faith in the story. Several years after Marilyn's death, it would successfully remake the original story as *Move Over, Darling*, with James Garner and Doris Day.

The movie's producer was to be Henry Weinstein — replacing David Brown — who seems like an odd selection, since his credits were primarily in theatre and television. However, Weinstein was a long-time friend and patient of Marilyn's psychiatrist, ever-helpful Dr. Ralph Greenson, who now appeared to be surrounding the actress with his friends and clients. As Greenson's influence over Marilyn was enormous at this time, some journalists have suggested that he may have hoped Marilyn would be more cooperative if someone she knew to be a good friend of his helmed the picture.

The director was to be the deservedly famous George Cukor. Marilyn may have accepted Cukor because of his fame as a skilled director of women. Many actors felt he slighted their contributions. Clark Gable had initially refused to play Rhett Butler in *Gone with the Wind* because he was reluctant to work with the openly homosexual Cukor. Dean Martin, in contrast, seems to have been comfortable with him as director.

Cukor had a way with comedy, and had directed some of Spencer Tracy's and Katherine Hepburn's most successful team-ups. Marilyn and Cukor had worked together on *Let's Make Love* and Cukor had even directed the original version of *Something's Got to Give* and *My Favorite Wife.* He seemed the ideal choice to direct the remake.

Even though Marilyn had personally approved Cukor as director of the picture, they were at odds before filming began and continued to grate on each other's nerves throughout the brief period before production was canceled. Cukor, for some reason, failed to come to the star's wardrobe test. This test is usually one of a director's prime prerogatives, especially in a lavish production where the look of the film is critical to its success.

Previously, the director's male stars had felt slighted; now, Marilyn felt slighted. She did not forgive Cukor, and their relationship was hateful and spiteful . . . with Cukor becoming even more ego-maniacal as time went on..

PRODUCTION BEGINS

Something's Got to Give began production on April 23, 1962. Some crew members joked that April 23 was also the last day they saw Marilyn Monroe. They were not far wrong. Out of the next thirty-six days of shooting, before the studio called a halt to filming and closed the production down, the actress appeared only twelve days — and was late on many of these.

Immediately after filming began, Marilyn became ill with a respiratory ailment. She missed the next several days of shooting.

Five days later, on April 30, Marilyn made an appearance on the set, but had a temperature of 101 degrees and a sore throat. Someone from the studio soon sent her home. However, David Bretherton, the film's editor said, "she looked beautiful."

Many journalists have speculated that Marilyn's illnesses were faked. They accuse her of lying in order to avoid having to go to the studio. Others acknowledge that she was genuinely physically ill, but say she probably created the illnesses in order to avoid going to the studio.

Certainly, Marilyn was physically ill. The studio's own doctors confirmed that. More than one psychologist, however, has pointed out that depression suppresses the immune system, and that the way Marilyn caught one illness after another suggests weakened immunity. The actress's symptoms also have an eerie resemblance to the recently discovered Epstein-Barr virus.

Cukor knew about Marilyn's notorious inability to be punctual, and filmed around her by shooting scenes in which she did not appear, and long shots where a stand-in could be used in her place.

On May 1, Marilyn made a third appearance on the set. The star arrived on time at 7:00 A.M., and left still suffering from her respiratory infection. *Something's Got to Give* was now two and a half days behind schedule.

By May 10, Marilyn had missed sixteen out of seventeen

days of filming. The studio's own doctor, Phillip Rubin, ordered her to bed on the basis of "sinus and virus complications."

Even when Marilyn felt well enough to work, her habitual lateness played havoc with the film's shooting schedule. Due on the set between 6:00 and 7:00 A.M., the star would often not appear until midmorning or later. Cukor continued to shoot around her, but everyone associated with the production knew that one day the director would run out of scenes that didn't require Marilyn's presence. What would happen then remained a matter of speculation.

Marilyn's famed inability to sleep may have been one cause of her lateness. Often, even after taking large doses of Nembutal or other sleeping medications, the actress would pace the floor restlessly all night. She would finally fall into an exhausted slumber only an hour or so before she was due at the studio.

Marilyn wasn't late only in getting to the studio. She was often late getting to the set when called to do her scenes. Frequently, cast and crew were left waiting for an hour or more while the actress remained locked in her dressing room, refusing to emerge.

Terry Moore has her own theory about why Marilyn was always late for her scenes. "I think she was afraid of the pressure. Studio pressure was very difficult on her. I think that's why she remained in her dressing room for hours. She was not narcissistic at all. But when she had to become Marilyn the star, all her insecurities came out — and she had a hard time trying to get away from the mirror. She would be three and four hours late, still not sure that she looked good enough to go on stage. I've seen them actually have to pull her away from the mirror. I think that was pressure."

HER INABILITY TO REMEMBER LINES

Production was also delayed because, when Marilyn did finally arrive on the set, she often had trouble remembering her lines. Terry Moore, who shared a makeup man with the superstar, offers a rare behind-the-scenes glimpse of the problems these lapses caused.

"They would take shots of Marilyn with Dean Martin doing a scene together. Then they would start to take the close-up of Marilyn repeating the same lines — and she couldn't remember her lines. So they'd stop and do Dean's close-ups, and come back to her — and Marilyn still had trouble. So they ended up with more film of Dean Martin than they did of Marilyn."

Most journalists who have written about the ill-fated making of *Something's Got to Give* have attributed Marilyn's inability to remember her lines to her declining mental and emotional state, and to the enormous quantity of sedatives she was said to be taking. However, the actress's friends offer a different explanation. They blame the problem on the film's troubled script.

Marilyn's friend Nunnally Johnson, one of Hollywood's wittiest screenwriters, had penned the remake. Both Johnson and the script met with the star's approval. But George Cukor felt the script still needed work and brought in a second writer.

By the time shooting was scheduled to start, the script was still under revision. New changes of dialogue would arrive on the set almost every hour. Often Marilyn would sit up late into the night, memorizing changes she had just been given for the next day's filming, only to arrive on the set and discover that her lines for the day had been changed yet again.

Marilyn began to view Cukor as an enemy. The director, she told friends, was deliberately trying to sabotage her career. Cukor, for his part, was equally unhappy with his leading actress. His assistant director, Butch Hall, despised Marilyn for reasons unknown. Had filming been resumed, it is likely that either Cukor or Marilyn would have had to leave the picture.

There is an untold side to the story of Marilyn's participation in the making of *Something's Got to Give*. Crew members report that when her lines weren't changed on her at the last minute, Marilyn worked well and did most of her takes in one shot. These crew members blame much of the movie's cost overruns on Cukor. They say the director, his powers declining with age, shot up to fifty different takes of each scene — unable to decide if he had what he wanted.

THE FILM FALLS BEHIND

Finally, Marilyn appeared for work three days in a row, May 14, 15, and 16. On May 17, a helicopter landed on the Fox lot to fly Marilyn to the airport. She was to perform in New York for President Kennedy's May 19 birthday gala.

This act seems to have infuriated the studio, which would later cite it as one of the reasons for terminating Marilyn's contract. But the fact is that the studio had given her advance permission to make the trip. The film's official production log for Thursday, May 17, contains a notation that Marilyn would not be present on the set that day, and would instead be in New York. However, the Fox board of directors rescinded permission at the last minute, after all the arrangements had been made, and Marilyn went anyway.

The studio's change of heart may be understandable: at this point, the film had been shooting for less than twenty days, and was already seven and a half days behind schedule. In retrospect, Henry Weinstein, the movie's producer, now believes he and Fox made a mistake. Marilyn's spectacular appearance before a glittering crowd of political dignitaries, including the president of the United States, could have reaped a windfall of international publicity for the studio, their star, and their film.

Back in L.A., Marilyn appeared on Monday, May 21, and put in a full day's work. But the next day, Dean Martin came in with a temperature of 100 degrees. Afraid of getting sick again, the star refused to work with him and went home.

On May 25, Marilyn enjoyed one of her rare days working with her male co-star. She phoned in sick again the next day.

By the end of May, Marilyn had been absent because of illness more often than she had been on the set.

HER THIRTY-SIXTH BIRTHDAY

On June 1, 1962, Marilyn was at the studio. It was her thirty-sixth birthday. The star was to celebrate the occasion on the set. Evelyn Moriarity, Marilyn's stand-in, had purchased a large cake and the entire cast had signed a birthday card.

But Cukor, fuming over her many absences and delays, wouldn't allow the festivities to begin, or the cake to be brought out, until after the day's shooting was completed. "I was told we couldn't bring the cake out until 6:00 P.M.," Moriarity recalled. "Cukor wanted to get a full day's work out of her."

Marilyn worked hard that day. She had important scenes with Dean Martin and co-star Wally Cox. No one knew it, but the camera was capturing the last moments the actress would ever put on film.

That night, Marilyn went to an Angels game held at Chavez Ravine (home of the Dodgers — at that time the Angels were using the Dodgers' field) and threw out the opening ball. Her appearance at this special charity event for the Muscular Distrophy Association was the final public performance of her career. Marilyn caught another cold from the chill night air. She was unable to report for the next scheduled day of filming.

On June 5, *Something's Got to Give* was sixteen days behind schedule and, according to Fox, one million dollars over budget. Word was circulating throughout the industry that the studio was planning to replace Marilyn with another actress. The rumor was correct. Fox was already conducting behind-the-scenes negotiations with several stars, including Lee Remick, Shirley MacLaine, Doris Day, and Kim Novak. But all had previous commitments.

Harrison Carroll, movie columnist for the *Los Angeles Herald Examiner* broke the story with a headline that screamed: "Studio in Crisis over Marilyn Monroe."

Marilyn was still unable to work on June 4, 5, and 6. Dr. Lee Siegel, the studio physician who attended her, stated that she was genuinely ill. "Her temperature had climbed to 102. Her sinus had flared up. She was unable to work."

On June 6, Dr. Greenson rushed back from Europe, his much-needed vacation cut short in response to an urgent summons from his friend Henry Weinstein, the movie's producer. The psychiatrist was surprised to discover that Marilyn was suffering from something more than bronchitis and a sinus infection: Fox was preparing elaborate plans to terminate her contract, and rumorswere rampant. Marilyn was in a deep funk.

FIRED

Dr. Greenson had hoped that his return would reassure Twentieth Century–Fox, and that they would give him time to exert his well-known influence on Marilyn. But he was too late. On June 8, the star received an official notice that she had been suspended and her contract terminated.

Ironically, the decision was handed down by the head of the studio, Peter Levathes, who was in Rome green-lighting further expenditures on *Cleopatra*. Internal Fox memos indicate that this decision had actually been reached on June 3 by Milton Gould, chairman of the board of directors. But the announcement had to made by Levathes, and several days were lost telegraphing messages back and forth across the Atlantic.

Internal Fox memos reveal that even as this decision to fire Marilyn was making its way through channels, her attorney was conducting last-minute negotiations in an attempt to save his client's role in the film.

On June 5, Rudin phoned the studio. He advised them that Marilyn was probably not going to make it to the studio that day, but asked if it would help "if she showed up in the afternoon." It was too late. Fox executives were ready to show their teeth. "I told him we had dismissed the company because of her non-appearances," one executive reported.

Rudin told the studio that Marilyn's psychiatrist, Dr. Greenson, was on his way back to the States to take charge of his patient. Rudin said he felt Greenson could handle Marilyn, and that upon his return they would be able to guarantee the star's appearance and performance.

Fox had its doubts, but agreed to meet with Greenson and Rudin on June 7. At this meeting, Greenson repeated Rudin's guarrantee to Fox and requested that the studio give Marilyn one more chance --— a three-day or two-week trial. Attorney and psychiatrist asked the studio to name any conditions it wanted, and they would jointly ensure their client's complete cooperation.

But Fox representatives told the two men they "were not convinced." The studio had no desire to resume production with Marilyn as the star until they were certain "she was able to finish and that we would finish with her; that we were not interested in starting on an experimental basis."

Rudin then officially advised Fox that his client was ready, willing, and able to go back to work. The studio advised him officially that she was in breach of contract, and that they "were not interested in progressing the conversations further." The studio wasted no time in replacing the star. At the same time that Fox announced Marilyn's dismissal, they told the press that actress Lee Remick had been signed to play Marilyn's role.

This announcement would prove premature. The studio had failed to consult Dean Martin. Martin's contract guaranteed him approval over his co-star.

Whatever others might have thought about the delays caused by Marilyn's illnesses and lateness, they didn't seem to have bothered the laid-back Dino. The singer told studio officials he "would not do the picture without Marilyn Monroe."

Allen "Whitey" Snyder, Marilyn's makeup man for sixteen years, was an eyewitness to Martin's initial reaction. "I was with Dean at the studio when the news broke. He said, 'No Marilyn, no picture.'"

In a closed-door meeting, the studio reminded Martin that they already had an investment of over two million dollars in the picture. Where, Fox representatives wanted to know, did that leave them? The unflappable Dino, considered the epitome of coolness, offered a typically laid-back reply. "It's not fair to ask me," he said. "I'm a nice guy. I got trouble with no one. And I don't want trouble with you."

Studio representatives urged Martin to reconsider his

position about Lee Remick. But the singer told them that: "I felt the chemistry between me and Marilyn was right. That was why I took on this picture — and for no other reason." The financially astute Dino added that Marilyn's name meant a lot more at the box office than Remick's.

Martin also felt that Remick would not be believable in the role. The point of the picture, the singer told Fox, was that he left Cyd Charisse for Marilyn. Martin did not feel audiences would believe that he would leave Charisse for Remick.

Fox attorneys immediately filed a one million dollar lawsuit against Marilyn for breach of contract. They followed this with a second half million dollar lawsuit against Dean Martin when he remained determined to exercise his legal right not to approve Remick as his co-star.

Marilyn was officially suspended from the Fox payroll on June 12, 1962. At that time, production on the picture was shut down. Marilyn had been fired by the studio where — over the course of a decade — she had made some of the most successful and popular motion pictures of all time.

DEPRESSED

Much has been written about Marilyn Monroe's state of mind at the time of her death. According to the Hollywood rumor mill the star was falling apart, her professional and personal life in a shambles. Filming had been suspended on her last movie, *Something's Got to Give*. Distraught at the thought of her motion-picture career ending in a blaze of lawsuits, Marilyn was said to have attempted taking her own life. But these rumors do not tell the real story.

For thirty years these rumors and this cloud have obscured the truth about Marilyn's final weeks. What few people knew is that less than a week before the actress died,

Fox had capitulated.

Dean Martin's refusal to accept any other co-star, and Mickey Rudin's relentless campaign in her behalf, had paid off. Marilyn was to be fully reinstated. The studio dropped its lawsuits, and slated production to resume in October when Martin would again be free for filming.

Rudin had Fox over a barrel. The studio now needed Marilyn if they were to see any return on the two million dollars they claimed to have already sunk into the picture. Rudin pointed out that Fox had terminated the star — making her old contract null and void. If the studio wanted his client, they couldn't expect to have her under the old terms. They would have to negotiate a whole new deal.

By the time Rudin finished with the studio, he had leveraged Fox executives into a substantial raise. Marilyn would now receive *five* times her original fee. From now on, the actress would receive not $100,000 but $500,000 for this picture.

Some of Marilyn's friends doubt it was solely Rudin's efforts that won the star her reinstatement. Shortly after Fox terminated her contract, Marilyn had called Bobby Kennedy for help. Bobby had told her not to worry, that he would take care of everything and use the Kennedy family's considerable influence with the studios in her behalf. Perhaps the two men reinforced each other's efforts.

Marilyn died before knowledge of her reinstatement became public. After her death, studio officials placed the agreement and the paperwork on it in their inactive files, thus burying vital evidence which could have helped clear the actress of the charge of suicide.

Much of the case for Marilyn having taken her own life is based on the widely held supposition that she was despondent over losing her role in *Something's Got to Give*. But it hardly seems likely that the star would have been despondent after bringing her studio to its knees and winning her job back at five times her original salary. It is even less likely that, after having fought for reinstatement and professional vindication all summer, she would kill herself over what was, after all, just one more relationship problem.

Jeanne Carmen is one of several close friends who believe that Marilyn's reinstatement removed all reason for suicide. "I don't think Marilyn was suicidal. I mean that is definitely a story that has gone around. That's a lie. When she was reinstated on *Something's Got to Give*, she was as happy as I've ever seen her. The last month of her life Marilyn was having a blast. She was enthusiastic. She never looked more gorgeous. . . . She looked better than I've ever seen her. I certainly don't think she was suicidal at the time of her death. I think something fishy went on."

Actress Terry Moore agrees: "Marilyn's career was certainly not over. I know that Twentieth Century–Fox had so much money tied up in this movie and her career that they wanted to go on with the movie."

But even if Marilyn hadn't been reinstated by the studio, she had no reason to be despondent. If Fox didn't want her, other studios and independent producers did. Offers and scripts began to pour in. Almost two dozen scripts for prospective movies were found in the star's house after her death.

One Las Vegas casino offered Marilyn $100,000 per week to star in her own review. Every seven days she would have earned as much as Fox was paying her for an entire picture. "There were many people waiting to give her offers," Moore confirms.

SLY AS A FOX

Some insiders believe that Twentieth Century–Fox's reinstatement of Marilyn would seem to eliminate them as candidates for complicity in her death. It doesn't seem likely that a motion picture company would want to kill a star whose performance they hoped would save a two million dollar investment.

Another theory holds that Fox's sudden about-face may not have been voluntary. This theory says that the studio reluctantly bowed to pressure from Bobby Kennedy, while secretly conspiring to bring about Marilyn's death and collect their three million dollars.

The Kennedys, the CIA, the Secret Service, the FBI, the Justice Department, the Mafia, an unsettling circle of advisors, and a studio desperate to cash in on any asset, even its stars — everyone seemed to have motives for wanting to see Marilyn dead.

Virtually the only person who didn't have a motive for the superstar's death was Marilyn herself. Reinstated at five times her original salary, with motion picture and television offers flooding in from all sides, the star's friends say she had never been happier. Certainly, if there is anyone whose name we can eliminate from the list of suspects in the death of Marilyn Monroe, it is Marilyn's.

And yet Marilyn's nude, lifeless body would be found on the morning of August 5, and the official verdict on the cause of death would be "probable suicide."

FILE #9

The Day MM Died

Saturday, August 4, 1962, would be Marilyn Monroe's last day. It was nearly dawn in the exclusive suburb of Brentwood. In her house at 12305 Fifth Helena Drive, Marilyn was wrapped in an old bathrobe, sitting at the kitchen counter, placing a phone call. She had been up all night, unable to sleep.

Pat Newcomb, the actress's publicist, was still asleep in the guest bedroom. Marilyn, who had difficulty falling asleep even when she took massive doses of sleeping pills, was envious. Eunice Murray, Marilyn's housekeeper-nurse, had spent the night at her own home at the star's urging. Marilyn was alone.

Marilyn had spent most of the night trying to track down Bobby Kennedy for a final confrontation. She had called me in Columbus, Ohio, late Friday afternoon, wanting to know if reports that Bobby Kennedy was spending the weekend in San Francisco were true. Marilyn, who believed her own lines were tapped, had made the call from a nearby pay phone.

She said Bobby's private line at the Justice Department had been disconnected, and that all her attempts to reach him had failed. Far from being despondent over the way Bobby was treating her, as many have claimed, Marilyn was angry. She felt Bobby owed her an explanation for all the lies he had told her, and for abruptly walking out of her life without even a goodbye.

I advised her to forget about talking with Bobby and to concentrate on preparing for her role in *Something's Got to Give*, the film she was scheduled to finish with Dean Martin when production resumed in October. But Marilyn was determined to talk to Bobby one last time, and make him face up to the way that he and his brother had used her. If he continued to avoid her, Marilyn said, she was going to expose the Kennedy brothers publicly for the hypocrites they were.

"I might just call a press conference and tell them about it," she threatened.

Marilyn's had chosen a dangerous target for her anger. She was willing to destroy the political futures and personal lives of the president and attorney general of the United States. The power they could wield if they became aware of her plans was awesome. Even more troubling was the fact that Marilyn had told others about the proposed press conference. It didn't seem likely that such a juicy item could remain a secret for long in Hollywood.

Except for frustration over her inability to reach Bobby, Marilyn sounded better than she had in months. She had called me a few times that week to discuss her growing excitement over all the offers for movies and personal appearances that had been pouring in since Twentieth Century–Fox had suspended production on *Something's Got to Give*.

Marilyn had also been excited by her plans for remodeling her new house, and the progress the workmen were making.

In that last call to me, Marilyn said she was going to call Pat Lawford — Bobby Kennedy's sister and then-current wife of Peter Lawford — to see if Pat would give her Bobby's present number.

Apparently Marilyn did make an attempt to reach Pat Lawford later that Friday night. Peter Lawford told reporters Marilyn called him and, unaware of her intentions, he gave her the number of the Kennedy compound in Hyannis, where Pat was visiting.

No one in the Kennedy family will discuss Marilyn's affairs with JFK and Bobby or say whether Marilyn Monroe tried to reach Pat Lawford at the family compound that night. But there is verification that she tried to reach Bobby Kennedy at the St. Francis, his San Francisco hotel. It is likely that Marilyn attempted to do so through Pat Lawford.

According to Elizabeth Francher, assistant to the celebrated crime reporter, Florabel Muir, her employer paid a telephone operator at the St. Francis for information about calls made that weekend. The operator told Muir that Marilyn Monroe had called the hotel several times leaving numerous messages for Bobby Kennedy each time.

Many journalists have suggested that Marilyn Monroe's inability to sleep that Friday night was due to frustration and anger over her failure to reach Bobby. But there may be more involved in the star's insomnia than that. There is some evidence that Marilyn may have been stood up by Bobby Kennedy on Friday evening.

Shortly after Marilyn's death, the Briggs delicatessen, which often delivered food to her home, presented a claim against her estate in the amount of $150 for champagne, hors d'oeuvres and assorted delicacies. They delivered this order about 7:00 P.M. on the night of August 3. Obviously,

Marilyn planned to entertain someone that evening. The question is: Who was to have been her guest?

If Marilyn mentioned her prospective guest to anyone, they have not said so. Nor has anyone claiming to be that prospective guest ever come forward. If Marilyn was expecting a visitor, she obviously felt she needed to keep both the visit and the visitor a secret. She even sent Eunice Murray home for the night.

The obvious conclusion, Marilyn's friends say, is she was expecting Bobby Kennedy. What other visitor, they ask, would she have felt it necessary to keep secret?

If Marilyn had been expecting Bobby Kennedy earlier for dinner, why would she have been frantically trying to reach him by phone? Or could Bobby have called the star later that day, promising to fly down and see her in the evening? If so, the attorney general must have not shown up.

Whatever Marilyn's intentions for the evening of Friday, August 3, her plans seem to have changed drastically by dinner time. According to Pat Newcomb, she and Marilyn dined together that night at a small neighborhood restaurant.

Billy Travilla, the wardrobe designer who created many of Marilyn's most memorable costumes, supports the restaurant story.

But Travilla places it several miles east, on the Sunset Strip, and adds Peter Lawford to the party. "I was having dinner at a restaurant on the Sunset Strip that night," Travilla recalls. "During my dinner I heard a lot of laughing coming from a nearby booth. When I finished, I got up and took a peek and saw Marilyn with Peter Lawford and Pat Newcomb.

As Travilla walked over to say hello, he noticed Marilyn's eyes were glazed from drinking. He greeted the star, but she looked at the fashion designer as if she had never seen him before. Travilla repeated his greeting. Then Marilyn shocked him by asking rudely, "Who are you?" Travilla says his "feelings were deeply hurt," and he walked away.

Some of those who have investigated those last fateful days of Marilyn Monroe's life believe Travilla must be mistaken about the date — that he ran into Newcomb, Lawford and Marilyn on a different night. But the costume designer is certain he could not be wrong. When he read about her death in the paper on Sunday, Travilla says, he thought about how sad it was that he had seen her only that Friday night.

Which of these accounts is correct: Travilla's or Newcomb's? The answer is — possibly both.

If Bobby Kennedy had stood up Marilyn Monroe that night, she and Newcomb might have gone out drinking after dinner. And if Marilyn had been despondent enough, either of them might have called Lawford to join their party.

Travilla may have encountered the trio later, after they had all tied on one too many in helping Marilyn get over her disappointment at Bobby's failure to show.

But there was a third reason Marilyn may have had trouble sleeping Friday night. According to Jeanne Carmen, Marilyn told her that she had been kept up all night by a series of disturbing phone calls. A woman, whose voice Marilyn did not recognize, had supposedly kept calling her, on her private line, from before midnight until almost 5:30 A.M., telling the actress to "Leave Bobby alone!" and calling her a "tramp."

If Marilyn was expecting Bobby Kennedy, did he cancel out at the last minute because Ethel had discovered his plans? Was Ethel so angry that she spent the night harassing the woman she felt was stealing her husband and threatening her family's future? If so, it would hardly be surprising that

Marilyn Monroe spent the night before her death restlessly pacing the floors of her Brentwood home.

HER LAST MORNING

According to Jeanne Carmen, Marilyn phoned about 6:00 A.M. on Saturday morning, waking her from a sound sleep. The doomed actress, who now had less than eighteen hours to live, had called to tell Carmen about the harassing calls she had received that night. The calls had stopped half an hour earlier. Since then the phone had remained silent. Marilyn said she hoped the calls were finally over.

"Marilyn sounded exhausted," Carmen told one journalist. The star begged her friend to come over and keep her company. Then she added meaningfully: "Bring a bag of pills." This worried Carmen, who refused. She told Marilyn she didn't have time for a visit, either. Carmen explained that it was her birthday, and a series of engagements would keep her busy until late that night. When Marilyn hung up, Carmen felt uneasy. Her friend's request for the bag of pills disturbed her.

A few hours later, around 10:00 A.M., Eunice Murray let herself in the front door of the star's home on Fifth Helena Drive. Marilyn was still up and still making phone calls. Whatever the actual events of Friday night, they apparently upset her enough to make her reach out to friends and acquaintances. Marilyn would continue to make phone calls throughout the day and well into the evening of her death.

Among those the actress is known to have called or spoken with that morning are: Arthur James, a life-long friend she had met through former amour, Charlie Chaplin Jr. (James was out of town and did not get the message until after her death.); her former father-in-law, Isadore Miller, who returned Marilyn's call but was told she was in the shower; her masseur, Ralph Roberts, who she phoned about a tentative dinner date they had for that evening; and Jeanne Carmen, who she called again to confirm a golfing date the following Monday.

The final call of the morning seems to have come from Sidney Skolsky, one of the few journalists Marilyn trusted. Weeks earlier, the actress had asked the politically astute Skolsky for advice about her troubled relationships with the Kennedy brothers. Like Marilyn's other friends, Skolsky was concerned about her involvement with the Kennedys and her lack of discretion in discussing her relationship with them.

Marilyn's revelations were becoming so sensational that Skolsky had asked his daughter, Stephanie, to listen in on his last few conversations with the star. He wanted a witness who could later confirm their content if it were ever questioned.

In the last conversation with Skolsky, Marilyn discussed his family. She had taken the same deep interest in them that she had with the families of all those with whom she formed close relationships. Marilyn always seemed to be trying to take part in family life, something she had never really known.

Next, the conversation turned to backstage Hollywood gossip. Finally, Skolsky asked Marilyn what her plans were for the evening. "I'm seeing Bobby Kennedy at Peter Lawford's house," Marilyn replied.

If Marilyn had a date with Bobby for later that Saturday, why would she have reminded Ralph Roberts of their tentative date for that same evening. Could Bobby Kennedy have called up after Marilyn talked to Roberts, and before she spoke to Skolsky, and arranged a last minute meeting for Saturday evening to make up for the one he had postponed the night before?

Further, if Marilyn really believed she was going to see Bobby Kennedy on Saturday evening, why did Pat Newcomb, Eunice Murray and Dr. Ralph Greenson tell reporters that she was restless, unhappy, and angry all day long? Why did Mrs. Murray say that she summoned Dr. Greenson that Saturday after one disturbing conversation with Marilyn?

As it is impossible to resolve these questions without a great deal more knowledge about that fatal Saturday, let's look at the events of the next few hours the way Eunice Murray, Pat Newcomb and Ralph Greenson described them.

Pat Newcomb was still asleep when Eunice Murray arrived around mid-morning. Murray noticed that when she mentioned Newcomb's name, Marilyn was curt and sounded angry. As the hours passed, the star seemed to grow more and more angry with the slumbering publicist.

When Newcomb finally emerged around noon, rested and refreshed, Marilyn's anger exploded. Exhausted from lack of sleep, the actress was furious at her publicist's ability to slumber the night away. The two women argued bitterly and loudly, according to Eunice Murray.

Many journalists have questioned this account. They don't believe two grown women would engage in a violent argument over so trivial an issue. Instead, they believe the argument was really over Pat Newcomb's growing attraction to Bobby Kennedy at a time when Marilyn was losing access to him.

Others have suggested that neither of these interpretations makes sense. They point out that at 4:30 P.M., when Dr. Greenson was summoned to the star's home, Pat Newcomb was still there. Would Marilyn really have allowed the publicist to remain all afternoon, they ask — and would Newcomb have stayed all afternoon — if either was seriously upset with the other?

Sometime late that afternoon, Marilyn Monroe is supposed

to have asked Mrs. Murray, "Is there any oxygen around?"
Oxygen is often used to resuscitate suicide victims, and
Murray's purpose in telling this story is clearly to indicate
that the actress was contemplating suicide as early as mid-
afternoon.

However, the whole story is absurd as it stands. Oxygen
comes in huge metal canisters and Marilyn knew it. She also
knew there wasn't an oxygen tank in the house and never
had been. So why would she suddenly ask if there was one
around, implying that it might be used to revive her if she
later tried to take her own life? The answer clearly seems
to be that Marilyn wouldn't ask such a question. But why
would Murray tell us this? Many who have sought to answer
this question believe Eunice Murray was lying. In an attempt
to conceal something about the events of that evening Murray
was, in short, engaging in a cover-up.

Worried by Marilyn's question, Mrs. Murray claimed she
phoned Dr. Greenson and asked him to come over.

When Greenson arrived, he supposedly found Marilyn
and her publicist still feuding. After talking with Marilyn for
a while, Greenson says he then took what seems to be the
day's most reasonable action: he told Pat Newcomb to go
home.

If Murray and Greenson are to be believed, Newcomb
jumped up and left without another word. Marilyn remained
in her room. The two friends never spoke again after that.
The next time the publicist spoke her client's name, it would
be to announce Marilyn Monroe's death.

HER LAST AFTERNOON

With Pat Newcomb's departure, Marilyn Monroe was left
alone with her psychiatrist and housekeeper-nurse. Most

of what we know about her activities during the remainder of that afternoon and evening is based on their testimony. Yet, almost exactly twenty-four hours later they, with the aid of Dr. Hyman Engelberg, would give an account of the actress's death so riddled with inconsistencies that it aroused the suspicion of every police officer who heard it.

According to Greenson and Murray, Marilyn spent more time in her bedroom talking with her psychiatrist after Pat Newcomb's departure. Greenson was apparently helping her work through some emotional difficulty. When asked what they discussed in those last few hours, he pleaded client confidentiality and refused to divulge the contents of the conversation.

Shortly after 6:30 P.M., Greenson is said to have left for home. Before he went, a curious exchange took place. Eunice Murray said she asked Greenson if he felt she should stay the night to "keep an eye" on Marilyn. Greenson told her he did not think it would be necessary. But Murray decided to stay anyway. Murray refuses to explain why she made this decision.

Two separate sources support this part of Saturday evening's timetable.

Ralph Roberts, Marilyn's masseur, called at about 6:30 P.M. to confirm their date for dinner. But it wasn't Marilyn who answered the phone. Dr. Greenson took the call. When Roberts asked for Marilyn, the psychiatrist told the masseur, "She's not in," and hung up the phone.

According to both Greenson and Murray, Marilyn never left the house that day. Perhaps the psychiatrist had just succeeded in settling his client down and didn't want to risk anyone upsetting her again. Marilyn may have wanted some time alone and had given orders that she was not to be disturbed.

But this was the second time that fateful Saturday that close friends of Marilyn's had been told she wasn't home. Joe DiMaggio Jr., who the star still thought of as her stepson, had tried to reach Marilyn twice that afternoon. Both times Eunice Murray said Marilyn was out.

Clearly, Murray and Greenson were lying. But were they lying when they told Joe DiMaggio's son and Ralph Roberts that Marilyn was out? Or when they told police and journalists that Marilyn had not left the house all day?

It is here that what would become the "official" version of Marilyn's final hours begins to come apart. It was contradictions like this that initially aroused my suspicions and led me to belive that the true story of Marilyn's death was untold. Over the next three decades, the contradictions in the statements and actions of all those who support the official verdict in Marilyn's death would feed these suspicions. In the last two years, a firestorm of expert opinion demanding an official investigation into the circumstances of her death has arisen.

Those who defend what was to become the official verdict of suicide say there is nothing suspicious about Greenson's and Murray's statements to Joe DiMaggio Jr. and Ralph Roberts. They claim that DiMaggio Jr. might have called at times when Marilyn was feuding with Newcomb and didn't want to be disturbed. But the actress's anger with Newcomb doesn't seem to have prevented her from taking and making numerous calls to and from others throughout the morning and mid-afternoon.

And why would Dr. Greenson have wanted to break Marilyn's date with Ralph Roberts? Wouldn't he have thought an evening out with a friend would help take the star's mind off her troubles?

Whatever the correct explanation, as soon as Dr. Greenson left, Joe DiMaggio Jr. got through to Marilyn Monroe. Marilyn's stepson lifted her spirits by telling her he had terminated a painful relationship. Eunice Murray said she heard the actress laughing and saying, "Oh, that's wonderful."

Murray told me that after this conversation Marilyn was in a much better mood. "It was hard to get the feeling that just a short time after that she might have been depressed," Murray said.

Dr. Greenson's family attests that he returned home from seeing Marilyn shortly after 7:00 P.M. The psychiatrist and his wife had a dinner engagement that evening. After cutting his European vacation short to nurse Marilyn through the emotional crisis she underwent during the making of *Something's Got to Give* — and after all the long sessions he devoted to helping her through the depression that followed her termination from the film — Greenson hoped his client would be able to get through one night without him. He felt he and his wife deserved a normal Saturday evening to themselves.

According to Greenson, Marilyn called him one last time that night, shortly after 7:30 P.M. The actress assured him that she was feeling better. Greenson later told interviewers his patient sounded much "more cheerful" than she had earlier in the day, and that he worried less about a crisis occurring while he was out for dinner.

According to Greenson, Marilyn then asked, "Did you take away my bottle of Nembutal?" The psychiatrist was supposedly taken off-guard by this. First, because he had not taken Marilyn's Nembutal. Second, because he thought the actress had recently cut down on her use of sleeping pills.

Here again, as with the story of Marilyn's question about having oxygen around the house, the implication seems to be that the star was preparing to take an overdose and couldn't find the Nembutals she needed.

Opponents of the "official" account of Marilyn Monroe's last day are skeptical of Greenson's story. If the actress was really thinking about killing herself, they ask, would she have tipped off her psychiatrist by asking where her pills were?

Those who defend the official verdict answer that this question is exactly what one would expect Marilyn to ask, given the pattern of her past suicide attempts. They claim the star had a compulsive need to attempt suicide and then seek rescue — perhaps because this pattern reassured her of her importance or fulfilled her need for attention. She had, therefore, deliberately made the implication that she was considering suicide, an obvious tip-off that would later send her psychiatrist running to her just in time for the rescue.

This explanation seems plausible enough, skeptics agree. But taken in the larger context — of contradictions, misinformation and outright lies which Greenson and Murray would later be found to have told about that evening — many feel the story sounds too pat to be true. Instead, they believe it was probably manufactured as part of a deliberate attempt to cover-up the truth, and support the appearance of suicide.

There is another troubling aspect of Greenson and Murray's stories. Both went to great lengths to describe how Marilyn's mood improved just before the psychiatrist left for dinner and Mrs. Murray retired for the evening. The point of such a story would seem to be that Greenson and Murray were conscientious in their assesment of Marilyn's "improved" mood and, therefore, justified in leaving the actress unobserved. Having emphasized their conscientiousness with respect to Marilyn's psychological state, they could hardly be blamed for not suspecting that "just a short time after that she might have been depressed," and taken her own life.

Shortly before 8:00 P.M., Marilyn Monroe is said to have

told Eunice Murray she was going to bed. The actress went into her bedroom, closing the door behind her. According to the housekeeper-nurse, the next time she saw Marilyn Monroe, the world's most famous body would be sprawled lifelessly across her bed.

HER FINAL HOURS

As far as the "official" story goes, 8:00 P.M. was the last time anyone ever saw Marilyn Monroe alive. Both Ralph Greenson and Eunice Murray felt her mood was so positive that neither of them worried about her again that night. If Marilyn took her own life, then sometime between 8:00 P.M. and the time of her death, something must have happened to tragically alter her mood.

No hint of such an event can be found in accounts of the half-dozen friends with whom Marilyn spoke by phone over the next two hours. But we do find other, more ominous clues — clues that seem to contradict the stories Greenson and Murray tell of Marilyn's final change of mood — indicating events which not only altered Marilyn's mood but culminated in her death.

The first call was made to Marilyn by Henry Rosenfeld, a wealthy dress manufacturer Marilyn had met at New York's legendary El Morocco club during her short-lived career as a model. Rosenfeld remembers calling her sometime prior to 9:30 P.M. He later told journalists that the star sounded "groggy."

Shortly after her conversation with her New York friend, Marilyn called Sidney Guilaroff, a film colony hairdresser she had gotten to know well. Guilaroff says she told him: "I'm very depressed." Then she rang off without saying good-bye. Next, José Bolanos, another close friend of Marilyn's, phoned her from a nearby restaurant. Bolanos refuses to disclose the content of their last conversation. He will only say that rather than hanging up after the call was over, Marilyn simply put the receiver down and stopped talking to him. But, Bolanos added, this was not unusual — she had done it before.

Later, around 10:00 P.M., Jeanne Carmen says Marilyn called her for the third time that day. "Are you sure you can't come over?" Marilyn asked. Carmen pleaded exhaustion. She recalls that Marilyn sounded nervous and on edge.

The next day, Ralph Roberts discovered that Marilyn had tried to reach him at around the same time. According to Roberts' answering service, a woman with a "slurred" voice called. Learning he had already gone out to dinner with friends, the woman hung up the phone.

Jeanne Carmen's phone rang again sometime before 10:30 P.M., but she was too tired to answer it.

According to Peter Lawford, he was the last person Marilyn contacted. Lawford claims Marilyn had already taken the overdose that would kill her. Her call to him contained strong clues that she was going to take her own life. Presumably she expected him to complete the pattern by rescuing her.

Peter Lawford's then-current wife, Deborah Gould, told television interviewers that Peter had told her Marilyn called sometime around 10:30 P.M., during dinner. The actress's voice was extremely slurred. She reportedly told Lawford she couldn't take it anymore. Marilyn closed by telling him to "take care of yourself." And then the phone went dead.

Lawford claimed he attempted to call her back, but her line was busy. Although aware of her past attempts to take her life, Lawford later stated he thought Marilyn's call to be reflective of her dramatic tendencies. Apparently, it never occurred to him that Marilyn Monroe might actually be in the process of committing suicide.

If Marilyn had already taken an overdose, when did she take it? She had been on the phone almost continuously from the time she entered her room until the time she is said to have phoned Lawford.

The star's voice is reported to have sounded "slurred" or "nervous." Neither to Jeanne Carmen nor Jose Bolanos did she give the slightest hint she was contemplating suicide, or that she was dangerously overdosed. Did Marilyn save this revelation solely for Lawford's ears because, as a member of the Kennedy family, she counted on him to phone Bobby immediately with the news?

The reports of all the individuals with whom Marilyn spoke between the hours of 8:30 P.M. and 10:30 P.M. unanimously concur that Marilyn's voice sounded "depressed," "anxious," and "slurred". Yet, both Dr. Greenson and Eunice Murray report her to have been in a positive mood only thirty minutes prior to the first of these calls. In fact, Marilyn's mood was characterized as being so much improved, neither Greenson nor Murray could imagine Marilyn taking her own life.

Is the Greenson-Murray story false? Or did Marilyn learn something during the half-hour between entering her bedroom and talking with Rosenfeld that brought on a renewed attack of depression? Does the explanation lie in Sidney and Steffi Skolsky's report that Marilyn told them she was expecting to see Bobby Kennedy at Peter Lawford's that night? Did Bobby renew a postponed date with Marilyn, only to cancel out on the love goddess a second time?

If Marilyn did expect to see Bobby Kennedy, why would she have been depressed and unhappy all day? If her motive for suicide came later, between 8:00 and 8:30 P.M., why did Marilyn ask her housekeeper-nurse about oxygen and her psychiatrist about sleeping pills — two to four hours earlier?

The RFK supposition requires Bobby to have called Marilyn during two very narrow windows of time. The first was in the morning after Marilyn's conversation with Ralph Roberts and before her conversation with Sidney Skolsky. The second was in the evening after Marilyn entered her bedroom and before the call from Henry Rosenfeld, a mere half-hour later. Are we to believe that Bobby Kennedy conveniently reached Marilyn twice when no one else was around and just in time to create a complete reversal of her mood?

Or might it be that nothing Dr. Ralph Greenson, Eunice Murray and Pat Newcomb said about that fateful Saturday is true? Are Marilyn's psychiatrist and housekeeper-nurse covering up an entirely different set of events . . . events that include Bobby Kennedy's arrival that afternoon and a quarrel, not with Pat Newcomb, but with Bobby — a quarrel that left Marilyn depressed, anxious and suicidal?

I believe that the entire official investigation by the LAPD, the coroner's office and the special Suicide Investigation Team — which resulted in an "official" verdict of suicide — and even the two district attorney's investigations, almost twenty-five years later, are all part of a cover-up.

This cover-up was designed to conceal Bobby Kennedy's visit that Saturday and all evidence of his affair with Marilyn. This cover-up concealed, perhaps inadvertently, a much darker secret as well: that Marilyn Monroe's death was not suicide, but murder.

More than a quarter of a century later the cover-up would be uncovered.

FILE #10

LAPD: *The Politics of Policing*

As Sergeant Jack Clemmons drove away from Marilyn Monroe's Brentwood home, the LAPD's official investigation was just beginning. In charge was Sergeant Robert Byron, a veteran detective with extensive experience investigating suicide and homicide scenes. Clemmons had discovered discrepancies in the stories that Marilyn's housekeeper and doctors told him, and contradictions in the physical evidence at the death scene. But Clemmons knew Byron's reputation and thought he was leaving the investigation in good hands.

According to the report filed by Sergeant Byron, Mrs. Murray discovered Marilyn's comatose body at approximately 3:30 A.M. She immediately contacted Marilyn's psychiatrist, Dr. Ralph Greenson, and, moments later, the star's personal physician, Dr. Hyman Engelberg. At 3:50 A.M., Marilyn Monroe was pronounced dead by Dr. Engelberg. Dr. Greenson told police that Marilyn had taken forty-seven Nembutals and an unknown quantity of chloral hydrate.

For almost thirty years, Sergeant Byron's report of the circumstances surrounding Marilyn's death was the basis of the "official story." At the time, the salient facts of the case, as reported by Byron, would become the keystone of the entire investigation. They would influence the way the pathologist evaluated the autopsy results, and affect the depth of the coroner's investigation into Marilyn's mental state at the time of her death — a state which, as determined by the coroner's investigating team, would become the justification for the official verdict of "probable suicide."

An accumulating body of evidence, however, does not support the "facts" as reported by Sergeant Byron. Rather, it reveals his investigation to have been seriously flawed; the evidence obtained therein is dubious at best. Byron now admits his efforts to have been perfunctory. The fact that he saw no evidence of foul play, and that the autopsy supported Greenson's story of a drug overdose, convinced him that a more thorough and responsible effort would result in the waste of department time.

In retrospect, Byron's management of the case appears to be negligent. He failed to notice important physical evidence at the scene of Marilyn's death. He overlooked significant contradictions in the witnesses' stories, and in the stories they told different investigators. Although aware of the star's affair with RFK through LAPD sources, and told that Bobby Kennedy had been seen at Marilyn's home on the day of her death, Byron made no effort to either contact or question the attorney general. He felt the issue of Marilyn's rapport with RFK to be outside the scope of his investigation. He even failed to interview Sergeant Jack Clemmons, the officer who had preceded him at the scene.

Jack Clemmons had no official involvement with the investigation of Marilyn's death. As the acting watch commander, he had visited the site only to ascertain the validity of the death report the LAPD had received in the early morning hours of August 5. He was not asked to divulge what the witnesses had told him or what he gleaned at the scene of

Marilyn Monroe's death. Over time, Clemmons says he forgot about the case because of the press of other duties.

Ironically, Clemmons would be the first person to discover discrepancies in the LAPD's investigation files. Clemmons says that a chance remark a few months after Marilyn's death sent him to the files. What he read surprised him. "I had never read the official report," Clemmons explains. "I was very surprised. It seems Mrs. Murray did not tell Byron and other officers that she had discovered the scene at midnight, as she had told me. She told them that she discovered it at 3:00 A.M.

There were other major discrepancies in the version of the night's events as Marilyn's housekeeper and the two doctors described them. Jack Clemmons believes that he knows the reason for those discrepancies. He thinks the witnesses deliberately changed their stories to cover the contradictions he had discovered in their first version. "Sometime after I left, I guess they got to talking about it, and they said, 'This is not going to fly; so we had better change our story.' " Unwittingly, the three conspirators merely created other contradictions in the account they told Byron, leading to further alterations in the stories subsequently given to later investigators.

THE DISCREPANCIES

The discrepancies in the stories told by Mrs. Murray, Dr. Greenson, and Dr. Engelberg to different investigators are so glaring it is difficult to understand how Sergeant Byron could have ignored them. The noticeable absence of any commentary on these inconsistencies is, however, more than ample evidence that Byron did not acknowledge their existence. These discrepancies include:

* how many times Mrs. Murray tried Marilyn's door before calling the psychiatrist;

* who first saw Marilyn's dead body through the window;

* who first called Dr. Engelberg; and

* alterations in the physical evidence supporting their stories, such as the lack of a water glass and the condition of the pill bottles. To understand just how glaring these discrepancies are, let us consider the following comparison.

The Time When Mrs. Murray First Noticed Something Wrong

WHAT THEY TOLD CLEMMONS
Mrs. Murray woke up about midnight.

FIRST OFFICIAL REPORT
Mrs. Murray woke prior to 3:30 A.M.

FOLLOW-UP REPORT
The same.

How Often Mrs. Murray Tried Marilyn's Door

WHAT THEY TOLD CLEMMONS
Seeing the light under Marilyn's door, Mrs. Murray tried once to arouse Marilyn by prolonged knocking on her bedroom door. Then she phoned Dr. Greenson.

FIRST OFFICIAL REPORT
Mrs. Murray tried knocking at the door twice, the first time prior to 3:30 A.M., on her way to the bathroom. She tried again at 3:30 A.M., when she noticed the light was still on and the door locked.

FOLLOW-UP REPORT
Twice: once before calling Dr. Greenson; then a second time after she had talked to Dr. Greenson, who told her to try again.

How Often Mrs. Murray Called Dr. Greenson

WHAT THEY TOLD CLEMMONS
Mrs. Murray called him once, after failing to get a response at the door.

THE FIRST OFFICIAL REPORT
Once, after seeing Marilyn dead through the window.

THE FOLLOW-UP REPORT
Twice: once after Marilyn failed to answer the door; a second time, after she had looked through the window in response to Greenson's instructions.

When Mrs. Murray Summoned Dr. Greenson

WHAT THEY TOLD CLEMMONS
Mrs. Murray called Dr. Greenson around 12:10 P.M.

FIRST OFFICIAL REPORT
Mrs. Murray summoned him at approximately 3:35 A.M., after she had looked through the window when Marilyn failed to answer her door.

FOLLOW-UP REPORT
Mrs. Murray summoned him at 3:45 A.M., when she called him a second time to report what she had seen through the window.

Who Saw Marilyn's Body Through the Bedroom Window

WHAT THEY TOLD CLEMMONS
Dr. Greenson arrived, and failing to arouse Marilyn when he knocked loudly at her door, went outside and looked in through the window.

FIRST OFFICIAL REPORT
Mrs. Murray, after Marilyn failed to respond to loud knocking at the door.

FOLLOW-UP REPORT
Mrs. Murray, following Dr. Greenson's instructions over the telephone, looked in through the window and then called him back to report that she had seen Marilyn lying face down on the bed and that her appearance seemed unnatural.

What Greenson Did

WHAT THEY TOLD CLEMMONS
Dr. Greenson tried knocking on Marilyn's bedroom door. When he received no response, he went out and looked through the window. Seeing her motionless, he broke the window.

FIRST OFFICIAL REPORT
Dr. Greenson arrived, went straight to the window, broke it, and found Marilyn dead.

FOLLOW-UP REPORT
The same.

Whether or not Marilyn Held a Telephone

WHAT THEY TOLD CLEMMONS
None of the three witnesses mentioned a telephone.

FIRST OFFICIAL REPORT
Dr. Greenson removed the telephone receiver from Marilyn's hand.

FOLLOW-UP REPORT
The same.

Who Called Dr. Engelberg

WHAT THEY TOLD CLEMMONS
Dr. Greenson called Engelberg after finding Marilyn dead.

FIRST OFFICIAL REPORT
The same.

FOLLOW-UP REPORT
Before leaving his home, Dr. Greenson told Mrs. Murray to call Dr. Engelberg and have him join them at Marilyn's.

When Engelberg Pronounced Marilyn Dead

WHAT THEY TOLD CLEMMONS
Dr. Engelberg pronounced her dead shortly after 12:30 A.M.

FIRST OFFICIAL REPORT
Dr. Engelberg pronounced her dead shortly after 3:35 A.M.

FOLLOW-UP REPORT
Dr. Engelberg pronounced her dead shortly after 3:50 A.M.

The contradictions in these three accounts of the night's events are obvious. Though Sergeant Byron only had the first official report and the follow-up report to work with, these should have been enough. It is not easy to believe that any of the three had difficulty remembering experiences as important as:
* who first looked through the window;
* whether Dr. Greenson came over immediately or first asked Mrs. Murray to check again and call him back; and
* whether Mrs. Murray or Dr. Greenson called Dr. Engelberg.

Byron's failure to notice, and subsequently investigate, these discrepancies is inexplicable. It is equally difficult to understand how he could have failed to notice that the sequence of events the three witnesses describe could not possibly have taken place in the time frame their testimonies established. In their longest version, from the beginning — when Mrs. Murray first summoned Dr. Greenson — to the conclusion — when Dr. Engelberg pronounced Marilyn dead — no more than twenty minutes passed. During this brief period the following events occurred:

(1) Dr. Greenson got out of bed;

(2) dressed;

(3) went out and started his car;

(4) drove three miles to Marilyn's house;

(5) saw Marilyn's body through the window, smashed the window and crawled inside Marilyn's room;

(6) examined her body and found her dead;

(7) called Dr. Engelberg, who then

(8) got up, dressed, and went out;

(9) started his car;

(10) drove two miles to Marilyn's house;

(11) went in, examined her, and pronounced her dead.

Could Byron really have believed all this activity transpired in just twenty minutes? If so, it would have required extremely fast action on the part of two men awakened from a sound sleep at 3:30 A.M.

In the earlier testimony obtained by Jack Clemmons, Mrs. Murray told Clemmons that the doctors had pronounced Marilyn dead shortly after midnight. When queried as to the reason for the delay in notifying the LAPD, the response given outlined a sequence of events which eliminated nearly three hours in the time frame established by later testimony. Remarkably, Sergeant Byron failed to notice that, in either version, there was a delay of nearly an hour prior to the LAPD's notification of Marilyn's death.

These shockingly obvious discrepancies raise serious questions about the evidence that Mrs. Murray, Dr. Greenson, and Dr. Engelberg gave the police. Why Sergeant Byron never queried either their existence, or remarkable significance, is yet another of the baffling mysteries surrounding

(1) Dr. Greenson got out of bed;

(2) dressed;

(3) went out and started his car;

(4) drove three miles to Marilyn's house;

(5) saw Marilyn's body through the window, smashed the window and crawled inside Marilyn's room;

(6) examined her body and found her dead;

(7) called Dr. Engelberg, who then

(8) got up, dressed, and went out;

(9) started his car;

(10) drove two miles to Marilyn's house;

(11) went in, examined her, and pronounced her dead.

Could Byron really have believed all this activity transpired in just twenty minutes? If so, it would have required extremely fast action on the part of two men awakened from a sound sleep at 3:30 A.M.

In the earlier testimony obtained by Jack Clemmons, Mrs. Murray told Clemmons that the doctors had pronounced Marilyn dead shortly after midnight. When queried as to the reason for the delay in notifying the LAPD, the response given outlined a sequence of events which eliminated nearly three hours in the time frame established by later testimony. Remarkably, Sergeant Byron failed to notice that, in either version, there was a delay of nearly an hour prior to the LAPD's notification of Marilyn's death.

These shockingly obvious discrepancies raise serious questions about the evidence that Mrs. Murray, Dr. Greenson, and Dr. Engelberg gave the police. Why Sergeant Byron never queried either their existence, or remarkable significance, is yet another of the baffling mysteries surrounding Marilyn's death.

Equally unfathomable as Byron's negligent investigation of the discrepancies in the testimony of key witnesses, was his extraordinary disregard for the physical evidence at the them, the bottles had been set back neatly upright with all the caps on tight.

Even without interviewing Jack Clemmons, Byron should have known from the physical evidence at the scene that there was more to Marilyn Monroe's death than suicide. The physical evidence of foul play that Byron said didn't exist was right under his nose — literally. Byron could have found one of those clues by simply looking down at his feet.

Mrs. Murray had told all three police investigators that she had first become concerned about Marilyn when she saw the bedroom light was still shining through the space beneath Marilyn's door. It was the one consistent element in her story. But workmen had installed new, deep-pile carpeting in Marilyn's bedroom only a few weeks earlier.

Police photos of the death scene show that this carpet's pile was so deep, the legs of Marilyn's bed disappear into the nap; the mattress appears to be lying on the floor. When I visited the site of Marilyn's death a few days later, I discovered the carpet piling was so high that it prevented any light from escaping under the bedroom door — a fact that was confirmed by others not long after.

Had Sergeant Byron been more observant and taken note of the carpeting's deep pile — if he had simply turned on the light, closed the door, and looked to see how much light actually escaped — he might have asked Mrs. Murray two key questions:

* How had she actually first learned of Marilyn's death?
* Why did she want to conceal the manner in which she had first become aware of Marilyn's death?

If he had posed these queries, we might know far more about how Marilyn really died.

There was another vital piece of evidence lying right at Byron's feet. Had he walked outside and bent over, Byron might have held one of the more significant pieces of evidence contradicting the testimony of Dr. Greenson and Mrs. Murray in the palm of his hand.

Dr. Greenson told police that he had gained entrance to Marilyn's locked bedroom by going outside and smashing a pane in the window of her bedroom. But on the same visit in which I discovered the depth of the bedroom carpet's piling, I found that the broken glass from the window pane was, curiously, all on the outside of the house. Only a blow struck from *inside* Marilyn's bedroom would have knocked all the glass to the room's exterior.

Byron might have canvassed the neighborhood, and asked Marilyn's neighbors if they knew anything that might shed light on her death. Byron appears to have contacted one or two neighbors, but seems to have put as little effort into that aspect of the investigation as he did into all the others. He failed to discover three neighborhood ladies — who had been playing cards the night of the death — and another neighbor, Abe Landau, all of whom had seen an ambulance parked next to Marilyn's home around midnight, a full four hours before her death was reported.

How could an LAPD detective with Sergeant Byron's experience have overlooked so many obvious clues? Some journalists believe Byron did not overlook these clues at all. They think the perfunctory, inadequate nature of his investigation and his report's arbitrary conclusion of suicide were part of a deliberate attempt to conceal the true circumstances of Marilyn Monroe's death — a cover-up that Byron may have carried out at the direction of Chief William Parker, the head of the LAPD.

PARKER'S AMBITIONS

A number of credible insiders have linked Los Angeles Chief of Police William Parker to a conspiracy and cover-up of critical facts in the death of Marilyn Monroe. In the early 1960s, this charge was ridiculed. Few would believe that the chief of police of one of the world's largest cities would take part in an effort to conceal important facts from the citizens he had sworn to serve. Now, after Watergate, Koreagate, Contragate — and even Daryl Gates — the charges against Chief Parker seem more credible.

Former LAPD officer Jack Clemmons was one of the first to discuss the possibility of a cover-up and Chief Parker's role in such a scenario. "There was a cover-up. The LAPD excuse was that national security was involved. Chief Parker had taken the records of Marilyn's last phone calls. For years LAPD denied he had them, but in 1985 they were forced to cough them up."

Milo Speriglio, CEO of the Nick Harris Detective Agency, has also been outspoken about this conspiracy and the LAPD's participation. "My investigation has led me to believe there has been a massive cover-up of the death of Marilyn Monroe. It involved the district attorney's office, the coroner's office, and other politicians and bureaus."

One victim of this cover-up was Parker's boss, former L.A. Mayor Sam Yorty. Incredible as it seems, Parker concealed the existence of the LAPD files on Marilyn's death from his own boss, the highest elected official in Los Angeles, and one of the most powerful politicians in California. This cover-up was still in effect years after Parker's death.

As Yorty tells it: "I don't remember what the year was, but Chief Parker was no longer chief; he was dead. I asked the police department to send me any records they had about Marilyn's death, and they said they didn't have any." Then Yorty discovered the truth. "Later I found out they did have records. And that surprised me. Because I had a very good relationship with them, and I really thought they didn't have any." Then the mayor pauses for emphasis. He wants what he says next to be remembered. "They must have had a secret they didn't want to come out," he says.

The extent of Chief Parker's participation in the cover-up, though it appears to have been substantial, can never be known; neither can all his motives. Some people believe part of the answer may lie in Parker's personal ambitions and close relationship with Bobby Kennedy after he became attorney general.

Sam Yorty attests to both Parker's ambitions and his friendship with the Kennedys. He was an eyewitness to the way Bobby received the chief on a trip to Washington. "He was very friendly with the Kennedys, and Bobby was very friendly with him. They got along very well. When we went to Washington, we stopped by the Justice Department to see Bobby Kennedy — and, of course, we went right in."

Yorty was well aware of Parker's political ambitions, ambitions only Bobby Kennedy could have fulfilled. "He would have liked to have been head of the FBI, and he certainly would have been good at it. But, of course, to get that job, you have to have Bobby Kennedy on your side."

POLICE PROCEDURE OR POLITICS

Increasingly, the evidence suggests that the LAPD made no real investigation of Marilyn Monroe's death. Important discrepancies in the stories told by Murray, Greenson and Engelberg — as well as important physical evidence at the scene — were ignored. Minimal effort to contact neighbors resulted in the failure to learn about the ambulance seen outside the actress's house shortly after midnight. Relying almost entirely on the inconsistent and duplicitous testimony of her housekeeper and her two doctors, the conclusions which formed the official LAPD report were egregiously superficial, if not erroneous.

The coroner, the pathologist, even the special team of psychiatrists who investigated Marilyn's state of mind when she died, relied on the LAPD report's assurances that there were no signs of anything abnormal at the scene of Marilyn's death. This suggests that the conclusions these subsequent investigators drew might be wrong as well.

Is the LAPD too professional an organization to mishandle an inquiry into the death of a high-profile celebrity? That they would have deliberately mishandled it without orders from the top seems unlikely. Could such a cover-up have been part of a larger conspiracy?

But what could this conspiracy be designed to cover up? Could the actress's last lethal cocktail have been accidental? Could Marilyn have been so far gone from pills that she no longer remembered how many she'd taken earlier, and so unknowingly gulped down one handful too many — as many people have suggested? Possibly. But if so, no one would have conspired to hide an accident, and thus tarnish the star's image with suicide.

Until very recently, few people have been willing to accept the incredible truth. The next obvious conclusion, though logical, seemed too far out, too incredible — the stuff of bad fiction or lunatic conspiracy theorists — to believe.

But suddenly it is being revealed in best-sellers, and has become the subject of many television reports. If the conspiracy to cover up key facts about the way Marilyn Monroe died was not to conceal suicide and was not to conceal an accident, then only one possibility remains . . . Murder.

THE OCID: LAPD'S SPY UNIT

Front page news in July, 1992, revealed the secret surveillance activities of the LAPD's Organized Crime Intelligence Division (OCID).

LA's new Police Chief, Willie L. Williams, who replaced the outspoken and controversial Daryl Gates, made a surprise move in closing down the operations of the OCID, sealing its offices and files, and launching an internal investigation.

Reportedly, Chief Williams' sudden move was precipitated by the recent publication of *L.A. Secret Police: Inside the LAPD Elite Spy Network*, written by a former OCID detective, Michael J. Rothmiller, with Ivan C. Goldman.

According to the authors, the LAPD has a long history of spying on high-profile Los Angeles citizens, actors, politicians, business leaders, celebrities, "subversives," and others deemed to be "of interest to the department." These intelligence-gathering activities were organized and operated under a variety of names, the OCID being the current designation.

Among those reportedly spied on by the LAPD are Mayor Tom Bradley, Dodger Manager Tommy Lasorda, Frank Sinatra, Barbra Streisand, Robert Redford, Rock Hudson, Sugar Ray Leonard, former Governor Jerry Brown, and many other notables . . . including Marilyn Monroe and Robert F. Kennedy!

I have long suspected that this information existed. As you can see from my collection of documents reprinted in the back of this book, I have asked for these files and have repeatedly received misleading responses from a protective LAPD seeking to hide its own involvement in intelligence-gathering. It seems that refreshing winds of change may now be clearing the murky atmosphere created by Chief William Parker, and so craftily perpetuated by Chief Daryl Gates.

Perhaps under this newly open and responsible leadership, some of those "lost" or "non-existent" files and photographs may finally surface. I expect even more explosive information regarding Marilyn and the Kennedys will erupt in the wake of this breakthrough at the LAPD.

FILE #11

The Inconclusive Autopsy

On the morning of August 5, Marilyn Monroe's body arrived at the basement morgue of the Los Angeles County Coroner's office. There it was prepared for an autopsy that would leave very little of the actress's legendary beauty untouched. The one photo of her face taken after the autopsy shows an unrecognizable ruin.

The police investigation had been badly bungled — some say deliberately so. Now the pathologist's scalpel would have its turn at exposing the secrets of the blond sex symbol's death.

Dr. Thomas Noguchi, a brilliant young pathologist on the coroner's staff, was called on to perform the autopsy. Noguchi would later head the coroner's office, gaining fame as L.A.'s flamboyant "Coroner to the Stars." Dr. Noguchi's peers would rank him at the top of their profession, electing him president of the National Association of Medical Examiners.

Still in his early thirties at the time of Marilyn's death, Noguchi's skill and talent were already held in high regard by the coroner's staff. Deputy Coroner's Aide Lionel Grandison, who worked in the department during the early 1960s, recalls the reputation that Noguchi had earned among the coroner's staff. "Dr. Noguchi was a very thorough doctor. Everyone in the coroner's office felt Dr. Noguchi was the best surgeon in the place. The talk around the office was: if you wanted an autopsy, and you wanted accurate information, you asked Dr. Noguchi to do it." Deputy District Attorney John Miner was the D.A.'s official observer at that autopsy. An attorney specializing in medical and psychiatric law, Miner's credentials are impressive. Miner, an associate clinical professor at the University of Southern California Medical School, has also lectured on the faculty of the Institute of Psychiatry.

Together the pathologist and the deputy D.A. would examine Marilyn's body for clues to the cause of her death.

Having read Sergeant Robert Byron's preliminary report, the two men would be particularly alert for evidence that the actress had killed herself by taking a massive overdose of barbiturates. Marilyn's stomach would be inspected for traces of pills. Her skin would be searched for needle marks. Her digestive system would be examined for signs of an overdose administered by suppository or enema.

Noguchi and Miner's visual examination would be supplemented by the toxicologist's report. The toxicologist, Ralph Abernathy, would test samples of the actress's blood, organs, and tissues. With reagents and microscopes, he would discover if Marilyn actually had taken drugs before she died — and if she had taken drugs, which drugs, and in what amounts.

If Marilyn had died of a barbiturate overdose, Noguchi would look to his autopsy and the toxicology reports to answer three vital questions:

* What specific drugs had she taken?
* How had those drugs gotten into her body?
* How long had it taken for them to kill her?

From these he hoped to learn whether Marilyn had deliberately taken her own life or consumed the lethal overdose by accident. Dr. Noguchi had ruled out homicide almost from the beginning, guided by Sergeant Byron's far from accurate report. The resultant autopsy report and the conclusions drawn from it may be a classic case of how expectations influence perceptions.

THE AUTOPSY

At 10:30 A.M., Dr. Noguchi was gowned, gloved, and ready to proceed with the autopsy. Deputy D.A. John Miner stood next to him. Noguchi's assistants hovered in the background, waiting eagerly to carry out his commands.

Today, John Miner is the only person who was present at that autopsy willing to talk. Miner's eyewitness account of Noguchi's dissection of one of the world's most beautiful women is all the more chilling because of the measured, clinical terms in which it is told.

Noguchi and Miner began the autopsy by inspecting Marilyn's body for puncture marks. They found no sign that drugs might have been injected through the skin with a hypodermic needle. Miner's memory is very clear on this point.

"We both examined the body very carefully with a magnifying glass for needle marks," he told me in an exclusive interview. "It would have taken a substantial dosage of barbiturates to kill her, and that would have produced a noticeable bruise. If drugs had been administered by way of injection, there would have been evidence of it. Any needle produces at least a small ecchymosis, a bruise."

The pathologist and the deputy D.A. even checked between the actress's "toes and orifices." Today John Miner is prepared to swear that: "There were no needle marks on the body. There was no indication that the drugs had been administered by way of a hypodermic needle. If there had been needle marks, they would have been apparent on such a very careful examination of the body."

Noguchi and Miner did find bruises on Marilyn's body, but Miner says all of them were minor, except for one large bruise on the star's left hip. "We saw a bruised area on the body," he recalls, "but it wasn't bad or extensive — nothing that could have contributed to death in any way." Marilyn's lack of needle marks proved that if she had died of an overdose, it had not been by injection. If Dr. Noguchi wanted to learn anything further about the cause of her death, it would have to be through dissection.

"The body was opened up," Miner recalls, "the rib cage removed. Then all of the chest organs were examined, weighed, and samples of each dropped in a jar of formalin to preserve them for examination. The same was done to the organs in the abdomen and the throat."

Noguchi removed Marilyn's liver in its entirety. The liver is one of the body's vital organs. It detoxifies dangerous substances by absorbing them from the bloodstream. The higher the concentration of a substance in the liver, the longer it has been in the body. In cases of drug overdose, the amount of the drug in the liver helps pinpoint when the drugs were taken and how long the victim took to die.

Next the pathologist slit open the actress's stomach, and the two men examined the contents for signs of the sleeping pills she was said to have taken. But here, too, they were to be disappointed. "There was a small quantity of liquid in the stomach," John Miner recalls, "but we did not detect any sign that would indicate it contained any heavy drugs or sedatives."

Continuing their examination of Marilyn's digestive system, Noguchi and Miner looked at the duodenum, the first section of the small intestine after the stomach. Sometimes, when pills have been in the body a long time, they will have moved through the stomach, but remains can be found in the duodenum. "The duodenum was felt all the way down to the ileum, which is at the end of the small intestine and the beginning of the large intestine," Miner says, "but there was nothing obstructive."

Noguchi knew he had not ruled out the possibility that Marilyn had swallowed sleeping pills. Many capsules dissolve quickly in the stomach. If the actress had not died immediately, all trace of pills might well have vanished.

The two men completed their search of the star's digestive system by inspecting the large intestine and rectum. But according to John Miner, they discovered none of the "discoloration or irritation" that suppositories create. The actress's large intestine also looked normal, with the exception of a "purplish discoloration of a portion of the sigmoid colon." At the time, neither Noguchi or Miner felt the discoloration was important.

Today, with the benefit of hindsight, Miner believes the discoloration of the colon should have been followed up: "I had seen autopsies of barbiturate overdose deaths at least a score of times, and I'd never seen that. I should have pursued it further, but I didn't." Miner feels his failure to pursue this issue was a "mistake." However, he was only the district attorney's observer. As a layman, he had no choice but to trust Dr. Noguchi's medical judgment over his own.

Noguchi's autopsy was to be much criticized in later years. But John Miner, who was an eyewitness to that autopsy, disagrees. In Miner's opinion, "It was a thoroughly professional autopsy." Yet before the week was over, Miner, the man who still praises Noguchi's work on that autopsy, would write a highly controversial memo completely contradicting the pathologist's conclusions.

Noguchi and Miner had learned nothing from the physical examination of Marilyn Monroe's body. They found no clues that would indicate what had killed her or how she had died. Their hopes were now pinned to the toxicologist's report.

THE TOXICOLOGIST'S REPORT

Samples of Marilyn Monroe's organs, tissues, and blood were dispatched to the toxicologist's laboratory by Dr. Noguchi. There toxicologist Ralph Abernathy subjected these samples to chemical tests and microscopic examination. The results were consistent with at least one part of Sergeant Byron's preliminary report: Marilyn's death was due to a massive overdose of barbiturates.

Abernathy found 4.5 milligrams percent barbiturates in the star's blood — ten times the prescribed dose. His tests also revealed 8.0 milligrams percent of chloral hydrate in the blood — twenty times the prescribed dosage. All together, there were enough drugs in the actress's beautiful young body to have killed a dozen Marilyn Monroes.

Abernathy's analysis of the liver shed further light on the actress's death. Her liver contained 13 milligrams percent barbiturates. This is a "high concentration," according to John Miner. "It indicates that however the drugs were administered, hours and not minutes were involved before she died." Toxicology had discovered the cause of Marilyn Monroe's death. It was now up to Dr. Noguchi to discover how that death had occurred.

THE PATHOLOGIST'S REPORT

Pathologist Thomas Noguchi's conclusions would be based on toxicological analysis. Noguchi's conclusions were the vital second link in a chain of evaluations that allowed the coroner to arrive quickly at the official verdict of "suicide" and preempt any deeper investigation into the actress's death. Thanks to Dr. Noguchi's own testimony, we now know how he arrived at those conclusions.

Sergeant Byron's preliminary report stated that Marilyn Monroe was a probable suicide whose death resulted from barbiturate overdose. Her body had been found in a room whose windows and doors were all locked from the inside. An empty bottle of sleeping pills, said by her physician to have contained forty-seven capsules of Nembutal the day before, lay on her bedside table. The toxicology report confirmed the barbiturate overdose — Marilyn Monroe's body had been saturated with the deadly drug at the time of her death.

Noguchi's own examination had ruled out injection, suppository, and enema. A half-empty glass of water had been discovered near Marilyn's bed. That suggested she had swallowed the fatal dose. True, Noguchi had failed to detect any trace of the pills in Marilyn's stomach. But that seemed a minor detail. The liver analysis showed that it had taken the actress several hours to die. All trace of the pills could have dissolved into her bloodstream by then.

To Dr. Noguchi, trying to correlate the medical evidence with the known circumstances of her death, it appeared that the actress had locked herself inside her room before taking the overdose. Noguchi had read that all the windows were also locked from the inside. This made it seem likely she had consumed the barbiturates while alone — precluding the possibility of homicide or anyone else's involvement in her death.

The empty bottle of pills found by Marilyn's bedside seemed to rule out accident. The actress might have become groggy and taken an overdose without realizing it, but it was not likely she could have consumed an entire bottle of pills in a few hours by accident.

Noguchi's final deductions are summed up in a few words

in the official report the pathologist would forward to the coroner. Under *Cause of Death*, Dr. Noguchi entered: "Acute barbiturate poisoning due to ingestion of overdose." Under *Mode of Death*, he circled "Suicide," writing the word "probable" after it in his own hand.

Noguchi's report, which he was to repudiate many years later, carried great weight in the coroner's final verdict in the death of Marilyn Monroe. The coroner would even emphasize Noguchi's findings in the press conference where the official verdict was announced. Had Noguchi's report on the autopsy been different, the coroner's verdict would have been different.

If Noguchi had concluded that the circumstances surrounding Marilyn Monroe's death were ambiguous, that the events of the death did not correspond as closely to the medical evidence as he might like, the coroner's investigation would have proceeded much differently. The coroner's office would have had no choice but to hold a full-scale inquest, summoning all who could offer information about that death to testify under oath, and before the public, to what they knew.

Yet Noguchi would question his own conclusions during a nationwide television interview. Ironically, it was the purplish bruise on the actress's left hip, the one that John Miner dismissed, that Noguchi felt should have been followed up. That bruise, Noguchi stated, "has never been fully explained."

Asked what might have caused the bruise, Noguchi stunned reporters: "There is no explanation for that bruise. It is a sign of violence."

"Did that mean Noguchi thought Marilyn Monroe might have been murdered?" one reporter wanted to know.

"Could be," Noguchi answered.

The man whose findings had been instrumental in helping bring about the original coroner's verdict concluded the interview by calling for a new official investigation. "I feel an inquiry or evaluation of the new information should be made."

Could it be that Noguchi, misled by Byron's highly suspect report, overlooked other vital clues as well? Noguchi doesn't think so. But those who have studied the curious death of Marilyn Monroe, while welcoming Noguchi's call for a new investigation, believe that Noguchi's heavy reliance on the facts as reported by Byron caused the pathologist to misperceive and misinterpret some of the autopsy's key findings.

Because Noguchi believed Dr. Greenson's now-suspect account of Marilyn dying in a locked bedroom, he may have dismissed two important but contradictory facts. First, Noguchi found a massive dose of barbiturates in Marilyn's bloodstream. Second, he found no trace in her stomach of the almost forty-seven pills she was said to have taken.

Since Noguchi mistakenly thought the evidence showed that Marilyn had locked herself in her room before taking the overdose, he assumed the pills might have already been dissolved. But would he have made the same assumption if he had known the truth? Or would he have felt there was greater reason to question the absence of residue in her stomach? We may never know.

We do know that Noguchi had second thoughts about his autopsy report not long after he had turned it in. The toxicologist had tested only Marilyn's blood and liver. After discovering evidence of overdose, he had not bothered to analyze the rest of the samples. Noguchi, his curiosiy aroused by something he has yet to disclose, asked for the remaining samples to be tested.

But Noguchi was too late. The samples had vanished. They, too, had become part of the official cover-up of the death of Marilyn Monroe.

Sound farfetched? Then consider this: according to former Deputy D.A. John Miner, organ samples have disappeared from the Los Angeles County Coroner's Office only twice in history.

Once in the death of Marilyn Monroe.

Once in the death of Bobby Kennedy.

FILE #12

The Coroner Wants a Suicide

Dr. Thomas Noguchi's autopsy report on Marilyn Monroe was forwarded to the Los Angeles County Coroner's office. At the time of Marilyn's death, the coroner was the powerful, controversial Dr. Theodore Curphey. Curphey was the medical official responsible for discovering the cause of death when accident, suicide, or murder were suspected.

To reach his verdict, Curphey could call on the resources of the police, the district attorney, and even the state and federal government. Where there was doubt about the cause of death, he could convene an inquest, subpoena witnesses, and conduct a full-scale inquiry.

In cases where suicide is suspected, the coroner must seek evidence about the deceased's state of mind. Friends, relatives, and colleagues are interviewed, along with physicians, ministers, and therapists. Every clue is gathered that might help the coroner's office find out whether the victim's mental makeup makes suicide a likelihood.

The results of these investigations are added to those of

the police investigation and the pathologist's report. The coroner must then decide if the total circumstances surrounding the victim's death support a verdict of suicide.

Members of the coroner's staff usually conduct the interviews into the decedent's state of mind when possible suicides are being investigated. But in the case of Marilyn Monroe, Dr. Curphey broke precedent and gave these tasks to outsiders.

To interview Marilyn Monroe's family and friends about her state of mind, Dr. Curphey picked members of the newly formed Los Angeles Suicide Prevention Center. To interview the actress's psychiatrist, the one man who could give the greatest insight into her mental state, Curphey chose Deputy D.A. John Miner, whom he knew had witnessed Marilyn's autopsy and concurred with its findings.

The Suicide Prevention Center's enquiry, which was heavily influenced by the now-suspect police and autopsy reports, would echo them in concluding that Marilyn Monroe had taken her own life. But Deputy D.A. John Miner, the man who had called Noguchi's autopsy thoroughly professional, would become the first to dissent from the prevailing evaluations of Marilyn's death. However, Miner's dissent would go completely unheard, suppressed by Coroner Theodore Curphey, who would make no mention of it at the press conference that presented his official verdict to the world. Miner's report would first be buried in the files, and then vanish from them, becoming another milestone in the conspiracy to cover up the truth about the death of Marilyn Monroe.

THE SUICIDE PREVENTION TEAM

The newly formed Los Angeles Suicide Prevention Center was the brainchild of Dr. Norman Farberow, a psychologist, and Dr. Robert Litman, a psychiatrist. Together, they and members of the center's special Suicide Investigation Team were asked to find out everything they could about Marilyn Monroe's personal life, and then tell the coroner whether, in their professional experience, she was a likely candidate for suicide.

Coroner Curphey's choice of the Suicide Center's fledgling Investigation Team was an odd one. Experienced in the prevention of suicide, the team's members were all therapists. They had no previous experience with investigations or investigative procedures. Considering the public stature of the deceased and the spotlight of attention that would be focused on her death, Curphey's motives in selecting a group of inexperienced investigators rather than seasoned professionals from his own office has drawn suspicion.

Critics of Curphey's investigation have suggested one possible motive. Dr. Farberow's Suicide Investigation Team had a number of plusses for anyone planning to conceal facts about the actress's death.

The team was a privately funded group of doctors acting on a volunteer basis. Its members were not a part of any government organization. If their findings were ever questioned, the coroner's office could not be held accountable. Curphey could sidestep any negative fallout by the classic political ploy of laying the blame on a well-intentioned idea gone wrong.

The Suicide Prevention Team's status as a private organization had another plus for anyone planning a cover-up: as therapists, all team members were bound by confidentiality laws. They could not ethically reveal the names of those they interviewed nor disclose the contents of those interviews. Only their conclusions could be revealed publicly.

The team had a final plus for conspiracy theorists. Those interviewed by the Team would not be required to testify under oath. If they perjured themselves or hid important facts in aid of a cover-up, they could not be prosecuted later in a court of law.

Sergeant Jack Clemmons, the first police officer to visit the scene of Marilyn's death, believes Curphey's appointment of the untried Suicide Investigation Team was part of a deliberate cover-up. "The case had gotten so hot the coroner appointed this panel of psychiatrists. If Curphey had gotten caught with his pants down, he could say, 'I relied on those guys, and they misled me.' He was one of the people covering his rear end."

Is Clemmons right? Were LA County Coroner Theodore Curphey's actions part of a conspiracy? Or was Curphey, like pathologist Thomas Noguchi, innocently misled by the highly inaccurate police report? There is reason to hope we can soon answer this question.

Coroner Curphey's decision to use the Suicide Investigation Team, like so many of his decisions about this case, was made hastily. On August 6, the day after Marilyn's body was discovered, Curphey held a joint press conference with Dr. Farberow to announce the team's appointment. Dr. Farberow and his associates, Curphey said, were ideally qualified to advise him on the star's mental state. Both Curphey and Farberow promised a major investigative effort.

The next day, August 7, Dr. Farberow held a second press conference. "We're interviewing anybody and everybody," he told reporters. "We will seek out all persons with whom Marilyn had recently been associated." Then, to emphasize his determination to be thorough, Farberow added: "Well go as far back in her life as necessary."

Many years after Marilyn's death, Dr. Farberow would be asked if the Suicide Investigation Team had questioned either Kennedy brother. His reply was the first indication that the team's maiden efforts had been less than promised. "No," he told reporters. "We did not."

Asked to explain this critical lapse, Dr. Farberow shrugged.

"I'm sure discretion entered into it," he said.

Only the years would reveal just how inadequate that investigation had been. The list of those who have told journalists that the Suicide Investigation Team did not interview them has grown into a Who's Who of Marilyn's life. It includes: Bebe Goddard, her childhood friend; Bebe's parents, who had raised Marilyn; Jeanne Carmen; Terry Moore; Peter Lawford; Norman Jeffries, Marilyn's gardener; Ralph Roberts, her masseur; and at least three of her four husbands. Altogether, the Suicide Investigation Team seems to have interviewed less than a dozen people, many of them not very close friends, while ignoring many more who were in a far better position to comment on her personality and behavior.

On August 8, two days after his second press conference, Dr. Norman Farberow and his Suicide Investigation Team were back in the headlines. Farberow again touted the thoroughness of their investigation. The team's inquiries had "no limitations," he assured the media.

Four days after this assurance, on August 13, Florbel Muir, a veteran police reporter with an enviable record for accuracy, made national headlines when she informed readers of "mystery pressures in Marilyn probe." Muir's article, which was not carried in any of the Los Angeles papers, revealed that "strange pressures are being put on Los Angeles Police . . . sources close to the probers said tonight . . . the purported pressures are mysterious." Then Muir gave those familiar with Marilyn's recent amours a strong clue to the purported source of these pressures.

They are apparently coming from persons who had been closely in touch with Marilyn the last few weeks, this veteran reporter stated.

August 14, the next day, Dr. Norman Farberow held a hurried press conference in Los Angeles. Although his Suicide Investigation Team had been on the job for little more than a week, Farberow told reporters he was ready to announce the team's preliminary findings. Interviews with those who knew Marilyn best, Farberow claimed, had convinced team members the star was "an emotionally disturbed person who suffered from deep inner conflicts."

One week later, on August 21, only fifteen days after it began, the investigation that "would go as far back as necessary" and "had no limitations" was over. Coroner Curphey and Dr. Farberow held another press conference. The Los Angeles Suicide Prevention Team was prepared to announce their results.

Marilyn Monroe, Farberow announced, had suffered from severe depressions and abrupt mood changes for many years. Evidence showed that she had tried to take her own life several times before. The actress had even been institutionalized briefly after one suicide attempt.

There had been a pattern to Marilyn Monroe's suicide attempts, Dr. Farberow said, and the way she died fit into that pattern. First the star would take an overdose of sleeping pills, then she would phone a friend for help. Marilyn's cries for help had always been successful before. Someone had always responded to her call, and she had been rescued. On the night of August 4, the Suicide Investigation Team's report ended. The same pattern was repeated except for the rescue.

During the press conference, Farberow cited the police report on Marilyn's death. "Its contents had guided and influenced his team's decisions," Farberow said. No matter what those interviewed told the Suicide Prevention Team, would Dr. Farberow have been as certain about its conclusions if he had known the truth about Sergeant Robert Byrons investigation? It's not easy to believe he would.

But there was still one voice to be heard before Curphey could safely deliver his verdict and close out the case: John Miner, the man he had assigned to interview Ralph Greenson,

Marilyn Monroe's psychiatrist. Greenson had found the actress's body. He had been the one who first told the police she had "killed herself." Curphey had every reason to assume Greenson's voice would be just one more in the growing chorus that said Marilyn Monroe was a victim of her own hand.

With this assumption, Coroner Curphey was due for a shock.

THE MINER MEMORANDUM

The LAPD, the Coroner, and the Suicide Prevention Center all concurred: the beloved screen personality had taken her own life.

John Miner was an acquaintance of Marilyn's psychiatrist, Dr. Ralph Greenson. Since Miner, an attorney, also held a degree in psychology and was a lecturer at the prestigious Institute of Psychiatry, he was the logical choice to interview Dr. Greenson about Marilyn's psychiatric history and mental condition.

As Marilyn Monroe's psychiatrist, Greenson ought to have known more about how her mind worked than anyone else alive. To give his investigation the appearance of completion, Coroner Curphey had to ask Greenson's opinion. Did her psychiatrist believe the actress had taken her own life? "That question needed to be answered," Miner recalls. "My interview with Dr. Greenson was an effort to achieve that objective. I knew Dr. Greenson personally. Dr. Curphey knew that, and so he asked me to interview Dr. Greenson."

Dr. Greenson imposed one condition. "A promise was exacted by Dr. Greenson," Miner explains. "I would not reveal the content of anything I learned. He imposed this condition by reason of his professional ethics and consideration for Miss Monroe's privacy."

Miner accepted Greenson's terms, promising never to disclose the specifics of their interview. "I gave him my word that I would not," Miner says simply. Dr. Greenson in turn agreed that Miner was free to report the conclusions he drew from their talk, and to discuss those conclusions within certain limits.

According to Miner, Greenson was still shaken by Marilyn's death at the time of the interview. The two men met in the doctor's office a few days after the funeral and talked for several hours. Greenson discussed "not only Marilyn's habits but also the private confidences she shared with her psychiatrist."

Like Curphey, Miner assumed his interview with the man who had said his patient had taken "forty-seven Nembutals was strictly routine." Whatever Greenson said about the actress's death could only further confirm the judgment Miner had been the first to make. What Miner learned from the star's psychiatrist must have stunned him as much as it would Coroner Curphey.

Greenson told Miner he never made tape recordings of his sessions with Marilyn. But he did play a half-hour tape that Marilyn had made at home on her own machine. On this tape, intended only for her ears and those of Dr. Greenson, the star felt free to talk about her innermost thoughts and future plans. What Marilyn said on this tape made Miner conclude she had not died by her own hand.

Miner remembers it this way: "Dr. Greenson very graciously extended me an opportunity for quite a lengthy interview, one in which I heard tapes that were made by Miss Monroe. Afterward, I wrote a very short memorandum for Coroner Curphey. It stated that as a result of the interview I had with him, it was my conviction that Miss Monroe did not commit suicide."

Did Dr. Greenson share this view? John Miner says he did: "Dr. Greenson was very strongly of the opinion that Miss

Monroe did not commit suicide. He was very much distressed by her death. The notion that she committed suicide added to that distress, because he firmly felt that she did not commit suicide. Very much so. Very much so. That I can state. He did not bar me from saying that."

But further than this, John Miner will not go. He will not discuss the contents of the tape he heard that day or the details of his three-hour conversation with Dr. Greenson.

Under what circumstances would Miner reveal those details? "I gave my word to the man and he's dead. So I don't expect ever to reveal it. It's possible that a judge could order me to reveal it and put me in jail for contempt of court if I refused. I hope I never have to cross that bridge."

WHAT MINER MISSED

Dr. Greenson died in 1979. Without a grand jury hearing or some other legal forum to compel John Miner's testimony, there is no way to persuade the former deputy D.A. to talk. But he may not need to. Through John Miner, Dr. Greenson may have told us more than he meant to.

A few mornings earlier he had stood in the midst of Marilyn Monroe's bedroom, directed a police detective's attention to an empty bottle of Nembutal capsules, and said, "She's committed suicide. She's taken all these." By the time of his interview with Miner, Dr. Greenson knew the results of Marilyn's autopsy. He knew the toxicologist had found her saturated with deadly barbiturates. He knew Noguchi had ruled her death a "suicide," the very word he had used that fateful morning.

Strangely enough only seventy-two hours later, in his interview with John Miner, Dr. Ralph Greenson, the man whose professional evaluation of the death scene had become the keystone of every single decision that had ruled Marilyn's death a suicide so far, said that he did not believe Marilyn had taken her own life.

How can we explain this turnaround? What had happened during the preceding three days that could possibly have led Dr. Greenson, to completely reverse his opinion? Could Greenson have learned something that made him change his mind, something that outweighed all he had told police of the circumstances of Marilyn's death? It couldn't have been a minor detail, and it must have been awfully convincing.

More to the point: If Greenson had learned something which convinced him that what he had told police that morning was wrong, why didn't he come forward and tell them what he had discovered? True, he was sworn to protect his client's privacy. But if Greenson had evidence, for example, that Marilyn hadn't intended to take her own life, that her death was accidental, how could it violate her privacy for her psychiatrist to tell the world she hadn't committed suicide . . . and why he thought so?

We would find it hard to answer these questions if we didn't already know there was something fishy about Greenson's story to the police. Though Sergeant Byron failed to notice them, that story was shot through with so many holes it practically screamed cover-up.

Even Byron had noticed that the stories Greenson and his two companions told had sounded a little strained: "My feeling was that . . . it had all been rehearsed beforehand," he recorded in his report. His failure to officially note this in his report or act on it is suspicious in itself. The detective had attributed the brevity of his investigation to the fact that he noticed no signs of violence at the scene of Marilyn's death. The questions then becomes, why did Byron base his report upon testimony which sounded arranged, pre-staged? Why didn't he investigate the testimony more throughly and find out why it seemed rehearsed, and for what reason Greenson and the others felt the need to orchestrate their stories?

The answers to these questions came when, on Sunday, Greenson told the police a "rehearsed" story designed to prove that Marilyn had committed suicide and, on Wednesday, recanted his position while interviewing with John Miner.

We now know that many elements of the story which Dr. Greenson, Dr. Engelberg, and Mrs. Murray told the morning of Marilyn's death were not true.

Could the story that Greenson and the others told the police have been part of the cover-up of Marilyn's death? Did it go back that far? Did it reach those she ought to have been able to trust the most — her doctor, her psychiatrist, and her companion? Such a scenario would answer many questions. It would explain why Dr. Greenson changed his story so rapidly.

Perhaps Greenson hadn't learned anything new. Instead, the psychiatrist may have decided that his conscience would not let him go along with the cover-up. That could have been why he had to tell John Miner the truth. To Greenson, Miner was more professor of psychology than assistant D.A. Dr. Greenson felt he had to justify his treatment of Marilyn to a fellow psychologist. A man of Greenson's professional standing couldn't bear to send a peer away believing that Greenson's ineptitude had caused a patients death.

Perhaps Greenson had decided to come clean — as much as he dared, anyway the moment Miner asked for the interview. Perhaps he decided not to carry out his part in the cover-up the morning of Marilyn's death — and was only awaiting the first opportunity.

Whatever his motives, Greenson gave Miner as big a clue as he dared. He told Miner he didn't believe Marilyn had killed herself three days after he had told the police she could only have died by her own hand. Probably he thought that clue was glaring enough. If it wasn't, Greenson didn't dare follow up. Dr. Ralph Greenson had taken a chance, possibly risked his life, considering all the wire-tapping going on around him. He would never be so bold again.

The thing Greenson knew that made him tell Miner the actress hadn't committed suicide remained hidden behind the pretense of protecting her confidentiality. It couldn't have violated Marilyn's privacy for her psychiatrist, a man charged with her well-being, to at least tell the police that something she had said to him in privacy convinced him that there was reason to believe the actress might have been murdered.

No, in all probability, Ralph Greenson kept his silence not to protect Marilyn Monroe but to protect himself. If what he told John Miner is true, then what he told the police was false. To have publicly made that admission would have resulted in Greenson's personal and professional disgrace.

There could have been a second reason why Ralph Greenson remained silent. His motives may have less to do with concern about the safety of his reputation than about the safety of his life.

Yet why would Greenson have lied about Marilyn's death that Sunday morning if he hadn't been part of the cover-up? It is not likely he would have agreed to the brief participation he had in this conspiracy, if he hadn't known who wanted Marilyn's death covered-up. Greenson's reason for not saying more may be that he knew someone who had talked too much — Marilyn Monroe. And Marilyn Monroe was dead.

Unless, of course, Greenson had murdered Marilyn himself, and persuaded Mrs. Murray and Dr. Engelberg to help him conceal his guilt. But then why would Greenson have changed his story? Why would he alert Miner by telling the assistant D.A. that he didn't think the star had killed herself? Did guilt overcome Dr. Greenson, burst out for this one three-hour period, and then never overcome him again? It seems unlikely.

Though Ralph Greenson said little to Miner, it should have been enough. That he completely contradicted his own earlier conclusions was a dead giveaway that something was wrong. Greenson was trying to tell Miner that Marilyn had been murdered, but he didn't dare say it out loud there might have been bugs anywhere in his office. Greenson's recantation was the entire smoking gun of the case. But investigators and journalists seem to have missed it for more than three decades.

The very fact that Greenson changed his story proved Marilyn hadn't taken her own life she had been murdered. There is no other reasonable explanation for his behavior.

Greenson needn't have worried; his secret was safe. John Miner was too straight-shooting to imagine that people as upstanding as Dr. Greenson, Coroner Curphey, Sergeant Byron, and Chief William Parker would take part in a conspiracy to conceal the murder of a world-famous motion picture star. Or that people in real life give complicated murder clues like they do in the movies.

All Miner wrote in his report to the coroner was that Dr. Greenson did not believe his patient had taken her own life, and that what Miner had learned caused him to concur.

Miner's memorandum to Curphey was a bombshell. If Marilyn's psychiatrist, the one indisputable authority on her mental state, was convinced that she would not have killed herself, then how could the Suicide Investigation Team's findings be explained? And where did Greenson's statement leave the police report that was based on this misinformed suicide investigation? In 1982, when news of Miner's memorandum surfaced again, it would give those who questioned Curphey's final verdict their first real ammunition in their campaign against the official verdict.

Miner forwarded copies of his memo to Coroner Curphey and his own superior, District Attorney Manley Bowler. The memorandum did not ask for an investigation. It was not

Miner's place to make such a suggestion. But at the back of his mind was the hope that after the two men read it, they might convene either a grand jury or a coroner's inquest to investigate the actresss death in greater detail.

THE CORONER'S VERDICT

Now that all the reports were in, Coroner Theodore Curphey moved swiftly to close the case. Whatever Curphey's private reaction to John Miner's report, his public one was simple. In neither the press conference that Curphey held to announce his verdict, nor in the official documents that contain that verdict, is Miner's memorandum even mentioned.

Instead, Curphey ignored Miner's memorandum. He cited the similarity of the conclusions arrived at by the police, the pathologist, and the Suicide Investigation Team — all of which were based on a story that Curphey now knew Greenson had all but openly repudiated — as the basis for his verdict. Marilyn had killed herself, Curphey told reporters, by impulsively gulping down a lethal dose of pills. He pronounced her death a "probable suicide."

Foul play was ruled out, Curphey implied, because Marilyn's bedroom door and windows had been locked from the inside. The high level of barbiturates proved that she had died from a drug overdose. The empty bottle of Nembutals indicated the source of the drug. The lack of bruises on her body or other signs of a struggle indicated she had taken them voluntarily. The suicide investigation had shown that the actress had made attempts on her own life before.

"On the basis of all the information obtained," Curphey announced, "it is our opinion the case is a probable suicide." By remaining silent about Miners report, Curphey had created the illusion of complete unanimity among those who had investigated Marilyn's death.

Was Coroner Curphey also playing his role in the conspiracy to cover up the actual facts about Marilyn's death? Many critics of his department believe he was. They cite Curphey's failure to ever publicly mention John Miner's memorandum, and its subsequent disappearance, as proof.

Curphey's verdict had its critics long before Miner's report was rediscovered. Even as the Coroner's investigation had proceeded, additional accusations of cover-up and conspiracy were added to those initially made by Florbel Muir. Some of those accusations came from within the Coroner's office itself.

FILE #13

The Grand Jury That Wasn't

If anything was designed to convince the public that there really was a high-level conspiracy to cover-up crucial facts about the death of Marilyn Monroe, it was Los Angeles County District Attorney Ira Reiner's handling of a proposed 1985 grand jury investigation into allegations that such a cover-up existed.

At my instigation, the Los Angeles County Board of Supervisors, the highest elected body in LA, voted unanimously to recommend that the LA Grand Jury make an official investigation of the circumstances surrounding Marilyn's death and the increasing evidence of a conspiracy to conceal those circumstances.

After examining all the evidence, the grand jury and its foreman, Sam Cordova, agreed there was reason to doubt the original coroner's verdict of "possible suicide" and found evidence of a cover-up as well. A press conference to announce the results of this offical inquiry was scheduled.

On the day of the press conference, District Attorney

Reiner announced the firing and replacement of the grand jury foreman. It was the first time in California history that this has ever occurred. The newly appointed foreman promptly shut down the investigation.

To many observers, Reiner's actions were further evidence of the cover-up the grand jury had been asked to investigate.

The Los Angeles Board of Supervisors had first recommended an investigation be made into Marilyn's death three years earlier, on August 11, 1982, but their efforts to pursue a grand jury investigation were preempted. While the Board of Supervisors was announcing its recommendation, the then LA District Attorney John Van de Kamp, held a hastily assembled press conference to announce that, by coincidence, his department had already started such an investigation a week earlier. Why Van de Camp had failed to disclose he was beginning the investigation, he did not say.

Once again the statement that "all relevant material" would be gathered was heard.

The investigation dragged on through the fall and winter months. Van de Kamp was engaged in a hard-fought campaign for attorney general of the state of California. Whatever his decision in the case of Marilyn Monroe, it was bound to anger some faction. Thus, no announcement was made until December 28, long after the election. With voters sunk in the trough of holiday exhaustion, the story would be lost in a welter of after-Christmas sales advertising.

Like all other officials who had investigated Marilyn's death before him, Van de Kamp announced that his findings supported the official verdict of "probable suicide." As for suggestions that the actual facts of the case pointed toward a darker explanation of the actress's demise, the district attorney told reporters: "The facts, as we have found them, do not support a finding of foul play." But the facts as Van de Kamp found them, we now know, were based on a story later re-canted and a perfunctory police report that overlooked important evidence.

As with previous investigations, District Attorney Van de Kamp's attempts had two flaws: those individuals whom the D.A.'s office interviewed were not required to testify under oath nor tell all that they knew. The D.A.'s twenty-two page confidential report on the inquiry reveals that, predictably, the four people still living whose testimony might have cleared up most of the central questions about Marilyn Monroe's — death Mickey Rudin, Hyman Engelberg, Patricia Newcomb and Eunice Murray — refused to talk to investigators.

One person who did come forward to talk was former LAPD Sergeant Jack Clemmons, who had been watch commander the night of August 4. But District Attorney John Van de Kamp told Clemmons he was mistaken, that the events couldn't possibly have happened as he described them. Clemmons' story was rejected out of hand.

"I came to tell the district attorney's office my story," Clemmons recalls. "They didn't even want to talk to me. So I showed up and the district attorney, and the deputy district attorney who talked to me, were very surprised. Their attitude was somewhat bemused. I gave him the story and they took every-thing down."

Throughout the interview, the district attorney's investigators kept telling Clemmons that his story had to be wrong. "They were refuting everything I'd said. When I told him about Mrs. Murray telling me that she discovered the body at midnight, he said I was mistaken. When I told him that it was impossible for anybody to have as large an amount of barbiturates in their bloodstream as Marilyn did, and have taken the barbiturates in sleeping pills without it showing up in her stomach, he said: 'That's out of the question that can't be.' Clemmons was blind. Clemmons was incompetent. Clemmons was hallucinating! Clemmons was imagining things. So the entire thrust of this so-called investigation was simply to refute, in one way or another, anything anybody said that disagreed with what was 'officially believed.' It was just a comic opera, a lot of nonsense."

But there are two additional facts about John Van de Kamp's investigation of Marilyn's death that are worth noting: the first is that Teddy Kennedy made a few appearances at fund-raising events for Van de Kamp that fall, throwing his endorsement and that of the Kennedy clan behind Van de Kamp's candidacy. The second is that John Van de Kamp became attorney general of the State of California.

Coincidence or cover-up? Or just the appearance of a cover-up? Whatever the answer, the actions of Ira Reiner (Van de Kamp's successor) when the Board of Supervisors bypassed the district attorney's office three years later, and recommended the grand jury look into the matter should convince most objective persons that something important about Marilyn Monroe's death was being manipulated and that Reiner was in on it.

REINER TAKES CHARGE

Three years later, I petitioned the LA County Board of Supervisors to re-open the inquiry into Marilyn Monroe's death. This petition raised eighteen points that suggested that vital evidence had been missed in both the original (1962) and subsequent (Van de Kamp's 1982) investigations into Marilyn's death. I argued that since this missing evidence might open an entirely new interpretation of the case, further investigation was surely warranted.

The LA Board of Supervisors agreed. They in turn petitioned the Judge of Criminal Courts, who also agreed. The judge passed these recommendations on to the six-man body of the Los Angeles County Grand Jury. Sam Cordova, the grand jury foreman, then presented this recommendation to the body of the grand jury, who immediately approved the investigation.

With the 1985 publication of Anthony Summers, "Goddess," a revealing BBC documentary, the impending ABC-TV "20/20" documentary on Bobby Kennedy's affair with Marilyn, and continuing revelations about CIA double-dealings during the 1960s and 1970s, the media and the public began to take the grand jury investigation much more seriously than they had in 1982.

LA County grand jury foreman at the time, Sam Cordova, became a controversial figure. Previous grand jury foremen had been content to let the police and district attorney's offices develop cases and present them to the jury for investigation. Cordova liked to take charge of investigations, often initiating them without waiting for other departments to develop them for him.

Cordova's activities alienated District Attorney Ira Reiner. Critics have accused Reiner of being jealous of Cordova's prerogatives. Cordova was muscling into the district attorney's territory and challenging his previously uncontested powers.

Sam Yorty, former mayor of Los Angeles, also believes Reiner resented Cordova's actions. "The district attorney really controls the grand jury. He's not supposed to, and sometimes they do what he doesn't want them to do. They call that a 'runaway grand jury.'"

Reiner may have feared that Sam Cordova was a one-man runaway grand jury in the making. If so, the case of Marilyn Monroe certainly gave Cordova reason to be so. Reiner had already joined his predecessors in stating that there was not enough evidence to reopen the case. Now the board of supervisors and the foreman of the grand jury were humiliating Reiner publicly by questioning Reiner's judgment over an issue that was gaining national attention.

Cordova took charge of the grand jury investigation immediately. Cordova did what no other public official who had investigated the death of Marilyn Monroe had ever done: he began following up some of the clues and contradictions that I and others who have studied the circumstances surrounding the star's demise had discovered.

Call it coincidence, but Cordova was also the first public official to conclude that the facts warranted a reopening of Marilyn's case and a full-scale investigation of her death. The grand jury foreman scheduled a press conference to announce his conclusions, hinting heavily to journalists that he planned to challenge the official verdict of "probable suicide."

"There is enough evidence to substantiate a special prosecutor to work with the grand jury on the investigation," Cordova told journalists. "A full investigation has never been done by the grand jury. People have not testified under oath. That should have been done a long time ago. It should have been done in 1962."

What Cordova couldn't know was that while he was holding his press conference at the Los Angeles Press Club, District Attorney Ira Reiner was holding his own press conference in his offices downtown and chopping the ground out from under the grand jury foreman's feet. Reiner announced that he had "removed" Sam Cordova from his position. The grand jury foreman had been fired.

Reiner's action was unprecedented. Never before in California history had a grand jury foreman been removed from office. Even political insiders were shocked.

"It's extremely unusual for a district attorney to go to a court and have the court dismiss the foreman of the grand jury," explains Jack Clemmons.

Reiner assured reporters that his actions had nothing to do with Cordova's press conference earlier that day calling for a thorough public investigation into Marilyn Monroe's death. "The decision had already been made before Cordova's call for the new investigation," Reiner asserted. Reiner had not initiated the foreman's ouster, he said, but had only acted in response to a petition by all eight other members of the grand jury. The jury members felt Cordova's abrasive, impulsive behavior was impairing the jury's ability to perform its duties.

The district attorney's office would investigate Marilyn's death, Reiner announced. They would make a fair and impartial investigation and release the results as soon as possible.

Reiner's investigation was swift all right. He announced the results at another press conference the very next afternoon. "New Marilyn Probe Nixed by D.A.," headlines summed up.

Reiner told the public he wouldn't seek a new investigation after all, rejecting claims that new evidence warranted reopening the case. His office, Reiner told journalists, had thoroughly examined the facts in the case and "no evidence new or old has been brought to our attention which would support a reasonable belief or even a bare suspicion that Miss Monroe was murdered."

"The star's death," LA County District Attorney Ira Reiner said, "was a matter of historical interest only." If Reiner could have foreseen the headlines his statements set off, he might have realized that to the world, Marilyn Monroe's was a matter of much more than historical interest.

A new foreman replaced Sam Cordova. He immediately informed reporters that "we are reluctant to see it go forward." There was no runaway grand jury this time. The remaining members of the jury concurred with their new foreman. They voted not to proceed with their own investigation and announced that they were dropping the matter once and for all.

Reiner's refusal to investigate the actress's death, following on his unprecedented firing of Cordova, lent fresh ammunition to those who claimed a cover-up of evidence surrounding the actress's death. After almost twenty-five years, they said, an honest man with no entrenched ties to the political establishment had investigated Marilyn's death and confirmed their own beliefs that a deeper inquiry was justified. Now, this man had been summarily removed from his office in an act without historic precedent, and by a member of the same entrenched bureauracy suspected of participating in the original cover-up. This, they felt, was proof beyond doubt of a high-level government conspiracy to conceal facts about Marilyn Monroe's death.

There appears to be more than some justification for this claim.

THE INVESTIGATION THAT WASN'T

Examined closely, a number of Ira Reiner's statements about his actions during the 1985 grand jury investigation into Marilyn Monroe's death appear open to question. Reiner's critics say the real behind-the-scenes story differs in significant detail from the one the district attorney presented to press and public. They say that Reiner was less than truthful in at least three key matters.

The first was his explanation of Sam Cordova's firing. Reiner told reporters the other members of the grand jury were united in their opposition to Cordova, and felt the foreman was impairing the jury's ability to discharge its duties. Yet, one of the eight jurors presented a much different evaluation of Cordova only two weeks later: "He was a good man; he was trying to do a good job. My feeling has always been he was doing the right thing. There were little squabbles that really didn't mean anything."

The second of Reiner's misstatements appears to have been his assertion that his decision to replace Cordova had nothing to do with the threatened grand jury investigation of the Marilyn Monroe case. One jury member disagrees.

Reiner had preempted that issue, the man told reporters, pointing out that most of the grand jury's present knowledge of the case came from the same members of the D.A.'s staff who had supported Van de Kamp's 1962 decision not to investigate the actress's death.

Reiner's critics charge him with one other critical misstatement. In large part, the district attorney justified his decision not to reopen the investigation on the grounds that no evidence had come to his attention that would support a reasonable belief or bare suspicion that she hadn't committed suicide. But such evidence had come to Reiner's attention. Former Deputy Coroner's Aide Lionel Grandison had brought it.

According to Grandison, he told investigators from Reiner's staff about the suspicious circumstances that convinced him a cover-up had been going on in the coroner's office at the time of Marilyn's death. Grandison thought he had made a favorable impression on the investigators. One even assured Grandison that because of what he told them that day, there would be a full investigation of Marilyn's death.

As Grandison remembers it: "The district attorney called me in when the determination was to be made on whether they should hold a grand jury hearing or not. We talked at length and I definitely told them I thought it was worth investigating. I also told them I would be more than ready to go before a grand jury and testify. As a matter of fact when I was leaving, the man from the D.A.'s office came and put my coat on me. "You're going to get your wish," he told me. "You're going to get the investigation."

But the promised investigation never came about. Lionel Grandison's eyewitness account of the cover-up within the coroner's office certainly seems to have provided grounds for at least a bare suspicion.

Grandison's story suggests that Reiner was not just refusing to look for evidence that Marilyn's death was more than just another tinseltown "suicide" but that he had such evidence and was actively ignoring it. In short, the District Attorney of Los Angeles County, like Dr. Theodore Curphey before him, was actively covering up facts that would contradict the official verdict in Marilyn Monroe's death.

THE COVER-UP'S COVER-UP

In refusing to act or publicly mention Lionel Grandison's testimony, was D.A. Ira Reiner attempting to cover up evidence of the earlier cover-up of the way Marilyn Monroe died? In addition to myself, there are at least three other people who think so.

One is the politically savvy Sam Yorty, LA mayor at the time of the star's death. "Well, I know that the board of supervisors wanted to reopen the case. They voted to reopen it. But the case was never reopened. There must have been somebody pulling the strings someplace to keep that from being opened up." Private investigator Milo Speriglio claims his own research convinces him Sam Cordova was fired to prevent him from pursuing Marilyn's case. "He called for a formal inquest and within a matter of hours, the District Attorney of Los Angeles County terminated him as the foreman. I believe he had a lot to say and I think he was silenced."

Jack Clemmons also believes Cordova's dismissal was part of a deliberate attempt to prevent him from proceeding with his investigation. "In 1985, we had a grand jury and the foreman intended to reopen the case and have the grand jury investigate it. Supposedly the grand jury is an independent investigative body — it can even investigate political and police corruption. Ira Reiner went to the courts and had the grand jury foreman discharged. That ended that."

Considering the public outcry that was sure to follow, it seems strange that if Ira Reiner's decision to dismiss Sam Cordova was unconnected with the threatened inquiry into Marilyn's death, Reiner didn't delay at least until Cordova's investigation was over. Surely a few weeks or months wouldn't have mattered. Why such a wily politician as Reiner would knowingly create the appearance of a cover-up, at the very moment he was denying that a cover-up existed, remained — in 1985 — a mystery.

The answers were hidden behind a wall of silence. Those who knew refused to speak. Without concrete evidence, the existence of the cover-up remained a matter of speculation. Until someone who had participated in it was willing to come forward and break that silence, the cover-up would remain safely in place.

Those who had engineered this cover-up had no way of knowing that that silence was just about to break. And when it broke, it wouldn't be by one voice, but a whole chorus, each eagerly rushing to unburden themselves of thirty years of silence and secret guilt.

The cover-up of Marilyn Monroe's death was about to come uncovered.

FILE #14

The Silence Breaks

No single act could have done more to convince the public that important facts about the death of Marilyn Monroe were being covered up by high officials than Los Angeles County District Attorney Ira Reiner's 1985 summary dismissal of Sam Cordova.

The public had not been able to follow all the intricate medical terminology in which other pathologists had disputed much of the original 1962 autopsy. As for the dozens of contradictions in the stories of Dr. Ralph Greenson, Dr. Hyman Engelberg, and Eunice Murray — upon which the police, the pathologist, the Suicide Investigation Team, and every other subsequent official inquiry based their conclusions — they were all a bit abstract.

Ira Reiner's actions were difficult to understand. Why, the public and media asked, would Reiner have fired the grand jury foreman in mid-investigation, knowing the accusations that action would be certain to produce? Didn't that firing constitute evidence and intensify speculation that such a cover-up not only existed but actively was still being enforced?

Plenty of clues pointed to a cover-up, but no actual proof acceptable in a court of law had been established. Without such proof, every official body refused to support a reopening of the investigation.

If the truth of Marilyn's death differed from the "official version," it was hidden behind a wall of silence. Unless someone broke the silence, the events of the evening of August 4 would always remain shrouded in mystery. And unless a participant in — or eyewitness to — the cover-up broke that silence, the cover-up's existence would forever remain a matter of speculation. Fortunately, the silence was broken.

Driven by a desire to see justice done to Marilyn's memory, participants in — and witnesses to — the cover-up did begin to speak out. Their testimony over the last six or seven years has provided convincing proof of a cover-up and has helped us to piece together a picture of that night's events.

Added to this testimony is that of people who would gladly have shared important information with investigators, but had never been contacted during any of the official investigations.

Much of this new testimony is now confirmed by the testimony of a major participant in the cover-up; someone who was on the scene at the time of Marilyn Monroe's death; someone who helped tell the lies that misled official investigators for almost thirty years: Eunice Murray, Marilyn's housekeeper-nurse.

MURRAY'S ADMISSION

Ever since the death of Marilyn Monroe, those who doubted the official version of her death have believed that Eunice Murray knew far more than she was telling. Murray, they said, could provide the key to the whole cover-up. Even with its subsequent emendations, her story of the night's events was full of contradictions and falsehoods. Murray might not know everything that occurred on the night of Marilyn's death, but if persuaded to talk, she should at least be able to explain why she stuck to the official story. Her explanation could either verify or disprove the existence of a cover-up.

That Murray's original story was a fabrication had been obvious from the beginning. Even the overly credulous Robert Byron, the LAPD sergeant charged with investigating Marilyn's death, felt that Murray was telling him "what she had been told to say . . . what had all been rehearsed beforehand." Sergeant Jack Clemmons, the first LAPD officer actually known to have interviewed Murray, noticed a number of "glaring contradictions" in her story. Some months later, when Clemmons read Murray's account of the night's events as told to Byron, he discovered that "she changed her story" to eliminate some of those inconsistencies.

Over the years, Eunice Murray provided investigators with at least six differing versions of how she first became aware something was wrong with Marilyn Monroe on the night of the star's demise — one such version involved psychic abilities.

In the first version, told to Sergeant Jack Clemmons at 4:40 A.M. on the morning after Marilyn's death, Murray said she had become alarmed around midnight when she noticed a bedroom light was still shining from beneath Marilyn's bedroom door.

In the second version, told to Sergeant Robert Byron and subsequent police investigators, it was still the sight of the light under Marilyn's door that alarmed Murray; she now fixed the time several hours later at 3:30 A.M.

In the third version, told after I pointed out that the high pile on Marilyn's newly installed bedroom carpet would have prevented any light from escaping under the door, she claimed to have been mistaken before: It was the sight of the telephone cord stretched under the bedroom door that had alarmed her, not the light. Marilyn was a light sleeper and always put the phones away in an adjoining room before going to sleep, Murray said.

In the fourth version, given in Murray's own biography, she recanted all previous accounts. Instead, Murray credited a "sixth sense" with sending her to the door of Marilyn's room. The three preceding versions having failed to satisfy journalists, Murray apparently felt safe in invoking the paranormal and blaming it all on precognition.

In the fifth version, which may begin to strike closer to the truth, Murray surprised researcher Justin Clayton. She told him that she had actually become alarmed at 3:30 A.M. because she "found Marilyn's door ajar."

Perhaps even closer to the truth is Murray's sixth version. In this rendition, Murray confirmed recently released police records that said Mickey Rudin, Marilyn's attorney, phoned Murray in the middle of that night to ask if Marilyn was "all right." And Murray, who claimed that Marilyn had been in a positive frame of mind when she went to bed, assured him that she was "fine."

Murray still stuck to the essential elements of her earlier stories. Rudin's question had seemed routine, Murray told journalists. It had not alarmed her and she had not bothered to check on Marilyn's condition at the time. Instead, Murray said she had dozed off, unaware that her employer's life might be in danger, until she awakened at 3:30 A.M.

Clearly, whatever the actual circumstances were that first led Eunice Murray to the discovery that all was not right with Marilyn Monroe, she had not yet told everything she knew about them.

Why was Eunice Murray lying? What did she actually see and hear on the night of Marilyn Monroe's death? And why was Eunice Murray covering up those facts? What secret was she concealing? Or what individual was she protecting?

Murray was not protecting Marilyn. If she had wanted to protect Marilyn, she would have claimed the star's death was accidental.

Was Murray protecting Ralph Greenson? Most likely she had strong personal ties to Greenson and had worked for him for over fifteen years. Their complex relationship involved real estate and other financial transactions, and even left-wing political activities. Greenson had often found work for other members of Murray's family.

The psychiatrist had done most of the talking when Jack Clemmons interviewed Greenson, Murray and Dr. Hyman Engelberg on Sunday morning. It was his account the house-keeper-nurse had been corroborating.

Could Murray have been protecting — as so many journalists have suggested — Robert F. Kennedy, the attorney general of the United States?

Those who support the results of the official investigation say the answer is "none of the above." They attribute Murray's lapses to the fading memory of an elderly woman. They also scoff at the idea of a cover-up or of Bobby Kennedy's involvement in any of the night's events.

Which side is right? Those who thought the contradictions and alterations in Eunice Murray's story evidence of a cover-up? Or those who dismissed them as signs of senility?

For over twenty-five years it appeared as if those seeking to prove or disprove the existence of a cover-up in the death of Marilyn Monroe would have to search elsewhere for answers. Then, in 1985, a historic and very public turning-point was reached in an unofficial investigation of the screen goddess's demise.

During an interview for a BBC television documentary, Eunice Murray suddenly threw in the towel. "Why, at my age, do I still have to cover this thing?" she asked irritably.

Until then, Murray had been repeating the official story: she, Pat Newcomb, and Dr. Ralph Greenson had been the only people present at Marilyn's home after noon that day. Now, after a silence of more than two decades, Eunice Murray wanted to tell someone the truth at last.

Murray's revelations over the next few minutes confirmed what every official report of the day's events denied: There was a cover-up — and one major fact it concealed was Bobby Kennedy's presence at Marilyn Monroe's home on the afternoon of her death.

At first, Murray explains: "I was not supposed to know the Kennedys were a very important part of Marilyn's life. But over a period of time, I was a witness to what was happening."

Asked point-blank if Bobby Kennedy had been present at Marilyn's house that Saturday, Murray revealed a secret that years of conspiracy, silence and cover-up had attempted to conceal.

She had always denied that Bobby Kennedy had been there and stuck to the official version of the afternoon's events. Now, her reply was unhesitating.

"Oh, sure! Yes!" she told the documentary crew — and through them hundreds of millions of television viewers worldwide.

"I was in the living room," Eunice Murray continued. "When he arrived, she was not dressed."

That admission was the concrete proof of a cover-up every one had been seeking. And it was all the more convincing because it came from someone whose efforts were an instrumental part of that cover-up.

Asked about the contradictions in her previous stories, Murray confessed: "I told whatever I thought was good to tell."

As far as most of the public was concerned, the claims of cover-up had been proved. Eunice Murray had become the first member of Marilyn Monroe's household to break the silence, admitting that the cover-up existed and describing her own active participation.

Critics of the official account of the star's death had been proven right. The stories Dr. Ralph Greenson, Eunice Murray and Pat Newcomb told of the afternoon's events were false. At least one other person had been present at Marilyn Monroe's house on Saturday: the attorney general of the United States.

However, reputable eyewitnesses place Bobby Kennedy hundreds of miles away that afternoon, at a ranch just south of San Francisco. Was Eunice Murray's earthshaking revelation nothing more than another fanciful product of an aging mind? Perhaps. But if so, what of the dozen other unimpeachable witnesses who would soon come forward to support Murray's story?

WHERE'S BOBBY?

Kennedy loyalists have long maintained that Bobby Kennedy could not have been in Los Angeles on August 4, 1962. Even today they dismiss Eunice Murray's story as nonsense. Instead, they place him at a ranch owned by John Bates, a wealthy campaign contributor who lived just outside San Francisco. According to this version of events, Bobby spent the night with his family before delivering a long-scheduled speech in the bay area Monday morning.

Some, who believe Marilyn's death was the result of something other than suicide, have charged Kennedy intimates with covering up the truth. They maintain that the attorney general paid a flying visit to Los Angeles that Saturday.

The priest whose parish includes John Bates' ranch says that Bobby and his family attended Mass that Sunday morning. But what about the hours prior to Bobby's appearance at Sunday Mass? By air, San Francisco is only an hour away from Los Angeles. Could RFK have flown down for a clandestine Saturday meeting with Marilyn Monroe, flying back again in time for Sunday morning Mass?

"Even Peter Pan would have a hard time doing that," John Bates told journalists. "It's mind-boggling."

Bates swears that he or members of his family were with Bobby Kennedy almost continuously throughout that Saturday — placing Bobby at the ranch at exactly the same time Eunice Murray tells us he was in Los Angeles meeting with Marilyn Monroe.

"The only time Bobby was out of my sight," John Bates says, "was when he went to bed at ten o'clock. He was with me all the rest of the time."

But Kennedy loyalists have also long maintained that Bobby Kennedy barely knew Marilyn and could not have had an affair with her — two statements we now know were not true.

Political supporters have been known to cover up for politicians before. What is rare is when political supporters refuse to go along with such a cover-up. Watergate and the Iran arms-for-hostages scandal are only two recent examples.

Against the word of Kennedy supporters and family, we now have the testimony of a dozen independent witnesses who confirm Eunice Murray's claim that Bobby was in Los Angeles that Saturday afternoon.

Who are these witnesses? They include, LA Chief of Detectives Thad Brown and his brother, Finis, a retired LAPD detective; Hugh McDonald, the officer in charge of the LA County Sheriff's Homicide Bureau; former Deputy District Attorney John Dickey; and LAPD Sergeant Robert Byron, who handled the official police investigation.

According to Sergeant Byron his investigation revealed

that "Robert Kennedy had come to see her" on the day of Marilyn's death.

Former LAPD Sergeant Jack Clemmons, who has publicly criticized Byron's investigation, does agree with him on this point. "We know that Bobby Kennedy was there at 7:45 P.M.," Clemmons confirms.

Another LAPD officer places Bobby in Los Angeles that afternoon: Daryl Gates, the controversial former LA Chief of police. "The truth is, we always knew Robert Kennedy was in town August 4. We always knew when he was here. He was the attorney general and we were interested in him, the way we were interested when other important figures came to Los Angeles. We had people at the airport — airline personnel, for instance — who could recognize a well-known person and alert us."

Private investigator Milo Speriglio supports the conclusions of these eight veteran officers: "Bobby Kennedy has been placed in the Monroe residence the night of her death."

Sam Yorty, former mayor of Los Angeles, also places Bobby Kennedy in Los Angeles that afternoon. "Several days after her death, Parker came to me and told me that Bobby Kennedy was in town, and that he was seen at the Beverly Hilton Hotel, staying at the regular suite that the Kennedys always used. I thought he was in San Francisco or someplace making a speech, like the papers said. But I know he was in town because Chief Parker knew him very well, and Parker would not lie to me."

According to Sergeant Jack Clemmons, investigative reporter Frank Capell also placed Bobby Kennedy in the Kennedy family suite at the plush Beverly Hilton Hotel on Saturday. "Bobby Kennedy had a room in his name at the Beverly Hilton Hotel. Frank Capell, who was a heck of an investigator, went over and checked the register. He got somebody to let him look at the register."

DAILY NEWS

NEW YORK'S PICTURE NEWSPAPER ®

5¢

Vol. 44. No. 36   New York 17, N.Y., Monday, August 6, 1962*   WEATHER

MARILYN DEAD

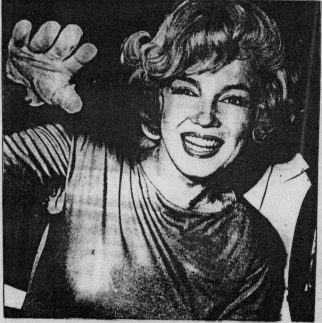

Marilyn Monroe: "I was never used to being happy."

THE MONROE SAGA: 7 PAGES OF STORIES AND PICTURES

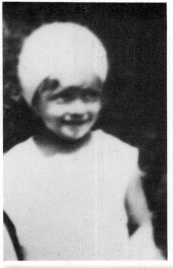

(clockwise from upper left) Little Norma Jeane at about age 4. In her early years, she boarded with a family in Los Angeles, and was visited by her mother. . . . By the time she was 9, she had lived in a series of foster homes and would spend two years in an orphanage. . . . At age 14, she was living with her beloved Aunt Ana in Westwood Village, and beginning to bloom into a confident young beauty.

(clockwise from right)
By 1952, Norma Jeane
was solidly established as
Marilyn Monroe, and
starring in major films like
Gentlemen Prefer Blondes.
Her favorite designer, Billy
Travilla, fits her for a
gown. . . . Marilyn also
began to take her business
seriously, even going so far
as to create a scrapbook
and guide to her various
facial expressions, which
she would study for lighting
angles, mood and character.
. . . Marilyn with her first
and long-time makeup artist,
Alan "Whitey" Snyder. He
would also apply her final
cosmetics for her funeral
years later.

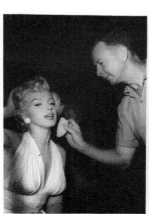

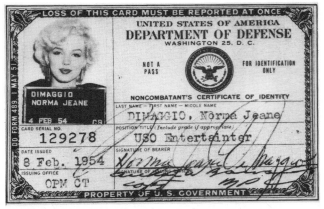

Marilyn's military ID card, used for her 1954 trips to Japan and Korea, where she entertained U.S troops in the field. . . . It was also part of her honeymoon trip with Joe DiMaggio, who wasn't quite as thrilled to see his bride on tanks and helicopters. For Marilyn it was a highlight of her career, and she reveled in he reaction of the troops to her singing and dancing.

Marilyn and Robert Slatzer at Niagara Falls in 1952, during a break in the filming of *Niagara,* her nineteenth movie role in five years and one that lifted her career greatly. . . . Marilyn and Joe DiMaggio vacationing in Florida in 1961, long-since divorced, but still close. Marilyn had recently completed *The Misfits* and divorced Arthur Miller.

One of Marilyn's favorite pictures, and her last formal portrait, taken in November, 1961. The dog is her new pet poodle, Maf, a gift from Frank Sinatra. She jokingly named it after the Mafia. Sinatra's reaction is not known.

Something's Got To Give, and a starry-eyed Marilyn looks ahead. The film's title would prove to be prophetic for all concerned. Principal photography began on May 7, 1962. The last filming was done on June 1, Marilyn's 36th birthday.

Sideline scenes from the set of *Something's Got to Give*. Marilyn and cinematographer Franz Planer proceed to set up a shot. She was comfortable with Planer, liked his style, and had worked with him before....
Paula Strasberg, her personal drama coach, was not a favorite on the set; and even Marilyn was beginning to realize that it was time for a change.

Something's Got to Give was being directed by the estimable George Cukor, a top-ranked director, but an effeminate taskmaster who became particularly abusive to Marilyn. He would often point 'the finger of blame' at her for his indecision. . . . but Marilyn was loved by the crew, many of whom tried to help her withstand the politics and pressures of a financially-troubled studio and hateful director.

While Marilyn was battling fatigue and the weakening effects of a severe sinus infection, Cukor and his new scriptwriter were continually rewriting the script on a daily basis. It became nearly impossible to learn the lines properly before filming began each day, adding yet another stress to the already deteriorating situation.

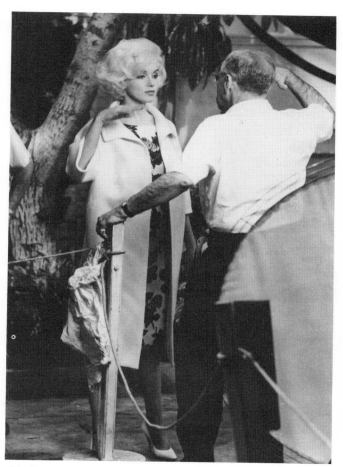

Marilyn and Cukor had worked together as actress and director on
Let's Make Love, in 1960. There was no love lost between them. But
with Cukor's reputation as a woman's director, Marilyn had hoped for
a better relationship this time. But it was even worse. Cukor's egotism
and malice raged relentlessly. He was determined to make her miserable.

When George Cukor wasn't angry, he was either petulant or patronizing with Marilyn. She saw through most of this and understood his prissy nature. For her, it was a matter of gritting her teeth and being professional or grinning and bearing it. She tried to make the film a happy experience, laughing at the problems whenever possible. But there was little to laugh about.

The most famous film footage in Marilyn's movie career was the nude swimming pool scene, shot on May 23, just days after her spectacular birthday singing salute to JFK. Marilyn spent most of the day in and out of the pool for repeated take after take—more than fifty of them. Co-star Dean Martin marveled at her beauty and endurance.

. . .Two weeks earlier, after a grueling series of takes, Marilyn collapsed on the set. Many felt that Cukor purposely ordered take after take to punish Marilyn for previous absences. Caring for Marilyn, Agnes Flanagan, her hairstylist stands next to her. To the right is Evelyn Moriarity, Marilyn's long-time stand-in.

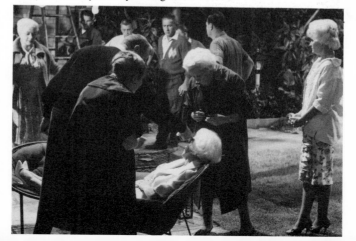

President John F. Kennedy and his brother-in-law, Peter Lawford, at Lawford's Santa Monica beach estate in 1961. The sprawling home was often the base of operations for the Kennedy's political and social activities on the west coast. The casual and informal lifestyle of Lawford had great appeal for Kennedy. Lawford also had great connections in the entertainment world — a world which provided Mr. Kennedy welcome relief from the rigors of Washington, D.C.

A view of the famed Lawford mansion at 625 Pacific Coast Highway, Santa Monica. Locals referred to it as the Western White House, or the Kennedy Playpen. It boasted the largest oceanfront lot in Los Angeles County—with a heated marble pool and nearly 30 rooms, more than 12 of them bedroom suites. . . .The Kennedy brothers and their FBI partner in crime-fighting, J. Edgar Hoover, in one of their typically awkward meetings. The Kennedys knew that Hoover had a secret file on them. RFK and Hoover had a special dislike for each other. Marilyn shared Bobby's distaste for this powerful, political rival.

Attorney General Robert F. Kennedy and his wife, Ethel and four children, arrive at San Francisco airport on Friday afternoon, August 3, 1962. Interestingly, RFK had recently been named Father of the Year, while rumors of his affair with Marilyn had begun to circulate among insiders with law-enforcement or underworld connections.

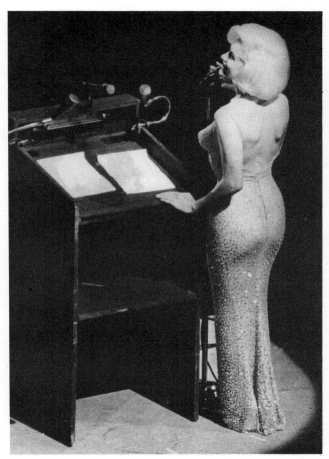

Marilyn sings Happy Birthday to President Kennedy for his 45th birthday party at Madison Square Garden, May 19, 1962. MM's extraordinary $12,000 silk, peek-through-nude gown by Jean Louis was described as "skin, air and beads." It made her front-page news around the world.

Marilyn's last public appearance, on a damp and chilly night, June 1, 1962, her 36th birthday. She had promised to help raise funds for The Muscular Dystrophy Association at an LA Angels baseball game at Dodger Stadium. Later that night, she had a relapse of her sinus and bronchial infections.

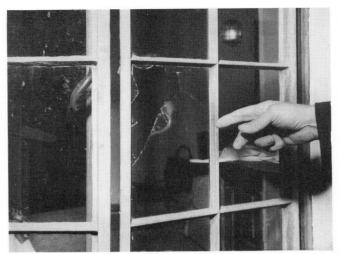

The famous broken window to Marilyn's bedroom, a revealing clue
that would launch a 30-year investigation by author Robert F. Slatzer.

. . . Marilyn's bedroom a few hours after her body had been removed.
This scene of confusion reveals evidence of foul play. Deliberate
arrangement of items in the room foreshadows the cover-up activities
that ensued.

Mrs. Eunice Murray, Marilyn's housekeeper/companion — possibly the last person to see Marilyn alive — later in the day of Monroe's death. Murray's testimony would change over the years, caught in contradiction and inconsistency, until finally revealing new evidence of the cover-up.

Miss Patricia Newcomb, Marilyn's friend and official publicist, as she leaves the Monroe house on the morning of August 5, 1962. Her activities during the last hours of Marilyn's life have never been fully accounted for. . . .she has continually refused to testify or cooperate with investigators.

Police security and journalists in front of Marilyn's Brentwood home on the morning of August 5. . . . Her body leaving the coroner's laboratory after the autopsy and toxicological tests were completed, August 6, 1962.

August 8, 1962: Dr. Theodore Curphey, county coroner, makes his official press announcement regarding Marilyn's probable suicide by means of a self-administered overdose. . . . Marilyn Monroe is put to rest in a crypt.

Dr. and Mrs. Ralph Greenson, at Marilyn's funeral services. An eminent psychiatrist, he was probably more aware of Marilyn's inner fears and wishes than anyone else. During those last months and weeks before Marilyn died, he saw her practically every day. Their relationship was much deeper than is typical of doctor and patient. His testimony has never been made public. He died in 1979. We believe that he had tapes and papers that could be valuable evidence.

Walter Schaefer, founder and owner of Schaefer Ambulance Company, in 1985. Over the years, Mr. Schaefer's testimony would also change, finally admitting the role of his ambulance on that fateful night. According to Schaefer, Marilyn died at Santa Monica Hospital, not at home. Experts dispute the logic of the claim. . . . Robert F. Slatzer, during a later visit to Marilyn's home, as part of his ongoing investigation into the contradictions in the case.

Robert Slatzer in front of the former Marilyn Monroe home at 12305 Fifth Helena Drive, in Brentwood. The house has undergone major renovation in recent years. . . . Mrs. Murray and Slatzer as he interviewed her in her Santa Monica home in 1973, for his earlier book, *The Life & Curious Death of Marilyn Monroe.*

Slatzer and Dr. Thomas Noguchi, 1975. Acclaimed as a brilliant
pathologist, Dr. Noguchi performed the autopsy on Marilyn. Based
on new evidence, he too, has some new opinions on this case and
could offer valuable assistance. . . . Author Slatzer and Dr. Hyman
Engelberg, Marilyn's physician, during a break in a television
interview, 1976. Dr. Engelberg is one of the few remaining witnesses
to Marilyn's last day alive, but still refuses to give a complete report
on what he saw or knows about the circumstances of Marilyn's death.

(clockwise from upper left) Witnesses and experts who have contributed to The Marilyn Files investigation: Terry Moore, actress and friend of Marilyn's; Alec D'Arcy actor and friend of Marilyn's; Milo Speriglio, author and CEO of Nick Harris Detectives; James Hall, the ambulance driver who claims to have nearly saved Marilyn.

(clockwise from upper left) Witnesses and experts who have contributed to The Marilyn Files investigation: Lionel Grandison, former Deputy Coroner's Aide in 1962; John Miner, former L.A. District Attorney; Dr. F. DeWitt Fox, neurosurgeon and consulting medical expert; Jack Clemmons, former LAPD sergeant, and first officer on the scene, August 5, 1962.

Jeanne Carmen, former actress, neighbor and one of Marilyn's best and closest friends. A witness to Marilyn's relationship with RFK and others and very knowledgeable regarding Marilyn's lifestyle, future plans and intimate thoughts during her last weeks. Does not believe it is possible that Marilyn would have committed suicide: "It was murder."

. . .Eleanor BeBe Goddard, Marilyn's foster-sister. She and Marilyn — then Norma Jeane — shared their teenage years together, living in the same home and attending Van Nuys High School. They became best friends from the day they met. Today BeBe remembers Marilyn as Norma Jeane and says that there was an inner strength in her that always helped her to survive, regardless of the circumstances.

Robert F. Slatzer, a Marilyn confidant—briefly her husband in October of 1952—and the leading author/investigator on this case for 30 years. He is at the forefront of the continuing *Marilyn Files* probe into the death of Marilyn Monroe.

This picture of Marilyn was taken in her dressing room by Robert Slatzer during the pre-production and wardrobe-fitting prior to the filming of *Something's Got to Give*. It is one of the author's especially favorite pictures of Marilyn.

In addition, several of Marilyn's neighbors claim they saw Bobby Kennedy entering Marilyn's house that day.

Several months after Marilyn's death, Sergeant Jack Clemmons began his own investigation of that Saturday's events. He soon discovered a group of women who regularly gathered to play cards on Fifth Helena Drive. They told Clemmons that "They saw Kennedy go into that house at about dusk. They were sitting playing bridge and Bobby Kennedy walked right by their window on his way into Marilyn's house."

The women told Clemmons that the attorney general had two other men with him. They also set the time at 7:45 P.M., shortly after the sun went down.

Asked if they were certain it was Bobby Kennedy, the hostess replied: "I've seen Bobby Kennedy go into that house a dozen times and that definitely was him. I don't know who the other two men were, but Bobby Kennedy went into that house."

Interviewed recently, the daughter of one of those women, Betty Pollard, supported her mother's story.

Ward Wood, one of Peter Lawford's neighbors also saw Bobby Kennedy in LA that day, this time entering Lawford's Santa Monica home. "A car drew up and I said, 'Oh, there's Bobby Kennedy.' I knew it was Bobby Kennedy." Wood had seen Bobby there several times before.

There is even further confirmation of Eunice Murray's story. Peter Lawford, the Kennedys' go-between in their relationships with Marilyn, told at least two credible witnesses that Bobby was in town Saturday, August 4.

One is photographer Milton Greene, a former partner in Marilyn's defunct production company. Greene claims Lawford told him Bobby "was in town. He saw her. He left. She got on the phone to Lawford." Lawford later told the same story to his wife, Deborah Gould. He also told her the attorney general had taken a helicopter back to San Francisco.

Patricia Conners, daughter of Hal Conners, the helicopter pilot whom Lawford and his intimates often chartered for special flights, admits her father was out late the night of Marilyn's death.

Conners once told his chief pilot, James Zonlick, that Lawford's neighbors called the police to complain about the noise when he had ferried Bobby Kennedy to the actor's Santa Monica home in the wee hours of the morning.

Pilot Ed Connelly, who also flew for Conners, remembers his boss describing this incident. "He had landed on the Santa Monica beach without lights," says Connelly. "It was uncharacteristic for Hal to do that sort of thing."

With the attorney general of the United States as his passenger, it's not surprising that Hal Conners felt safe in breaking a few regulations that night.

Once the information became public, the belief in a cover-up of the events surrounding Marilyn's death was fortified — this in spite of Kennedy loyalists' efforts to maintain the status quo.

But what was being hidden? And why are certain people still struggling to conceal it today?

The fact that Bobby was having a liaison with Marilyn Monroe, or was unfaithful to his wife, might have been explosive information before his death. But Bobby's infidelities have been chronicled as thoroughly as all of JFK's. Any damage that revelations about his relationship with Marilyn Monroe might have done has long since passed.

If his presence that afternoon was the extent of Bobby Kennedy's involvement with the events surrounding Marilyn Monroe's death, surely the conspirators would have simply admitted it by now — as Eunice Murray did — and let the matter drop. Such an admission would attract less notoriety to the

Kennedy name than the speculation, rumor and innuendo the current silence generates.

Even without the assistance of Kennedy loyalists, the cover-up is coming apart. It now seems beyond doubt that Marilyn's former lover, Bobby Kennedy, paid a visit to her house on Saturday, August 4. But for years this secret was concealed behind the same wall of silence that has hidden so many other vital truths about Marilyn Monroe's death. Those who helped break this silence were bringing the cover-up into the open. But many others still have to come forward, and many other pieces of evidence still have to be unearthed before the mystery that is Marilyn's death is solved.

By the late admissions of Murray and their subsequent substantiation by others, the existence of the cover-up has been disclosed. . . but the cover-up itself is still in effect.

FILE #15

The Mysterious Ambulance

THE NEGLECTED NEIGHBORS

As the silence about Marilyn Monroe's death began to break, and the cover-up started to come uncovered, more and more of the mysteries that surrounded the star's last night have been solved. It took the combined statements of three people, spread over a quarter of a century, to shed light on one of the case's biggest puzzles. But by following up a clue the LAPD did not think it worthwhile investigating, we now know a great deal more about what appears to have been Marilyn's final minutes.

Not long after the official investigation into the death of Marilyn Monroe closed, rumors began to circulate that neighbors had seen a mysterious ambulance outside the star's home several hours before her death was reported to police. The LAPD had chosen not to conduct extensive interviews among Marilyn's neighbors. Sergeant Robert Byron, who headed the investigation, felt the lack of evidence of foul play at the scene of Marilyn's death made further inquiry a waste of department time.

Byron's conclusion that there were no signs of foul play was based on the testimony of Dr. Ralph Greenson, the man who discovered Marilyn's body. Yet Sergeant Byron told one journalist that he felt Greenson was "giving us wild answers, wasn't telling us the correct time or situation, and that there was a lot more he could have told us." Inexplicably, he never pressed Dr. Greenson for answers that were less "wild," or for the "correct time or situation," or for the "lot more" the psychiatrist could have told.

Byron also didn't question Marilyn Monroe's neighbors. And there was much they could have told him. He might have learned about the visit of a certain very important person to Marilyn's home the night of August 4th also. He, might have learned that at 1:00 A.M., more than three hours before Marilyn was officially pronounced dead, Abe Landau and his wife, who lived right down the street, noticed an ambulance and several other vehicles parked outside her house.

If Byron had followed up that clue, he might have discovered rumors circulating among responding ambulance drivers that an ambulance had taken Marilyn to Santa Monica Hospital late that night and that she allegedly died there at approximately 2:00 A.M. This mysterious ambulance was then said to have taken Marilyn back to her home, where she was placed in her bed . . . all this more than two hours before the official discovery of her body by Jack Clemmons.

Milo Speriglio was one of many to verify this rumor. "Based upon our investigation, we know Marilyn's body was taken to the Santa Monica Hospital comatose, was returned back by, or under the direction of, a movie actor. It's possible they used an ambulance for that; that could have been the ambulance the witness had seen. The time could have well been around 1:00 A.M. because we know Marilyn was already dead at that time."

Had Byron followed up the ambulance rumor, he might have located the ambulance company that was said to have carried Marilyn to the hospital. By interviewing its owner and drivers, he might have saved other investigators twenty-five years of work. This would have authenticated or disproved the story of the mysterious ambulance and Marilyn Monroe's frantic, last-minute round-trip to death.

WHAT THE NEIGHBORS SAW

Abe Landau was Marilyn Monroe's neighbor at the time of her death. After the star's death, police failed to interview Landau or his wife. Yet, when journalists and others conducting unofficial investigations into Marilyn's final hours interviewed Landau, he had a remarkable story to tell. However, Landau both refused to be quoted and to reveal either his or his wife's name.

Landau never explained his reasons for keeping his identity secret. Those who interviewed him at the time all noted that he seemed scared. Landau told interviewers that if they used the story with his name "anytime soon," he would deny it.

Former LAPD Sergeant Jack Clemmons, who has conducted his own personal inquiry into Marilyn's death, talked to Landau a few months later. Landau admitted having seen an ambulance parked in the driveway outside Marilyn's house the fatal night. Landau said that there had been an ambulance at the scene, Clemmons now confirms.

As long as Landau declined to testify publicly to what he knew, there was no way to substantiate journalists' stories that a neighbor who refused to be identified had seen a mysterious ambulance parked in Marilyn's driveway that night. Even as recently as the LA County district attorney's so-called 1985 investigation into Marilyn's death, officials dismissed the ambulance story as mere rumor and refused to waste their time investigating it.

After years of silence, Abe Landau agreed to an exclusive interview only a few months before the publication of this book. At the time of the interview Landau admitted there had not only been an ambulance at Marilyn's home around 1:00 A.M. the night of her death, but also a police car and several other cars. Here, for the first time anywhere, is his own personal account of what he and his wife saw that night.

"Marilyn Monroe was my neighbor," Landau explains. "Everyone was excited about her moving in, so there was a lot of conversation about it. We used to see her come by in the limousine from the studio. She was very beautiful."

Like everyone else on the block, the Landaus couldn't help watching the star's home for a sight of her or one of her famous visitors. They also saw the remodeling of Marilyn's home in progress.

"She did the house over. She brought in Mexican workmen who made sort of a Mexican hacienda out of the living room. As a matter of fact, after it was done, we asked if we could see the place. Mrs. Murray said yes. And she did a beautiful job."

Landau says that on the night of August 4, he and his wife were returning home from an evening with friends. "My wife and I were out to a party. We came home quite late. It must have been close to 1:00 A.M. There was the ambulance. There was a police car and quite a few other cars."

Landau admits he and his wife speculated on what might have been happening. But it wasn't until the next morning that they discovered the meaning of all the activity they had seen outside Marilyn Monroe's house that night. "We didn't know what happened until we found out she was dead, on the news."

A few days later, Landau and his wife encountered Eunice Murray, Marilyn's housekeeper-nurse. At that point, Murray told them a curious story. This story adds another curious contradiction to all the other strange contradictions this woman was to tell about her employer's death.

"Mrs. Murray told us that Marilyn had taken an overdose of sleeping pills. She said Marilyn would take pills. Then she would wake up, forget that she had taken some, and take some more. And that's what Mrs. Murray said happened."

Surely this is an astonishing statement, and one that might have aided the police investigation of Marilyn's death, if the LAPD had bothered to interview the Landaus. Only a day or two before, Murray had joined Dr. Greenson and Marilyn's physician, Dr. Engelberg, in assuring police and media that the actress had committed suicide — a story she would maintain for the next twenty-eight years.

But within this same time frame, Murray was telling the Landaus that Marilyn's death was accidental. Was this one of those slip-ups which the housekeeper-nurse would make over the years, lending credence to the charge of cover-up? Was accidental death the story the trio had first decided on, or had been instructed to give, only to finally settle on suicide at the last minute? Surely the cause of her employer's death isn't something Murray could have difficulty remembering so soon afterward.

THE MYSTERIOUS AMBULANCE

In the mid-1980s, a man named Ken Hunter said he could name the company whose ambulance had been parked outside Marilyn Monroe's home at 1:00 A.M. the night of her death. Hunter claimed the ambulance belonged to the Schaefer Ambulance Company and that he was the ambulance driver. He identified his partner that night as Murray Leibowitz.

At first the owner of the ambulance company, Walter Schaefer, denied that any of his vehicles were at Marilyn's house the night of her death. He did admit that Hunter had worked for him. He also admitted that Leibowitz had been Hunter's partner.

But a quarter of a century later, during a personal interview with me, Walter Schaefer changed his story. Schaefer admitted one of his ambulances had been called to Marilyn Monroe's house that night and had driven the dying star to the Santa Monica Hospital. Curiously, he identified the main driver as Murray Leibowitz and the assistant as Ken Hunter. Schaefer explained that his company had probably been called because they had transported the star to the hospital before, when she had overdosed.

"I guess I can tell it," Schaefer began. "I came in the next morning and found on the log sheet we had transported Marilyn Monroe. I understood that she had overdosed. She was under the influence of barbiturates. They took her on a Code Three, an emergency, into Santa Monica Hospital, where she terminated."

Asked what he thought about the news which reported the star had been found dead in her bedroom with no mention of either the ambulance or the hospital, Schaefer replied: "Anything can happen in Hollywood."

Walter Schaefer said he had no idea why Marilyn's body had been returned to her bedroom. Schaefer hadn't asked. He had long ago discovered that ambulance companies that don't stay out of their clients's affairs don't receive recommendations for further business.

Unfortunately, it is impossible to verify Schaefer's story. Long ago, both the Schaefer Ambulance Company and Santa Monica Hospital destroyed all records from the year 1962 to make room for newer files. Ken Hunter suddenly broke off relations with the press and police; while Murray Leibowitz still declines to discuss the subject of Marilyn Monroe for publication.

Is the two ambulance drivers' refusal to talk about their activities on the night of August 4, 1962, part of the cover-up of the events surrounding Marilyn's death? Journalists have speculated that it might be. If Schaefer is mistaken about the identities of the two drivers, or if his story were fictitious, wouldn't Hunter and Leibowitz simply have told reporters their former employer was wrong, that they had not picked up the star's comatose body that night?

Jim Hall, a driver for the Schaefer Ambulance Company at the time of these events, has reason to believe that Hunter's and Leibowitzs's silence is a part of a cover-up. As Hall tells it: "Murray Leibowitz denies that he was ever there. He's been interviewed by numerous people and he won't talk. Subsequently, Halls reports, on a radio talk show, an attendant that rode with Leibowitz later, called in and said that every day Leibowitz would stop at a series of six different car washes. Finally this attendant said to him: "What are you, a car wash fetishist? Why are we going to these car washes all the time?"

Murray Leibowitz is then supposed to have said: "Well, you remember I told you I'd tell you what happened to Marilyn that night? Well, I'm not going to tell you that, but I will tell you this: After her funeral, I came into a very large sum of what you would call hush money, and I bought these car washes. I own them. And the only reason that I'm still working at Schaefers is to keep up appearances."

If this story is true, then it provides additional proof that a cover-up actually exists. The ambulance attendant's story would also be the first evidence that at least some of those who have kept silent about how Marilyn Monroe actually died have been bribed to do so.

Unfortunately, the ambulance attendant who called in that night has neither come forward nor identified himself. Without either his cooperation or that of Murray Leibowitz, this story has yet to be substantiated.

During an interview with Sergeant Jack Clemmons a few months later, Walt Shaefer offered even more telling evidence of a cover-up. Clemmons had interviewed Schaefer immediately following Hunter's allegations, but Schaefer denied Hunter's story and said that, of his own personal knowledge, no ambulance from his company had gone to Marilyn Monroe's house the evening of August 4.

Schaefer admitted he'd lied to Clemmons the first time and confirmed his story to me. According to Clemmons, Schaefer then explained why he had remained silent all those years. His statement was that he was afraid to say anything at that time because eighty percent of his business came from various city and county agencies. The Kennedys were involved and he knew his business would be ruined if he talked.

This was a moment without historic precedent in the investigation into the death of Marilyn Monroe. Walter Schaefer's admissions provided three major breakthroughs, breakthroughs that have continued to be ignored by those officially charged with determining the causes of Marilyn's death for almost a decade.

For the first time, someone whose silence had kept the truth hidden from the public for over a quarter of a century had broken silence and told the truth. His courageous admission would encourage others to come forward and tell what they knew as well, creating a landslide of facts that would allow investigators to come closer in solving the mystery of Marilyn's final, doomed hours.

More importantly, he became the first participant in the cover-up to confirm that such a cover-up existed. The cover-up was no longer a matter of logic and supposition. Walt

Schaefer put the lie to twenty-five years of conspiracy and deception on the part of those who helped conceal the actual circumstances of Marilyn Monroe's death. There was no longer any basis for ridiculing those who championed the charge of cover-up.

Walt Schaefer's admission points conclusively toward an explanation for at least one aspect of the cover-up: the attempt to keep Bobby Kennedy's involvement with Marilyn Monroe from the public and press. And, more important, to keep Bobby Kennedy's presence at Marilyn's home on the evening of August 4 from public knowledge and scrutiny.

WHO SUMMONED THE AMBULANCE?

Although Walt Schaefer's admission answers many of the questions that have puzzled journalists and other investigators over the years, it creates as many questions as it answers.

The fact that an ambulance was called seems to suggest that Marilyn's death was the result of suicide or accidental overdose. Would murderers call an ambulance to rush their dying victim to the hospital where she might be successfully revived?

What if the murderer or murderers were already gone when the dying star was first discovered? Maybe those who called the ambulance company, finding her comatose, and having no reason to suspect murder, had merely assumed she had overdosed and, in a natural attempt to save her, summoned an ambulance to rush her to the hospital.

But whatever the reason for sending Marilyn to the hospital, why bring her back? If someone who wanted to save her life had called for the ambulance, why didn't the drivers follow the usual procedure as soon as they arrived at the hospital and summon a doctor from inside to pronounce the actress dead and take official charge of her body?

If Marilyn's friends didn't call the ambulance, who did? Some journalists have suggested a possible answer. They believe that Marilyn's death may have been due to an accident caused by someone else. The person who caused that accident then directed that an ambulance be rushed to the scene to try to save the dying actress.

When Marilyn died on the way to the hospital, the party or parties responsible for that death became afraid to be seen at the hospital and ordered the drivers back to the star's house, where they could decide on the best course of action.

The key question then becomes: Who called the ambulance to Marilyn's house that night? The answer to this query might well illuminate the final mysteries of Marilyn Monroe's death.

In 1985, almost twenty-five years later, Walt Schaefer swore he did not remember by whom the call to his company had been placed. If any of those who claim to have driven in the ambulance that night know who called the Schaefer Ambulance Company and ordered them to the scene, they have never mentioned it. No records now survive that might offer a clue to the identity of these mysterious figures.

Fortunately, Walt Schaefer's statement helps narrow the number of people who could have made that call down to a very small list. Schaefer said that he felt his company was chosen because they had transported Marilyn to the hospital previously when she had taken an overdose. Whoever summoned the ambulance to Marilyn's home had probably known that.

It is not likely that friends or strangers would have been aware of the name of the ambulance company that had taken Marilyn to the hospital on previous occasions unless they had been on the scene and had either summoned or seen the ambulance. People rarely discuss the names of their ambulance companies the way they do the names of their fitness trainers and hair stylists.

The three people most likely to have been present during such a crisis and to have been familiar with the name of the ambulance company previously used are: Dr. Ralph Greenson, Dr. Hyman Engelberg, and Eunice Murray. It is hard to imagine who else could have known to call the Schaefer ambulance services the night of Marilyn Monroe's death.

If one of these three called the ambulance company, the searing question is: Why did they make the call? Did they accidentally cause the actress's death? If so, why rush the body back to her home? By doing so, were they attempting to cover up their guilt?

If Greenson, Murray and Engelberg were not responsible for an accident but had found Marilyn's body and were just trying to save her life, again, why would they rush her body back home?

Were they summoned to the dying star's bedside by someone else? And if they were, did that person find Marilyn dying of a self-administered overdose? Or did that person accidentally cause that overdose? Or was there a more sinister secret? Could that overdose have been administered deliberately? Or had that person been framed by a cunning trap sprung by clever, remorseless enemies who had bided their time for months until just the right moment? Were they just covering up that other party's involvement?

FILE #16

The Coroner's Cover-Up

If Los Angeles County Coroner Theodore Curphey's official verdict of "probable suicide" was intended to put an end to questions about Marilyn Monroe's death, it failed. Instead of quieting doubts, Curphey's verdict — as the investigations that preceeded it — only intensified them.

Those who reject the official verdict maintain that the coroner's judgment was hasty and perfunctory. Glaring contradictions were ignored and critical facts, if not covertly concealed, were obscured.

Some critics have claimed that Curphey's official verdict was part of a larger, high-level cover-up of the circumstances surrounding Marilyn's death. Rumors of such a cover-up, many of them emanating from within the coroner's office, have continued to this day. Dr. Curphey is dead, and former employees of the department who might have been able to substantiate or dispel such rumors have proven reluctant to talk. Without their corroboration, the complicity of the coroner's office in this cover-up has remained a matter for dispute.

Finally, a former member of the coroner's staff, Lionel Grandison, has joined the ranks of those breaking the silence that has, for so long, cloaked this conspiracy. At the time of Marilyn Monroe's death, Grandison was a deputy coroner's aide who played a key role in the department's investigation.

As a result of what he observed and learned during this period Grandison became convinced that the coroner was actively covering up the true cause of Marilyn Monroe's death. According to Grandison, Dr. Curphey suppressed evidence and ordered files rewritten that would otherwise have contradicted the official verdict.

"As I analyze my participation, my conversations with other staff members, and the things I've seen," Grandison has said, "there's no doubt in my mind that the Marilyn Monroe case, as we know it now, is not the true case. Some very sensitive areas have been covered up. Evidence was suppressed, paperwork was taken from the files, and people who have knowledge of what happened have not been listened to or sought out."

Grandison's accusations are very weighty, because he was among those privy to the inner workings of the coroner's office during its investigation into Marilyn's death. He was the man who maintained the department's master file on Marilyn. He was also the man who signed the death certificate when the coroner at last reached a verdict.

THE WRONG MORTUARY

Grandison's responsibilities included locating next of kin, and working with them to make arrangements for burials. He worked the early-morning shift, and generally arrived around 6 A.M.

Grandison recalls his thoughts on the morning of August 5: "Going through the calls that had come in the previous night, I saw the name of Marilyn Monroe. I knew by previous experience that in cases involving high-profile people, you have to watch what you do, and follow all the regulations. High-profile cases needed special attention to details because of increased inquiries about the death and the circumstances surrounding the death from the public, the insurance companies, the police departments, and the possible heirs."

Grandison had been employed in the coroner's office long enough to realize that under such intense public scrutiny, even the smallest mistake was likely to draw heat. He would have to handle the superstar's death strictly by the book. "I sensed that this was a case where we needed to bring the body down to the Hall of Justice and have a complete report with all of the laboratory tests."

Grandison sought out the deputy coroner's aide who had worked the previous shift. He wanted all the details available on this case: the circumstances surrounding Marilyn's death, whether the body had already been brought to the morgue, whether they had received the report from the police department — anything that might affect his handling of the case.

Almost immediately, Grandison faced the first of many irregularities in the handling of Marilyn Monroe's death that would lead him to suspect a cover-up was in progress: Marilyn's body was in the wrong mortuary. He recalls the manner in which he made this discovery: "When people die of natural causes in hospitals, their body is generally held there while arrangements are made for transporting it to a mortuary. For those who are not so fortunate, we had official on-call mortuaries designated for each section of the city where the body would be held temporarily until we could determine its proper disposition. But when the death involved a suspected suicide, or murder, or accident, or the causes were simply unknown, the law said the body had to be shipped to the downtown mortuary in the coroner's office for evaluation."

Grandison discovered that the body had not been brought to the morgue. Instead, it was being held at the Westwood Memorial Park. "For that to happen," Grandison explains, "someone would have to have called the mortuary, and specifically asked them to come and pick up the body, and take it back to their mortuary. Therefore my very first question was, who had called the mortuary? I asked the people on the night shift why the body had been sent there and who had okayed its release. No one at our department knew; there was no record in the file. So I put the matter aside for further investigation."

Grandison received his next shock when he called the mortuary holding Marilyn's body. As a courtesy, he phoned to tell them that the coroner's office was sending a team to collect the body and bring it downtown. There should have been no problem. Instead, the mortuary was reluctant to release the body to the coroner.

The mortuary's reluctance was unprecedented. Grandison kept his cool. He knew he had the authority to enforce his request. "They began to squawk. They didn't want to let us have the body. But ultimately there was nothing that they could do because they were under my orders. They worked for the county of Los Angeles like I did."

Grandison questioned the mortuary staff. He asked them who had released Marilyn's body from the death scene and directed it to the mortuary. The staff evaded his questions. No one there would admit to having received the call, and no one seemed to know who had.

Grandison was never to know the solution to this particular mystery. "We subsequently made quite an investigation into that. We talked to the mortuary, and they didn't know or wouldn't tell. We talked to the Los Angeles Police Department. We talked to the housekeeper. We tried to talk to

Marilyn's doctors, but they would not cooperate with us in any way. "

Many people believe that had it not been for the watchful eye of Lionel Grandison, there might never have been any further investigation of Marilyn Monroe's death. With her body at the wrong mortuary, far from the coroner's watchful eye, anyone could have given an order to embalm or cremate her remains, destroying any evidence her body might provide the pathologist before an autopsy could be performed. It was only Grandison's quick thinking that preserved her body for Noguchi to autopsy.

The body's presence at the wrong mortuary may have been intended to be the ultimate cover-up. If her body had been destroyed first, there could have been no subsequent investigation. This was Grandison's first clue that an attempt was being made to conceal evidence about Marilyn's death. It would not be his last.

CURPHEY INTERVENES

The next clue Grandison encountered was the first that involved Dr. Curphey directly. According to Grandison, the coroner began to intervene between his own staff and the data they needed to evaluate Marilyn's death.

The administrative branch of the coroner's office, where Grandison worked, is charged with the responsibility to investigate all circumstances pertinent to the occurrence of a death. If the victim had taken an overdose, as Marilyn had, the coroner's staff would try to discern facts such as: who the victim's physicians were; what drugs had been prescribed; the amount and type of drugs found at the scene; what treatment the victim was under at the time of death; and any other details which might help round out the autopsy.

But when the investigation of Marilyn's death began,

Coroner Curphey announced that he would personally question the star's doctors. "·Dr. Curphey said he would handle the conversations with the medical people. It was the administrative branch's responsibility but we backed out of that. We never even knew the names of the doctors he was interviewing."

Curphey's act was exceptional. As his position was administrative, he never did investigative work. The day-to-day work was delegated to others. His interference in this instance was unprecedented.

Curphey didn't just come between his department and Marilyn's doctors. The information he saw fit to pass on to his subordinates "changed from day to day, as if it were being tailored to fit a scenario in need of constant revision by its authors."

Why would Dr. Curphey have prevented his own investigators from interviewing Marilyn Monroe's physician and psychiatrist? Why would he keep even their identities from his staff? Why did the information he gave change from day to day? Curphey may merely have wanted to exercise personal control of what was sure to be a highly scrutinized investigation, one that would require contact with powerful, sensitive people. Or he may have wanted to spare the actress's private life from the glare of scandal and publicity.

Curphey's exceptional interference might have been a sign of a cover-up in action, the coroner personally orchestrating his department's end of the conspiracy in the same manner as LAPD Chief William Parker had with the police. Whatever Curphey's motives, his actions aroused suspicions that have dogged his reputation to this day.

THE MISSING FILE PHENOMENON

Grandison's next shock came with his discovery that someone in his department was removing and rewriting key material from Marilyn's file. Over the years, those who have investigated the death of Marilyn Monroe have cited the loss of many vital records and much physical evidence as strong proof of a cover-up. Lionel Grandison was the first to encounter this "missing file" phenomenon.

"I observed information leaving the file. Much of the information was taken out of the file and was never replaced. Now, who was taking that information or where it was going, I haven't got the faintest idea."

Grandison believes that the information which remains in the coroner's file on Marilyn Monroe's death today is nothing more than "a watered-down version." He claims the actress's file was doctored to support "what someone wanted the public to think."

Grandison also remembers the disappearance of one document that might have answered questions that have haunted investigators for thirty years. There has long been a rumor that many, and far more severe, bruises were found on Marilyn's body than the official documents reveal. Lionel Grandison says this rumor is true.

Standard morgue procedure, Grandison explains, requires any body brought into the mogue to be inspected immediately by a medical assistant. The location of all scars, bruises, cuts, or other marks are indicated specifically on a form that depicts front and rear views of the body. This form is then added to the official file. In fact, the medical assistants who filled out these original reports were likely the first individuals to examine Marilyn's dead body in an official capacity. Their examination took place before any rumors of impropriety had circulated, even before the autopsy report. Since their examination took place as routine and immediate examination, it is likely this was an independent and "unsupervised" effort.

Lionel Grandison saw this form on the morning of August 5.

According to Grandison, the form included the hip bruise publicized in the autopsy press conference and also revealed bruises in addition to those included in Dr. Noguchi's autopsy report. "There were bruises on the back of her leg that indicated that there might have been injections given to her. This form was a part of the file that disappeared as the case began to expand."

Of course, the disappearance of material from the coroner's files might be explained away as mere bureaucratic inefficiency. But Grandison asserts that the files that remain have been altered as well. "The reports that I saw were not the reports that ended up in the file that is now a part of the county records."

Lost files might be an accident. But altered files take a deliberate act. These alterations, if Grandison's story is true, seem to be irrefutable evidence of a conspiracy to conceal important facts about the death of Marilyn Monroe.

THE LITTLE RED BOOK

There is one document whose disappearance from the coroner's office Grandison will never forget: the little red diary in which Marilyn recorded details of her affair with Bobby Kennedy and the government secrets he divulged during their amours. This diary was not found among the effects turned over to Marilyn's estate by the police or coroner's office nor was it found at her home. Grandison believes the coroner's office allowed Marilyn Monroe's diary to be stolen; and that one or more senior officials were involved.

Grandison came into possession of the diary through his attempt to locate the actress's next of kin.

I told two of our drivers to go to her home and pick up whatever materials they found that might give us any type of lead on her relatives. The two men returned, Grandison claims, with a red-covered book.

Opening that book, Grandison discovered he was holding Marilyn Monroe's personal diary. The diary, which covered the events of only 1962, offered no clues to the star's next of kin. But Grandison was learning more about Marilyn's private life than he ever dreamed he'd know. Grandison says Bobby Kennedy's name appeared frequently, as did comments about government figures and activities. Most of these meant nothing to him at the time. Many still hold no meaning for him now.

A few of these entries would take on greater meaning for Grandison later, when future events made the subjects they discussed almost household names. Grandison remembers seeing the names of both Kennedy brothers. Reading someone's personal account of the president is not easy to forget. Grandison also remembers seeing the words CIA and Mafia. These stood out in his mind as unusual because these were names that rarely appeared in the media during the early 1960s. He remembers familiar names like Jimmy Hoffa, Fidel Castro, and Frank Sinatra.

Grandison would not understand the full import of what he read in Marilyn's diary for years. When he did at lastbegin to understand, Grandison realized what a critical piece of evidence it would have been.

Grandison put Marilyn's diary into the department safe. He planned to keep it secure until he could find out who was entitled to custody of the diary, and release it to their care. But when Grandison went back to the safe to retrieve Marilyn Monroe's little red book a day later, it had vanished.

Grandison says only three other people had a key to the safe: Richard Rathman, who headed up the administrative section of the coroner's office; Phil Schwartzberg, the coroner's administrative assistant; and Dr. Theodore Curphey.

Grandison believes it's possible that one of these individuals may have been approached by an outside agency and pressured into opening the safe.

If Grandison had had a little less regard for regulations, and had tossed Marilyn's diary into a desk drawer instead of the department safe, it might not have been discovered and removed by those "senior officials" until after Grandison had read further, and had made its contents too widely known for its theft to conceal them. On the other hand, perhaps Grandison is lucky he didn't read any further — or he might not have lived much longer either.

Marilyn's diary was one of the most important pieces of evidence in the case. From Grandison's statements alone, we know if it had been preserved, its entries would have supplied more than enough motive for the murder of Marilyn Monroe and more than enough material to force Coroner Curphey to convene a full inquest into the circumstances of her death. It would have proved to the disbelieving 1960s that Marilyn Monroe's affairs with the president and the attorney general were not the irresponsible rumors that the Kennedy camp claimed they were. Those facts alone would have created a clamor for a complete public investigation into Marilyn's death. But Grandison played it safe. And playing it safe is one thing anybody investigating the death of Marilyn Monroe should never do if they want to arrive at the truth.

ORDERED TO SIGN THE DEATH CERTIFICATE

As the man who first processed Marilyn's paperwork, it was Grandison's duty to sign her death certificate after the official cause of death was announced. But when the death certificate arrived on Grandison's desk, important documents were missing.

Grandison remembers the incident this way: "Three months

after Marilyn Monroe's death, the file came back to my desk. The death certificate was inside. "The standard procedure when we were about to close a case was that all the reports, charts, and other paperwork on the case were there in the file. It would contain the conclusions drawn by the pathologist; the determination of the police; and whatever other agencies made any type of investigation of the case. This file had none of that information in it."

Puzzled by the absence of so many key documents, Grandison decided to ask Coroner Curphey for an explanation. "I went to see Dr. Curphey, and asked about the missing paperwork," Grandison recalls. "I voiced my concerns about the lack of information in the file. This was maybe the third or fourth time I had been to him about missing paperwork."

Curphey's response was to hand Grandison what were only a few of the pages from the complete autopsy report. When Grandison looked at them, he found the report was not just incomplete, it had also been altered. "Now, I had seen the initial autopsy report, and this wasn't the same report. The report had been completely changed."

When Grandison asked Curphey what had happened to the original report, Curphey flew into a rage.

"He got very angry about it. He said, 'Listen, you sign the death certificate. That's the paperwork for the file.'" Then Curphey added what Grandison took as a threat: "Or else, I'm gonna do something."

The implication, Grandison believes, was that Curphey would see that he lost his position with the coroner's office if he did not sign the death certificate immediately. Grandison was a young man with a wife and children to support. He felt he had no choice but do as he was ordered.

"I left and went back to my desk," he told me, "signed the death certificate, put it in the file, and allowed it to be filed with the health department. If the county coroner insists it's suicide, who was I to say that it's not?"

CURPHEY'S MOTIVES

The way Dr. Curphey steered department investigators away from Marilyn's doctors, the missing and altered documents, the circumstances under which the death certificate was signed all convinced Lionel Grandison that Dr. Curphey personally orchestrated the cover-up of Marilyn's death from within the department. Grandison even believes that the coroner's verdict of suicide was a vital part of that cover-up.

"The one thing that stopped this investigation from going any further was the fact that it was determined to be a suicide. That stopped any chance of an inquest. As long as it was a suicide, as long as they kept that suicide verdict on the death certificate, there could never be any other investigation. That left it in the hands of Dr. Curphey."

As the coroner of the county of Los Angeles, Curphey had enormous resources at his disposal if he had actually wanted to conduct an in-depth investigation into the star's death. Lionel Grandison considers Curphey's failure to call on those resources and make that investigation to be additional proof of the cover-up.

"Curphey had the whole city and county investigative system at his disposal," Grandison explains, "to get additional information, to determine how this woman was killed. He could have called in all the investigation tools that the state has to offer. But he didn't."

Is Grandison right? And what might be Curphey's motives for taking part in the conspiracy? The answers may lay in the special nature of the Los Angeles Coroner's office at the time. As Grandison remembers it:

"The coroner of the county of Los Angeles was a very

powerful position. It was appointive. To get it, and keep it, you had to already be known to the politicians and the powerful factions that backed them — the wealthy, large corporations, the movie studios — as someone who could be counted on to cooperate in a sticky situation, to overlook, to keep your mouth shut."

Curphey is rumored to have cooperated in bringing in verdicts of accidental death in order to spare powerful families the humiliation of a verdict of suicide. He has also been accused of hushing up embarrassing circumstances surrounding the deaths of influential politicians. Critics have even charged Coroner Curphey with a systematic pattern of verdicts favorable to the police in controversial officer-related shootings.

Grandison is convinced this view of Curphey is correct. "There's no doubt in my mind that anyone who holds the position of coroner is susceptible to those kinds of things. It's that type of position. Curphey was no more susceptible than anyone else. Dr. Noguchi found that out when he became coroner. National and local government, police agencies, important people from the private sector come into your office and say, 'They're the dead, and we're the living. Listen, I want you to do this or else.'"

Grandison believes that some staff members may have disapproved of the way Curphey ran the coroner's office, but were afraid of losing their jobs if they spoke out.

"Very few people in the office questioned his decisions or what he did. Everyone was career, the civil service. If you made a determination according to regulations, and Dr. Curphey came in and said, 'Scratch this. Were going to change this,' even if you had followed regulations, you changed it."

Before Lionel Grandison came forward, the involvement of high-level government officials in the conspiracy to cover up Marilyn Monroe's murder could be no more than supposition. Grandison's testimony makes it fact.

These facts should call for a re-evaluation of the official investigation into Marilyn Monroe's death. We already know those reports were highly suspect. Now we have proof that the men who headed those departments deliberately conspired to cripple the investigations that led to those reports.

How many more voices will have to break the silence about Marilyn Monroe before we begin to call her death a murder? Grandison may have been one of the earliest to air long-hidden truths about the way Marilyn died, but he is not alone. Many others have stepped out of the shadows in recent years to join him. Increasingly, their stories add to the pool of facts that point to an unavoidable conclusion: Marilyn Monroe could not have taken her own life, but was a victim of premeditated murder.

FILE #17

"We Had Her Saved!"

On November 23, 1982, a new twist was added to the unfolding saga of Marilyn Monroe's death. A former ambulance driver named James Hall came forward with a dramatic and controversial story. Hall claimed that he and his partner had driven the mysterious ambulance seen at Marilyn's house the night of her death — and that they made an unsuccessful attempt to resuscitate her. Hall also claims that he was an eyewitness to Marilyn's murder, and that he knows the identity of her killer.

Jim Hall's story begins shortly after 3:30 A.M. on the morning of August 5, 1962. Hall was working as an ambulance driver for Schaefer's Ambulance Service at their Santa Monica office. His partner was Murray Leibowitz. What follows is Hall's uncensored account of the events of that night.

"We were returning from a run to the UCLA hospital, when we received a call to rush to 12305 Fifth Helena. We were told it was an emergency. We were real close, practically right around the corner. We were at the house within two minutes."

When Hall and his partner arrived at the house, there was a woman standing outside the house in a nightgown. The woman appeared to be "very hysterical, very distraught." She kept screaming over and over: "She's dead. She's dead."

Hall and Leibowitz tried to reassure her. "We'll do the best we can," they said.

The two ambulance drivers asked the woman who she was and what was wrong with the patient. The woman, whose name Hall would later learn was Pat Newcomb, replied, "I'm her publicist."

Hall, who was 22 years old at the time, had never heard of a publicist and didn't know what the word meant. He asked the woman again, "What's wrong with the patient?"

The woman told them, "I think she took some pills."

Hall and Leibowitz grabbed their first-aid kit, and followed the woman inside to a guest bedroom set off from the rest of the house. Marilyn was lying nude, face-up on the bed. She was unconscious, and appeared to be in obvious distress.

"Wow!" Hall thought. "Marilyn Monroe, you gotta be kidding me." Hall and his partner asked the publicist what she thought was wrong with Marilyn. "I think she took some pills," the woman replied.

The two ambulance drivers observed Marilyn carefully. Her pulse was very weak and rapid. Her respiration was almost nonexistent. They were the classic symptoms of overdose.

Hall and Leibowitz decided to apply CPR. But CPR requires a strong support under the patient's back. The two men knew they would have to move her. At first they thought about laying her down on the bedroom floor, but the bedroom was too small. They decided to carry her out to the foyer instead.

What Hall claims happens next may explain one of the more puzzling aspects of Noguchi's autopsy report. "We picked her up," Hall remembers, "and started to move her. Of all the patients I carried the whole time I worked as an ambulance driver, the only patient I ever dropped was Marilyn Monroe. We dropped her right on her fanny. On the autopsy there were two bruises they couldn't explain. One was on her upper arm — that's my fingerprints. One was on her fanny — that's where we dropped her. Dead bodies don't bruise. She was still alive." The two ambulance drivers picked up the actress and moved her to the foyer without further incident. Hall put an airway, a tube that would make breathing easier, into her throat. Leibowitz brought in the resuscitator from the ambulance and hooked it up.

THE DOCTOR'S ORDERS

The CPR, Hall says, was effective almost immediately. "I was getting a perfect exchange of air. It was really working good. Her color was starting to come back. I felt she was doing well enough that we could safely take her on in to the hospital. I said to Murray, 'Get the gurney.'"

At that moment, Hall remembers, a man came in carrying a doctor's bag. The man identified himself immediately. "I'm her doctor," he said. "Give her positive pressure."

The doctor's order surprised Hall. "I thought, 'Hey, turkey, what do you think we're doing? The machine's doing it perfect.' But you never argue with a doctor at the scene of an emergency. Never. You'd lose your job. So I took the resuscitator off, put an extension on the airway, pinched her nose, and began giving her mouth-to-mouth resuscitation. That's as positive as you can get." While Hall gave Marilyn resuscitation, the doctor began to give her CPR. However, according to Hall, the doctor did not apply it correctly. Instead of applying it to the chest, the doctor seemed to be applying it to the actress's lower abdomen.

Hall became concerned. "Look, Doctor," he said, "you blow and I'll push." The doctor ignored Hall. Instead, he opened his bag and pulled out a hypodermic syringe, with a heart needle already affixed to it. Hall wondered at the time why he would already have a heart needle prepared. Hall distinctly heard the doctor mutter, "I have to make a show out of this."

At about this time, "two men entered the room. One was wearing a Los Angeles police officer's uniform. The other, a tanned, handsome man, was wearing a suit. I figured he was also a police officer, possibly a plainclothes detective."

Throughout the attempt to resuscitate Marilyn, the publicist had been sobbing hysterically: "She's dead! She's dead!" As soon as they arrived, the man in the suit went over to her, put his arm around her, and began to calm her down.

The doctor took a pharmaceutical bottle out of his bag. He inserted the needle into the bottle and filled the syringe. Then he said, as if repeating something out of a textbook: "We have to inject this between the sixth and seventh ribs." The doctor's next move was chilling. Hall was shocked; what happened was so unexpected that he did not think to intervene until it was too late. "He counted down the rib cage, pushed her breast to the side, and stuck the needle into her chest. He did it wrong; it was at an angle, and the needle stopped. Instead of backing it out and starting over, he just leaned on it — and it went, 'Snap!' The needle broke her rib, and he just shoved it right into her heart." Hall knew Marilyn was dead right then.

The doctor leaned over, put the stethoscope on her chest, and said, "You can leave. I'm going to pronounce her dead."

Hall says he was sick at heart. "I mean, we had her

saved."

The time was 3:45 A.M. Only fifteen minutes had passed. But to the two ambulance drivers, it seemed like hours.

The policeman walked into the living room, where the two ambulance drivers saw him pick up and dial the telephone. They could not hear what he said.

Hall and Leibowitz filled out their call sheet, then gathered up their equipment to depart. "When we left the house, it was between ten minutes to four and four o'clock. As we went out the door, we saw the first-call ambulance from a local mortuary parked next to ours. It was there to pick up the remains."

Both men were puzzled. Hall asked his partner, "Hey, how'd they get here so quick? I mean she's only been dead ten minutes."

Leibowitz shrugged. It was the only answer Hall would get.

THE DOCTOR AND THE ACTOR

For years James Hall puzzled over the identity of the doctor who he feels killed Marilyn Monroe. He also wondered about the man he had thought was a plainclothes detective. Something about this man's face seemed elusively familiar. Now Hall believes he knows who both men were.

Twenty years later, Hall was reading about Marilyn's death when he saw a picture of the tanned, handsome man who had accompanied the police officer to Marilyn's death scene. The caption below the picture told him the man was Peter Lawford, the Kennedy brother-in-law. "It was Peter Lawford when he was a younger guy," Hall confirms. "That's who he was."

What about the identity of the mysterious doctor? The man Hall saw kill Marilyn Monroe by plunging a hypodermic needle into her heart? "I subsequently discovered who he was, too," Hall says.

Hall first learned the man's identity when he was hypnotized by Henry Coater. A forensic hypnotist, Coater has worked with the police for twenty years. Coater, a former police officer, is an expert at helping witnesses to remember details they think they have forgotten.

"Coater hypnotized me," Hall remembers. "He regressed me back in time to the night of Marilyn's death. He had me remember the face of the doctor, what he looked like. Afterward, when they brought me out of the hypnosis, we did a police identi-sketch. At that time one of the reporters walked by, and said, 'Hey, I know that guy.' They pulled pictures of Marilyn's psychiatrist, Dr. Ralph Greenson — and that's who it was."

Then Hall pauses, his cherubic face becoming serious. It is obvious Hall is convinced he has solved the mystery that has haunted investigators for three decades. And he repeats it again with emphasis, as if driving the point home to convince a disbelieving world. "I absolutely believe that Dr. Ralph Greenson murdered Marilyn Monroe," Hall says today.

TRUE OR FALSE

Hall's story is highly controversial. If true, it answers many troubling questions about Marilyn Monroe's death. But it also raises others that are equally troubling.

First, it supplies a dramatic explanation for the presence of the ambulance the neighbors saw at Marilyn Monroe's house earlier in the night.

Second, Hall's account of dropping the actress as they moved her to perform CPR explains the bruise on her hip that has puzzled Noguchi and other investigators for so long.

Third, it dovetails with Deputy Coroner's Aide Lionel Grandison's account of discovering that Marilyn's body had been transported quickly and rather mysteriously to the Westwood Memorial Park, instead of the coroner's office downtown.

However, there is a major difficulty with Hall's story — the discrepancy in the time factor. Hall claims Marilyn was still alive when he and his partner arrived on the scene at 3:30 A.M., and that she died only fifteen minutes later, at 3:45 A.M In contrast, the most likely version of the various stories told by Mrs. Murray, Dr. Greenson, and Dr. Engelberg places the death at around midnight, perhaps earlier. This is consistent with the fact that the men who handled Marilyn's body at the mortuary that morning reported that *rigor mortis* was already well advanced; since it takes about five or six hours for rigor mortis to set in. Consequently, Marilyn would have been dead for three or four hours before the events Hall describes.

Moreover, the ambulance that neighbors report seeing that night was parked outside her house shortly after midnight. Although consistent with the timing of *rigor mortis*, it is hours before the events Hall describes.

Hall might have remembered the time incorrectly, in spite of his insistence to the contrary. No amount of evidence can persuade him to change his story about the time element.

Is Hall simply wrong about the time, but unable to accept it? Perhaps there were three ambulances that night: one at midnight, that took Marilyn to the Santa Monica Hospital and then brought her back to her home alive; a second ambulance driven by Hall and his partner, that made a last desperate attempt to save her; a third, that transported her body to the mortuary. Such a hypothesis seems unlikely.

There is another difficulty with Jim Hall's story. According to Hall's eyewitness account, Marilyn was dead by 3:45

A.M. Her body was in a small guest bedroom. Yet forty-five minutes later officer Jack Clemmons would find Marilyn's body's in her own bedroom.

How did Marilyn's body get from one room to another? What happened during those lost 45 minutes? Jim Hall thinks he knows. "They moved her," he says with conviction. "They put her into the master bedroom." Jack Clemmons, the first officer at the scene, has said that she looked exactly like what she was — a dead body that had been arranged in that position on the bed, facedown, covered with a sheet.

There's a final problem with Hall's revelations. He claims that when he and Leibowitz arrived, the pill bottles were capped and arranged neatly on the dresser. But when Jack Clemmons investigated the scene, the caps were off, and many were lying on their sides in disarray.

There is indirect support for Jim Hall's account of Marilyn's death. The national tabloid that broke Hall's story claims that James Hall "took and passed six different lie detector tests confirming his eyewitness account."

Hall remembers the grueling ordeal clearly. "Yes, I was given a lie detector test. They took me to Florida. The polygraph examinations were conducted by John Harrison, who is the co-inventor of the polygraph. The initial question was: 'On the evening of August 4, 1962, did you attempt to administer life-saving techniques to Marilyn Monroe?' The results showed that there was no deception whatsoever. It's all truthful."

Sergeant Jack Clemmons believes that Hall's story clears up several mysteries about the events surrounding Marilyn's death. "What he's telling us fits in with what I already know. And they gave the man six lie detector tests, one of them by the man who originated the polygraph. He passed all of them with flying colors."

Clemmons feels there is another detail of Hall's story that

also lends it credibility. "Jim says that while he was trying to revive Marilyn, two men walked in, one in the uniform of a Los Angeles police officer. They witnessed Dr. Greenson giving Marilyn a shot and killing her. Then that Los Angeles policeman, whoever he was, got on that telephone. Now, I've told this story many times to policemen, retired and active. At the end I ask, 'Now, when that ambulance crew left, what would you have done?' I get one answer. 'I would have picked up the telephone and called my superiors, and I would have asked for instructions.'" And making a phone call is exactly what Hall says this officer did. He was calling his superiors in the LAPD and saying: 'What do you want me to do now?'"

Marilyn's childhood chum, Bebe Goddard, also believes Jim Hall's story. "Jim Hall and I met at the Hollywood Roosevelt in 1987. We had a very lengthy discussion, and I felt total sincerity and truthfulness from him. What he was saying was so logical — I think that was the most important thing. It was the most logical thing I had heard. For the first time Marilyn's death began to make sense to me. I felt that this was really the truth. This was really something that happened."

There is other indirect confirmation as well. Although some have suggested that Hall made up his story recently for publicity or personal gain, Hall's father, a retired police surgeon whose reputation is beyond reproach, has told interviewers that Jim Hall told him the same story within a day or two of Marilyn's death.

Even Hall's ex-wife, who has little reason to lie for him, claims to have heard the story from him at the time.

On the other hand, Hall's story has been challenged by none other than Walter Schaefer, owner of Schaefer's Ambulance Service. Schaefer has denied that James Hall ever worked for him.

Hall disputes Schaefer's denial vehemently. "I worked for him for about three years," Hall says with feeling.

Who is telling the truth?

Social Security records conclusively prove that Hall was on the Schaefer Ambulance company's payroll during August 1962. Nick Harris Detective Agency head Milo Speriglio has also verified Hall's employment by Schaefer at the time. "Jim Hall was indeed an employee of Schaefer's Ambulance Service during the period of Marilyn's death."

If Jim Hall worked for Schaefer, why would Schaefer deny it? Hall has his own explanation for Schaefer's failure to admit the truth. "I absolutely believe that there was a cover-up in Marilyn's death. I think Walter was part of the cover-up, too. I think he was told to discredit me."

There are no other witnesses to the events Jim Hall describes. Ralph Greenson died in 1979. Peter Lawford passed away in 1984. Pat Newcomb refuses to comment. Eunice Murray has no recollection of Jim Hall. Murray Leibowitz, Hall's alleged partner at the time, has never spoken publicly about what he knows.

Jim Hall seems sincere. But there is really only one way to prove his story. If Marilyn's body were exhumed, it would be easy for pathologists to find out whether there was a cracked rib that might have been broken by a needle.

If the broken rib were found, it would overturn most other theories of her murder and of her murderer. Until such an investigation is carried out, Jim Hall's account of his attempt to resuscitate Marilyn and of Dr. Greenson's fatal actions, murder will remain another of the many baffling mysteries that surround her curious death.

FILE #18

Creating the "Official" Story

Sorting out the discrepancies in the various accounts of how Marilyn Monroe spent her last day is difficult. Sorting out all the contradictions in accounts people tell of how she spent her last night is nearly impossible.

Until recently, lack of evidence about these last hours handicapped investigators' attempts to unravel the mystery of those missing eight hours. Today, now that the wall of silence concealing the night's events has been cracked, an excess of conflicting evidence has become an equal handicap.

Pieces of testimony we can safely trust about that night are those of Marilyn's friend, Jeanne Carmen, and her masseur, Ralph Roberts. According to them, Marilyn was still alive shortly after 10:00 P.M. Carmen spoke to her around that time, while Roberts says the actress tried to reach him a few minutes later, only to be told by his answering service that he was out for the evening.

Another reliable chunk of testimony we have is that of LAPD Sergeant Jack Clemmons, who arrived at Marilyn's house eight hours later, on Sunday morning, in response to a call from Dr. Greenson officially reporting her demise.

Ten days after Marilyn's death, actor Peter Lawford told reporters he had spoken to the actress around 7:00 P.M.

Lawford, a man of divided loyalties, was both one of Marilyn's closest friends and a Kennedy-in-law. Lawford asserted that, "Marilyn said she was happy and was going to bed."

Yet, as with so many of those whose testimony was responsible for the official verdict of suicide, Lawford would later recant this story. Lawford's new version of his phone conversations with Marilyn that night would place him as the last person to talk to the dying star.

As others who had important stories to contribute about that night's events came forward, Lawford's role would be seen, as that of a central player.

Even today, with the testimony of over a dozen witnesses to various aspects of the night's events, it is still not possible to say that we know all that occurred that night. Although several key periods are still hidden in a maze of contradiction and silence, it is possible to fill in an increasingly detailed outline of many of the events that transpired that night.

THE LAST EIGHT HOURS

Peter Lawford kept silent about actual events of the night of August 4, 1962, for more than thirteen years. Until 1975, the LAPD had never interviewed Lawford! Faced with official investigators for the first time, the handsome British actor told them a different story, one that illuminated many of the mysteries that have baffled journalists for years.

Lawford informed police that he had talked to the star twice that evening. The first time was at 5:00 P.M. when he phoned Marilyn. Lawford said she sounded depressed and despondent.

This is within thirty minutes of the time Eunice Murray claims to have been so concerned over Marilyn's emotional state that she summoned Dr. Ralph Greenson. Lawford's statement, fits with the timetable Greenson, Murray and Pat Newcomb later gave police.

However, Lawford's new story added an important difference. Lawford told police investigators that Marilyn had been depressed, but claimed it was over being fired from *Something's Got to Give*. Newcomb, Greenson and Murray, on the other hand, told police Marilyn had been upset over the publicist's ability to sleep while she had paced the floors all night.

More importantly, new information from Fox archives reveals that Marilyn had actually been reinstated on the picture a few days earlier, at a large increase in salary. She could not have been depressed over the loss of her job on the night of her death. Nor is it likely she would have told Lawford she was.

Lawford's slip seems to reveal precisely the secret he wanted to conceal — the same secret Greenson, Murray and Newcomb were trying to cover-up with their equally unlikely story of a fight over sleeplessness. All four agree Marilyn was depressed and unhappy that final Saturday. All four seem equally bent on concealing what had caused the depression.

The only secret in Marilyn's life important enough to unite four such very different individuals as Lawford, Greenson, Murray and Newcomb would be the actress's relationship with Bobby Kennedy, attorney general of the United States. Perhaps Lawford was unaware of, or had forgotten, what had been decided as the official explanation for Marilyn's depression twenty years earlier. Clearly, however, the aging matinee-idol cast around quickly for something that would justify his account of her depression. The thought of Marilyn's earlier troubles with Fox over *Something's Got to Give* seemed to fulfill this immediate need for a viable explanation.

The rift between Marilyn and the Kennedys had put a strain

on Lawford's relationship with the star. Lawford had no way of knowing his lie would be uncovered, and its purpose revealed.

Lawford told his LAPD interviewers that Marilyn had called him back about 7:30 P.M. to tell him she was even more depressed. Her speech sounded "slurry," he said, implying that she was already feeling the effects of an overdose. According to Lawford, Marilyn then uttered what may have been her last words — if we can believe his story.

"Say good-bye to Jack [Kennedy] and say good-bye to yourself. You're a nice guy."

Lawford said Marilyn's voice became less audible and then trailed off. He never heard her hang up the receiver.

Lawford claimed he tried to call Marilyn back several times but the phone was always busy. Lawford concluded it had been left off the hook.

Like most stars, Marilyn had two phone lines at Fifth Helena: a private number for friends and a second for business. If Lawford's story is true, he would certainly have gotten through to Eunice Murray on that other line as had Mickey Rudin a few minutes later.

What Lawford says he did next set off a complex pattern of interconnected phone calls. The British actor called Milton Ebbins. Lawford told Ebbins about Marilyn's call and said he was thinking about driving over to check up on her condition. Ebbins reminded Lawford that he was the president's brother-in-law, and should not become personally involved if there was something wrong with the actress. Instead, Ebbins said, he would call Marilyn's attorney, Mickey Rudin, and let Rudin handle the situation. Ebbins phoned Rudin and advised him of Marilyn Monroe's call to Lawford.

Quizzed shortly after Lawford's disclosure, Ebbins says he reached Rudin around 8:45 P.M. But this makes no sense in terms of what we now know of the timetable of phone calls

Marilyn Monroe made and received between 7:45 P.M. and approximately 10:30 P.M. that night.

If Marilyn had called Lawford at 7:30 P.M. (as he told LAPD representatives in 1975), while passing out from an overdose, she could hardly have been on the phone with Joe DiMaggio Jr. at 7:45 P.M. laughing and discussing the break up with his girlfriend.

And Marilyn would have been in no shape to talk to Henry Rosenfeld, Sidney Guilaroff, José Bolanos, Jeanne Carmen and Ralph Roberts' answering service over the next three hours.

If Lawford kept getting a busy signal when he tried to call Marilyn back after 7:30 P.M., it wasn't because she had passed out leaving the phone off the hook. It was because she was on the phone talking to someone almost every minute of the time.

Lawford had no way of knowing about those calls even as recently as 1975. He undoubtedly felt safe in placing Marilyn's call to him at 7:30 P.M. The fact that the other calls had been made brands Lawford a liar. Why was Lawford lying?

The answer was not to come for more than a decade, when Lawford's former wife, Deborah Gould, broke her own silence about the events of that night. According to Gould, Lawford told her he had received the second call from Marilyn not at 7:30 P.M., as he had told police in 1975, but sometime after 10:00 P.M. If true, that would be perfectly consistent with the actual timetable of Marilyn's known activities, and place her call to Lawford shortly before or after her unsuccessful attempt to reach Ralph Roberts.

In 1975, Lawford had been protecting a secret. He had been trying to alibi someone's timetable. But whose? His own?

That's possible. According to Gould, Lawford finally ignored Ebbins' advice and drove to Marilyn's house. He was joined there by a private detective he had called. Together the two men destroyed all evidence of Marilyn Monroe's involvement with the Kennedy brothers.

Others who were with Lawford that night support this timetable. His dinner guests, Joe and Dolores Naarr, say Lawford neither made nor received calls during the evening; or was there any sign that he had received disturbing news.

Around 11:00 P.M., after they had returned home, the Naarrs say Lawford called them and said that Marilyn might have taken too many pills. He then asked Bob Naarr, who lived near the actress, if he could drive over and make sure everything was all right. While Naarr was dressing, Lawford called back. He told the Naarrs it was a false alarm, and they then went to bed.

What made Lawford change his mind? He may have decided to check on Marilyn himself. Or Lawford may have phoned brother-in-law Bobby Kennedy and received instructions from him.

There is a third possibility. Lawford may have received an erroneous report that temporarily lulled him into thinking he had misinterpreted Marilyn's call. The person who gave Lawford this impression may have been Mickey Rudin.

When Milton Ebbins phoned Rudin to tell him of Lawford's conversation with the actress, Rudin, in turn, phoned Eunice Murray to ask her if everything was all right. According to Rudin's brief 1962 interview with the LAPD, Murray told him that the actress had been in a somewhat despondent mood earlier that evening, but had gone to bed in a much improved frame of mind.

Reassured, Rudin would have called either Lawford or Ebbins, or both, and told them there was no cause for alarm.

As for Eunice Murray, she says Rudin neither told her about Lawford's call nor his concern that Marilyn might have taken an overdose. Murray says Rudin gave her the impression he was making a routine inquiry. Had Rudin explained why he was calling, Murray implied, she would have checked on Marilyn immediately — with the result that the star's life might have been saved.

Instead, Murray told investigators, she fell asleep believing Marilyn to be in no danger. It was only when she awakened at 3:30 A.M., and noticed the phone cord under Marilyn's door that she became concerned, and discovered there was something seriously wrong with the star.

Rudin's and Lawford's relief was not to last very long. Before the night was over, both men would learn Marilyn had overdosed on sleeping pills. Both men would find themselves at the star's house, helping to orchestrate the cover-up that has shrouded the circumstances of her death in mystery for almost thirty years.

Before this latter event occured, however, one of Hollywood's most successful publicists would already be present, directing the opening moves of that cover-up.

JACOBS ON THE JOB

At the time of Marilyn Monroe's death, her publicist, Arthur Jacobs, owned one of the largest public relations companies in Los Angeles. The star's personal publicist, Pat Newcomb, was one of Jacobs' senior employees. The care, handling and feeding of Jacobs' highly impulsive client was Newcomb's main assignment.

On the night of Saturday, August 4, 1962, Arthur Jacobs and his fianceé, Natalie, were attending an outdoor concert at the Hollywood Bowl. It was Natalie's birthday and a celebration had been planned after the concert at Chasen's, the ultra-deluxe celebrity watering-hole.

What happened next would remain a secret until 1985 when Natalie, now Jacobs' widow, became the first to place her husband at the death scene later that night. According to

Natalie Jacobs, this is what happened: "We were enjoying the concert when this man came to our box and whispered into Arthur's ear that he had an urgent phone call. Arthur left and, when he came back, looked very pale and flustered. He told me he had to leave immediately; that there were problems at Marilyn's house. Arthur said I was to stay for the rest of the concert, take a cab home and he would call me later."

Natalie Jacobs says: "It wasn't until two days later that he called me. I asked him what happened that night. But Arthur just said, 'I had to fudge the whole thing.' He wouldn't say anything more."

Natalie is not certain as to exactly when her future husband left the concert, but places it somewhere between 10:00 and 10:45 P.M. (Hollywood Bowl concerts traditionally end before 11:00 P.M.)

Natalie Jacobs' revelation means the story Eunice Murray told Sergeant Jack Clemmons of waking at midnight to discover something was wrong with Marilyn, and the one she told Sergeant Robert Byron of waking to make the discovery at 3:30 A.M., are both false. And so are the stories Dr. Ralph Greenson and Dr. Hyman Engelberg told police and journalists in support of her timetable.

With Natalie Jacobs' information, the entire original story upon which the coroner's verdict of suicide was based, collapses like a house of cards. The stories that Greenson, Engelberg and Murray told (with variations) to every investigator and journalist who interviewed them for almost three decades are also fabrications. This official story became what Byron accepted, and served as the basis upon which all subsequent investigations into Marilyn's death, and their results, were founded.

Is Natalie Jacobs' account of Arthur's activities that evening reliable? I believe so. Several of Arthur Jacobs' former employees support it. Juliet Roswell, who worked for his public relations firm at the time of Marilyn's death, recalls his telling her, a few days later, that "I went out there at eleven o'clock."

A second employee, who insisted on confidentiality, told me that Arthur Jacobs was the "architect of the cover-up."

Another who confirms Jacobs' presence at Marilyn Monroe's house the night of her death is Milo Speriglio. But Speriglio's version adds a sinister twist to Natalie Jacobs' story. It also casts confusion on the question of whom that cover-up was designed to protect.

"Arthur Jacobs knew, and Fox studio knew by 10:30 or 10:45 P.M., that Marilyn was in danger. Marilyn was alive at that time. The studio did nothing to save her."

Jack Clemmons backs up Speriglio's story. "The studio seems to have been exclusively concerned with collecting on an insurance policy they had on Marilyn. Even though she had been reinstated on her film, soon after her death, the publicity department began making disparaging remarks about her."

Truth? Supposition? Or just innuendo? Arthur Jacob died in the early 1980s, and cannot defend himself from these charges.

But consider this: A little over a year after his client's death, Jacobs sold his public relations firm for top dollar and went to work for Fox as a producer. His first assignment was *What A Way To Go*, followed by *Doctor Doolittle*, and then *The Planet of the Apes*; the latter a huge money earner that spawned several lucrative sequels and a television series.

Who was Jacobs protecting and what was he covering up? Certainly not Marilyn. He would have attributed her death to an accident, not suicide, if his interest was in protecting her.

Was Jacobs protecting the studio? Were they somehow involved in Marilyn Monroe's death? It seems unlikely. Was the publicist simply managing events to ensure that if Marilyn did die that evening, the circumstances in which she was found would not keep the studio from collecting their three million dollars in insurance?

The one person who might be able to answer these questions is Pat Newcomb, who apparently joined Jacobs at Marilyn's house later that night. As Jacobs' employee, Marilyn's friend and a Kennedy supporter, Newcomb may have been privy to everybody's secrets.

Natalie Jacobs thinks she was. "If you want to know what really happened that night," Natalie Jacobs says, "ask Pat Newcomb. She knows the whole story."

THE REST OF THE CAST

Arthur Jacobs, Mickey Rudin, Peter Lawford and the private detective he had brought to help clean up any evidence of Marilyn Monroe's involvement with the Kennedys, weren't the only people now known to have entered Marilyn's house that night. In an exclusive interview, Inez Melson, Marilyn's long-time friend and former business manager, admitted to me that she and several others were at Fifth Helena during the early morning hours of Sunday, August 5. Melson saw representatives of the Twentieth Century-Fox publicity department, including Frank Neill, Johnny Campbell, and two studio guards.

According to Melson, all those present were engaged in the same activity: they were removing anything that the press might use "to tarnish Marilyn Monroe's memory." (It has been rumored that correspondence, contracts and other related materials were also removed, including a packet of love letters written to Marilyn by Bobby Kennedy on Justice Department stationary.)

Melson also saw Eunice Murray, Dr. Ralph Greenson and Dr. Hyman Engelberg three hours earlier, and in significantly different circumstances, than those the physicians reported to police.

One of those Melson did not mention, who may also have been there that night, is Pat Newcomb.

Throughout the years since Marilyn Monroe's death, Pat Newcomb has always denied that she was present at Marilyn's house on the night of August 4, 1962.

But Newcomb was willing to place Mickey Rudin there. In 1973, she told me that she had been awakened at 4:00 A.M. by a call from Rudin. He told her that Marilyn Monroe was dead. According to Newcomb, she asked Rudin where he was, and he said he was calling from Marilyn's home.

Peter Lawford's former business manager, Milton Ebbins, the man who first alerted Rudin to the possibility that Marilyn might have taken an overdose, also places Rudin at the scene of the star's death in the vicinity of 4:00 A.M. Ebbins told one journalist that Rudin had called him at about that time to inform him of Marilyn's death. As with Pat Newcomb, Rudin told Ebbins he was speaking from Marilyn's house and that she was dead.

Strangely enough, Sergeant Jack Clemmons would be summoned to the scene only twenty-five minutes later. By the time he arrived. there was no sign of the many people who had been at the star's home during the night. Only the two doctors and Eunice Murray would be waiting for him. In the account they would give him and other LAPD officers, there was no mention of Rudin, Jacobs, Newcomb or the rest of the Fox studio entourage.

Were the stories Greenson, Engelberg and Murray told part of the "fudging" Arthur Jacobs had to do that night? There is every reason to believe they are.

It is possible that Pat Newcomb was present at Marilyn's house, possibly in the detached guest bedroom, while Clemmons was interviewing Dr. Greenson, Dr. Engelberg and Eunice Murray. Newcomb may have been coaching them on the last minute details of their awkward and obviously hastily prepared stories. She may also have been the one who advised them on the changes they made when they told those stories later to Sergeant Robert Byron.

In that same 1973 interview, Newcomb told me that after hearing Rudin's news, she dressed quickly and drove straight to Fifth Helena. That would have placed her at the house some ten to twenty minutes before Clemmons could have arrived. Yet Sergeant Jack Clemmons saw no sign of her while he was there.

However, television news footage shows Newcomb emerging from the house with Eunice Murray — though the site was supposed to have been sealed off by Sergeant Iannone immediately after Clemmons returned to the station.

Could Newcomb's story of having first learned of Marilyn's death at 4:00 A.M. be yet another part of the cover-up? Had she actually been at the house all night, helping Arthur Jacobs to orchestrate the cover-up? Had Pat Newcomb simply remained — rather than arrived — for that last minute briefing?

We can easily assume she did. It's not likely that Arthur Jacobs, after having his evening interrupted just before his fiancé's birthday celebration, would have driven to Marilyn Monroe's home and orchestrated a massive cover-up without calling his trusty aide; Jacobs had been responsible for Newcomb's assignment as Mariyln's personal publicist. In fact, there is every reason to believe that Pat Newcomb may have been the mysterious person who called Jacobs at the Hollywood Bowl and first told him there was "trouble at Marilyn's house."

Pat Newcomb, as one of Marilyn's close female friends and a professional at giving the right spin to difficult situations, would have been a logical person for Eunice Murray, Dr. Greenson or Peter Lawford to call, if they had found the star comatose and apparently suffering from an overdose. Newcomb would have known instantly that the power of the studio would be needed, both to get Marilyn the fastest care, and to prevent the situation from mushrooming into a major scandal. Jacobs was her immediate superior; he knew how to protect his high-priced clients' images, and he had contacts at every level of city and county government.

It's hard to believe that Jacobs is the first person Eunice Murray or Dr. Ralph Greenson, or even Peter Lawford, would have called — if they had called him at all.

Clearly, whoever had phoned Jacobs at the Hollywood Bowl must have done so within minutes of the time Mickey Rudin had called Eunice Murray and asked if Marilyn was all right. Only Pat Newcomb would have been likely to think of Arthur Jacobs that fast, and only Pat Newcomb would have been likely to know where her boss could be found at the Hollywood Bowl at 10:30 P.M. that evening.

THE OFFICIAL STORY DEBUNKED

Those who have come forward to tell what they knew about the events surrounding Marilyn Monroe's last hours have helped us to fill in many missing gaps in our picture of the events surrounding her death. As a result of the testimony of Natalie Jacobs, Milton Ebbins, Juliet Roswell, Joe and Dolores Naarr, Peter Lawford, Johnny Campbell, and many others, we can see a frightening pattern of distortions, discrepancies and blatant lies . . . the so-called "Official Story."

We now know that Eunice Murray's account of how and when she first became concerned about Marilyn, as well as the story of Dr. Ralph Greenson breaking into a locked bedroom after seeing Marilyn's motionless body through a window, could not be true.

Clearly, someone discovered something very wrong with Marilyn shortly after her last call to Peter Lawford at 10:30 P.M.

In all probability, that someone was Eunice Murray, checking on Marilyn in response to Mickey Rudin's questions about the actress's condition.

We also know that Eunice Murray did not sleep through the hours from 9:00 P.M. to 3 A.M., as she long maintained. Instead, during those hours, Marilyn's house was a beehive of bustling activity. Arthur Jacobs and nearly a dozen others were there attempting to conceal important facts about Marilyn's demise, remove her papers and documents, and mislead the world about how that death had occurred.

But what about Dr. Ralph Greenson's story of being summoned at 3:30 A.M. to find Marilyn Monroe dead in a locked bedroom? Could it be true? Might Greenson be the victim and not a perpetrator of the cover-up? Could Eunice have called Greenson as part of Jacobs' cover-up? Could the death scene have been carefully prepared to convince Greenson that Marilyn had taken her own life? Possible — but not likely.

There's still Greenson's failure to mention Mickey Rudin's presence at 4:00 A.M., only minutes before the psychiatrist reported Marilyn's body to the police. If Rudin's presence was innocent, why conceal it at all? There was certainly nothing embarrassing about an attorney being summoned to a client's death scene.

And why would Greenson join Eunice Murray in a transparently false story about Marilyn's miraculous upswing of mood following her conversation with Joe DiMaggio Jr. Saturday evening? A mood swing that is contradicted by the testimony of every single person who talked with Marilyn during the ensuing three hours?

If anyone there that night was an innocent dupe, it may have been Dr. Hyman Engelberg. The physician, after all, was the last to arrive. Engelberg never testified to more than arriving at the house and finding her dead. He may well have simply accepted Greenson's and Murray's story of how they had discovered Marilyn's body at face value. Engelberg was a trained doctor, not a trained detective. The broken glass outside — instead of inside — the bedroom window, and the other discrepancies in Greenson's and Murray's account of the night's events, may have gone right over Engelberg's head.

A great deal about what actually went on at Marilyn Monroe's home during four of those missing eight hours has now been made clear. But it still leaves many questions unanswered. One of these questions is: at what time did the star's death actually take place?

Marilyn was still alive as late as 10:30 P.M. when she called Carmen, Roberts and Lawford. Sergeant Jack Clemmons said he observed post mortem lividity when he inspected the star's dead body. This suggests Marilyn had died several hours before.

Clemmons' statement seems to narrow the time of the actress's death down to the period between 10:30 P.M. and 2:30 A.M. This still leaves four hours which are unaccounted for. Marilyn's death might have occurred at any time during that period.

Knowing exactly when Marilyn died is a necessity if any answers are to be found among the many mysteries surrounding her final hours.

Determining when Marilyn died might point to the individual who was with Marilyn at the time of her death. This information might, in turn, reveal the circumstances in which Marilyn died.

No witnesses have yet come forward to verify the time of Marilyn's death with the kind of breakthrough testimony that has cleared up so many of the other mysteries surrounding the night's events.

But there is circumstantial evidence that may tell us what those who were there that night will not tell us: the hour, if not the minutes, of Marilyn Monroe's death.

FILE #19

Countdown to Murder

Few questions have baffled serious investigators as much as the exact time of Marilyn Monroe's death. In fact, pinpointing this time will likely provide vital clues to the circumstances immediately surrounding her death. These clues might, in turn, help determine how she died and, possibly, who was with her during and before the time of her death. They are the sort of important details that could lead to final answers in the larger controversy over whether Marilyn was murdered or a victim of suicide.

Over the years many different timetables have been suggested. Some have had the dying star resuscitated at the last minute, only to be deliberately murdered within minutes of reviving.

According to the first version of that night's events as described by Dr. Ralph Greenson, Eunice Murray and Dr. Hyman Engelberg — the version they told Sergeant Jack Clemmons — Marilyn must have been dead by or around midnight. That's when Eunice Murray, discovering something was wrong with Marilyn, summoned Dr. Greenson who found her dead. This would narrow the period during which she might have died down to the hour and a half between 10:30 P.M. and midnight.

However, the version they later told Sergeant Robert Byron had Murray making her discovery and summoning Dr. Greenson at 3:30 A.M. — meaning Marilyn might have died anytime from 10:30 P.M. to 3:30 A.M., a period that encompasses most of the night.

The story told by former Schaefer ambulance driver, Jim Hall, has Marilyn still alive around 3:30 A.M. but dead among a battery of onlookers only a few minutes later. However, there are some investigators who are not convinced by Hall's account.

If we have no reliable testimony that might help us fix the time of Marilyn's death, perhaps we can learn something from the medical evidence.

One way doctors determine the time of death is by the extent of *rigor mortis*. Over the first ten to fourteen hours after death, the muscles of the body contract to rock hardness, and then relax. By determining how far *rigor mortis* has progressed, physicians can estimate the time of death to within one or two hours.

In 1962, a man named Guy Hockett owned Westwood Memorial Park. Hockett's company picked up Marilyn Monroe's body from her Brentwood home the morning of Sunday, August 5. During an exclusive interview shortly after Marilyn's death, Hockett detailed to me his part in the events of that morning.

Unfortunately, Hockett was unable to clarify one of the day's most puzzling mysteries: Who had called Hockett and authorized the body's release to him.

Something else Hockett said during that interview, however, may offer the most substantial clue yet as to the time of Marilyn's death. "My son and I — we were the coroner's representatives — picked up the body that morning, about 5:30, at her house in Brentwood. When we put Marilyn's body on the gurney to move it outside and into the hearse, we had to do quite a bit of bending to get the arms into position so that we could, you know, put the straps around her."

Assuming Hockett's memory is accurate, and this seems like something most people would remember if they had transported a celebrity's body, then we may now be able to estimate the time of Marilyn's death to within a few hours.

According to John Miner: "If they found *rigor mortis*, she would have been dead at least two hours, maybe more. Say two to four hours to be safe."

Dr. J. DeWitt Fox, a leading Los Angeles neurologist and medical consultant, adds an hour to that time frame and sets the probable time of Marilyn Monroe's death at two to five hours earlier. "*Rigor mortis* is based entirely on the outside temperature. If the body is in a warm atmosphere, it may take longer for the *rigor mortis* to occur. In a warm bedroom such as this was, I would give an estimate of up to four or five hours before *rigor mortis* sets in. That would date death back to approximately midnight or 1:00 A.M. Otherwise, *rigor mortis* would not have been present at the time her body was picked up at 5:00 A.M."

Sergeant Jack Clemmons' eyewitness observations at the death scene seem to support this timetable. Clemmons reported seeing signs of postmortem lividity, a bluish-purple discoloration on the underside of a body caused when blood settles as the result of the pull of gravity. Like *rigor mortis*, postmortem lividity takes several hours to develop. This would also seem to fix the time of death at no later than 1:30 A.M.

There is another story that places the time of Marilyn's death before 1:30 A.M. This involves a report of Marilyn Monroe's supposed round-trip ride to the Santa Monica Hospital in one of Walt Schaefer's ambulances.

It is here that the testimony of Marilyn's neighbor, Abe Landau, assumes critical importance. Landau places the time he and his wife saw the ambulance parked in Marilyn's driveway at 1:00 A.M. But was the ambulance there because it was picking up the star to rush her to the Santa Monica Hospital, or because it was returning her from there?

THE POST-MIDNIGHT RIDE OF MARILYN MONROE

If Marilyn Monroe died during or shortly after that fateful ambulance ride, as now seems possible, when did that ride take place?

In order to answer this question, we have to first answer the question of when the first doctor was called to the scene.

It is not likely that whoever found the comatose star waited very long to summon a doctor. In all likelihood, that person was Eunice Murray, immediately responding to Mickey Rudin's phone call to her. If Murray summoned a doctor to a dying Marilyn's bedside, it would undoubtedly have been Dr. Ralph Greenson. As a psychiatrist, Greenson had first been required to earn an M.D. He was qualified both medically and psychiatrically to deal with suicidal patients.

This much of the story that Greenson and Murray told officials and journalists seems true: Ralph Greenson was the first person Murray called after she discovered there was something wrong with her employer.

Since Rudin's call had first alerted Murray to a possible problem, it is also safe to assume that he was one of the first to receive confirmation that Marilyn had, indeed, taken an overdose. Now we have to consider something Walt Schaefer told me. He said that Marilyn Monroe did not expire in her home; she was taken comatose to the Santa Monica Hospital, where she died. We now know that her body was taken back by a famous actor. That could have been the ambulance the witness had seen. The time could well have been around 1:00 A.M.

The "famous actor" could only be Peter Lawford. Assuming that Lawford had been notified by someone soon after Dr. Greenson had arrived at Fifth Helena and confirmed that Marilyn Monroe showed all the symptoms of having taken a dangerous overdose, Lawford could have driven to her home within half an hour.

This means he could not have arrived at Marilyn's house until at least 11:15 or 11:30 P.M. Whenever the star's round-trip ambulance ride began, it can not have been much before 11:30 P.M.

I have made a careful study of the events of that night, and I believe that journey may have started even later. I think that Dr. Greenson, aware of the adverse publicity that would be generated if Marilyn was hospitalized after taking an overdose, even if it were proved to be accidental, might first have tried to revive the comatose actress himself. He might possibly have done this with the assistance of her internist, Dr. Hyman Engelberg, who lived only a short distance away.

Dr. Greenson's career depended on discretion. His clientele, including many high-profile celebrities, expected it. Considering that Marilyn's entire professional career may have been at stake, it is hard to imagine that he would have rushed his patient immediately to a hospital unless her life clearly depended on it. If, in fact, he did make an abortive attempt to revive her himself, possible remedies for an overdose of barbiturates could have taken up to an hour or more, and would have included pumping her stomach or otherwise inducing her to expel its contents. If this scenario had transpired Greenson would have called the ambulance not much earlier than midnight. This theory would explain why Thomas Noguchi, the pathologist who performed her autopsy, found no trace of the barbiturates in her stomach.

Further, this scenario might also explain Jack Clemmons having found the washing machine and dryer operating at the time of his arrival later that morning. Certainly it is possible that Greenson had managed to pump Marilyn's stomach, causing her to regurgitate and soil the linen upon which she may have been placed. Clearly seeing that his efforts had failed, Greenson may then have cleaned Marilyn, removing any sign of vomitus — a fact noticed by Dr. Fox.

Another distinct motivation for discretion on the part of Greenson was the appearance of an attempted suicide or overdose to Marilyn's studio. Greenson had negotiated with Twentieth Century-Fox on his patient's behalf, and even guaranteed her behavior with his professional reputation. He knew the keen concerns of the studio regarding Marilyn's emotional stability. He would have been concerned that the publicity surrounding an apparent suicide attempt would result in the studio deciding Marilyn to be too unstable to work, and then firing her from the picture a second time.

If Dr. Greenson didn't think of these things, then Arthur Jacobs, who was certainly there by then, would have . . . or Peter Lawford would have. Certainly, Mickey Rudin would have thought of these implications regarding his client. He was one of the first to learn that Marilyn had actually taken an overdose and was at the scene sometime during the night.

As a conscientious attorney, it is not likely Rudin would have delayed long before driving to the home of a dying client. Thus Rudin could have been at Marilyn's house from shortly after 11:00 P.M. till shortly after 4:00 A.M.; had he phoned both Milton Ebbins and Pat Newcomb and told them he was there.

Greenson could not have arrived much before 11:00 P.M. by all accounts. Assuming that he spent a half hour or more trying to revive his patient, no one could have called an ambulance much before 11:40 P.M.

If so, Peter Lawford would certainly have had time to arrive and accompany the comatose Marilyn to the near-by Santa Monica Hospital and back before the Landaus saw the ambulance parked outside the actress's home at 1:00 A.M.

But could the ambulance drivers have been preparing Marilyn for the trip to the hospital, instead of bringing her back? Perhaps. But it would have taken at least a few minutes for them to strap the star into a stretcher and at least a few more minutes for them to question Dr. Greenson and the others at the house. The drive to the hospital then could not have begun much before 1:30 A.M.

Unless Marilyn died immediately after the ambulance pulled out of her driveway, she would have died somewhere enroute to the hospital, or upon arrival. This scenario would fix the time of her death at close to 2:00 A.M. But all the medical evidence indicates that Marilyn died at least an hour earlier!

This means Marilyn Monroe would have been dying, or already dead, by the time the Landaus saw the ambulance parked in the driveway. If Walt Schaefer is right and Marilyn Monroe died during the ambulance trip, then the ambulance had already made its fabled trip to the Santa Monica Hospital and back.

That narrows the time of Marilyn's death to the one hour period between 11:30 P.M. on the night of August 4, and 12:30 or 12:45 A.M. on the morning of August 5.

This time frame assumes that what the principals said about the night's activities can be trusted. I believe that practically everything Rudin, Murray and Greenson said about this night's activity to be a fabrication — part of publicist Arthur Jacobs' orchestrated "fudging" of the actual circumstances surrounding Marilyn Monroe's death.

According to that interpretation of events, no one stumbled onto the dying actress's body. Instead, Marilyn was callously murdered, and Jacobs, Greenson, Murray, Lawford, Rudin, and the others were forced to participate in the cover-up by

Marilyn's murderer.

In still another scenario, Marilyn may have been murdered, but the murderer convinced Jacobs, Greenson, and the rest that Marilyn's death was accidental. They attempted to help cover-up that person's identity and involvement as protection from the ordeal of a public investigation.

No certainties exist with any of the scenarios discussed here. At most, there are possible, logical inferences based upon the few facts we have ascertained. One certainty does exist: Marilyn died and she did not die the way the "official story" tells us.

FILE #20

The Experts and the Evidence

SUICIDE, ACCIDENT OR MURDER?

For thirty years, the controversy over the official verdict of "probable suicide" in the death of Marilyn Monroe has refused to abate.

Seven official investigations have found that verdict to be correct, but the public is not satisfied. An examination of the facts of the case and their subsequent investigation have led many to believe what journalists have long maintained: Marilyn Monroe may have been murdered.

A third and much smaller group has suggested that instead of suicide, Marilyn's death may have been the result of an accidental, not intentional, overdose.

John Miner, the Los Angeles County district attorney's official observer at Marilyn's autopsy, believes the latter two groups may be right. He rejects the official verdict. As a result of what he saw at the autopsy and learned during an interview with the actress's psychiatrist, Miner is convinced Marilyn did not take her own life.

"In my opinion," Miner declares, "Miss Monroe did not commit suicide. If it's not suicide, there are two possibilities: it could be an accidental death or it could be a homicidal death — a criminal killing of this lady. If it's not suicide, it's one of those two things."

Was Marilyn Monroe murdered? Was her death an accident? Is it possible that, though her doctors and her housekeeper-nurse lied about the circumstances of her death and about Bobby Kennedy's presence that day, they told the truth about the possible cause of her death?

Namely, that the star killed herself in a fit of despondency after some sort of disagreement with Bobby Kennedy and that the cover-up hid nothing more sinister than his affair with Marilyn?

There is this to consider: those who defend the official verdict are, almost without exception, government officials themselves on either the local or national level. Those who criticize it are, almost without exception, investigative journalists, licensed private detectives, retired government officials and others with no personal axe to grind.

Over 200 books about the screen legend have been published, and thousands of articles have been printed in publications around the world but no journalist who has thoroughly investigated Marilyn Monroe's death has ever concluded that the actress took her own life.

WAS IT SUICIDE?

The now discredited official story says that Marilyn Monroe committed suicide on the night of August 4, 1962. Despondent over the break-up of her affair with Bobby Kennedy, the actress was said to have deliberately taken an overdose of sleeping pills. Some supporters of the original verdict concede she did not actually intend to commit suicide when she took the fatal barbiturates, but was making a play for a dramatic last-minute rescue either by Peter Lawford, who would be sure to tell Bobby Kennedy of the night's events, or by Bobby himself.

Perhaps the strongest case for this scenario is made in the report which the Los Angeles Suicide Investigation Team made to Coroner Theodore J. Curphey after their inquiry into Marilyn's death, as follows:

"Miss Monroe had suffered from psychological disturbance for a long time. She experienced severe fears and frequent depressions . . . Miss Monroe had often expressed wishes to give up, to withdraw, and even to die. On more than one occassion in the past, when disappointed and depressed, she had made a suicide attempt using sedative drugs."

However, few of Marilyn's close friends at the time of her death believe the star took her own life. Interestingly, most of the people who told the original LAPD investigators that Marilyn was suicidal were business associates, doctors, attorneys, and entertainment industry figures. Pat Newcomb, the actress's publicist, was the closest acquaintance whom police interviewed who suggested the possibility of suicide was valid. We now know that almost everything Pat Newcomb said about the events of that last day were lies designed to cover-up Bobby Kennedy's visit.

Marilyn's long-time friend, Terry Moore, concedes that Marilyn may have been despondent enough over her relationship with Bobby Kennedy to have wanted to end her own life. "I think her heart was broken, I think she was still depressed over the broken romance. One thing that makes me think she was depressed is that she was taking a lot of sleeping pills. Another thing that makes me feel she must have been depressed is that when they buried Marilyn, her nails weren't done, her roots had grown out and her hair was broken off. That's a sure sign of depression. A woman keeps herself on high-maintenance grooming when she's feeling good."

However, like Marilyn's other confidantes, Moore ultimately rejects the suicide scenario. "I was living just a few blocks away from her, and I just couldn't believe it. I was just in shock. I broke out in tears. I did not expect it. She was too happy moving into the new house. I did not think that she was ready to kill herself. Even though I think she was depressed, vulnerable, and could be driven to it, I did not think that she was ready to take her life."

Bebe Goddard, who grew up with Marilyn and knew her well, believes the star a survivor, far too strong to take her own life. "I was very bewildered. I really could not imagine how it could happen. Our personalities were so much alike and so many of the same things happened to us in our different spheres of activity. But she was basically inwardly much stronger than I was. And if I was still going, then I just could not see any reason at all why she wouldn't."

Jeanne Carmen is another of Marilyn's close friends who insists the actress was not a candidate for suicide. Carmen insists Marilyn wasn't despondent and was looking forward to a golf match they were planning the next day. Carmen, who spoke with Marilyn on the morning of her death, says the star's mood was upbeat, even after a night filled with a series of harassing phone calls.

"I just don't think that it was suicide," Carmen says. "I will never think that. Marilyn had bought me some golf clubs. My birthday is August 4. On August 5, which was a Sunday, she had made reservations for us to play golf in Monterey. The last time I talked to her she was very enthusiastic about our golf game. She couldn't wait to see me use the clubs that she had bought me. So I can't believe that she was suicidal and on the same day, she was telling me: 'Let's go. I can't wait to go to Monterey.'"

In 1975 the LAPD Organized Crime Intelligence Division

(OCID) issued what the police and district attorney's office still consider the definitive answer to those who claim Marilyn was not deeply despondent at the time of her death. Daryl Gates even cites this in defense of the official verdict in his recent autobiography, *Chief, My Life in the LAPD.*

"FACTS: Dr. Ralph Greenson, her psychiatrist," the OCID rebuttal began, "had met with Monroe twice on August 4, the evening of her death. According to handwritten notes recorded by LAPD investigators on the death scene, Dr. Greenson had asked Eunice Murray (the housekeeper nurse) to stay with Monroe that evening because she was very upset.

Almost ten years later, it would be discovered that Greenson had recanted his story to Deputy District Attorney John Miner only days after Marilyn's death. Eunice Murray followed suit, recanting her version of this story shortly thereafter. Perhaps its time for the LAPD, its Organized Crime Intelligence Division, and Daryl Gates, to take a new look at what the "facts" really are in the case of Marilyn Monroe. If, as the evidence suggests, Marilyn Monroe didn't commit suicide, how did she die? Could her death have been an accident?

ACCIDENT

Over the years, a number of people have suggested that Marilyn Monroe might have been the victim of an accidental overdose. They believe the actress did not take her own life. Instead, they feel that she was groggy from having taken a large dose of sleeping pills, and unwittingly swallowed a second dose.

Daryl Gates has spoken eloquently for this point-of-view. "It is my opinion that her death was accidental. So many times people lose track of how many pills they take, especially if they are drinking or enjoying the good feelings the pills bring on; they just keep taking more."

John Miner believes it is possible that Gates is right: "We are all familiar with the way individuals who have taken drugs over a period of time forget, by reason of the action of taking the drugs, that they have taken them. Or, they have not gotten the result they want, so they take more. This goes on to the point where they take a lethal overdose. That can occur. And that, we would term to be an accidental death."

Bebe Goddard doesn't believe Marilyn took her own life or that her death was the result of an accidental overdose. "I absolutely knew that it wasn't suicide. And I knew that it was even more impossible for it to have been an accident because she did have a high tolerance for drugs. It could not have been a couple of extra pills taken by mistake that killed her."

Furthermore, if Marilyn Monroe's death were an accident, why would her doctors and housekeeper-nurse have covered it up? Surely they could have concealed Bobby Kennedy's presence at her home on the day of her death, and still have said Marilyn's death was the result of an accident rather than tarnishing her memory forever with the charge of suicide.

MURDER

Could Marilyn Monroe's death have been a murder? A number of leading pathologists and forensic pathologists believe there is medical evidence that it was. Among these distinguished gentlemen are: E. Forrest Chapman, M. D. medical consultant; Sidney Weinberg, M.D., former coroner of Suffolk county, New York; and J. DeWitt Fox, M.D., medical consultant. After reviewing the official reports and documents relating to her death, this specialists concluded that Marilyn Monroe could not have taken her own life.

Dr. Fox frequently testifies as an expert witness in personal injury cases and cause of death cases. "I've made a thorough study of the autopsy and other documents with regard to

Marilyn Monroe's death," Dr. Fox explains, "and I have arrived at certain conclusions. I do not feel that she died by her own hand, but rather that other factors were present, which made her death inevitable."

What are those "other factors?" One is the fact that Marilyn was found nude. Fox believes that this is almost conclusive evidence that she did not commit suicide. "It's very unlikely that she would have taken her own life without a nightgown, a robe, or something on. Women are very vain, and in the history of pathology, are very rarely ever found totally naked from suicide. They always have a nightgown or some other clothing on, and to find a girl such as this totally nude is almost out of the question."

Another reason Fox believes Marilyn did not take her own life is the discolorations found on her back and buttocks. "There's what we call postmortem lividity, which is a bluish discoloration of the body caused by gravity pulling the blood downward in the body after death. If someone dies face down, then most of the blueness is going to be over the front of the body, whereas if they are face-up, it'll be over the back. In her case, the blue occurred over the front part of the body. I think that she was initially prone. This would certainly be an indication of foul play, because afterwards she was found face-up, which means that the body was moved. Somebody must have thought that was the way that it should be. So they turned her over and put her face-up."

Dr. Fox also believes Marilyn did not die of an overdose of sleeping pills because of the lack of vomitus at the scene or around her mouth. "The presence of vomitus in agonal cases is always present. In other words, a brownish secretion is usually present as a last gasp as the patient dies. That brownish agonal vomitus is usually present in the nose, on the mouth, on the tongue or some place. In her case, this was not present . . ." As a result, Dr. Fox is one of many who believe Marilyn Monroe's death was neither accident nor suicide. In addition to the signs of "a hand other than her own accounting for the lack of vomitus, the fact that she was found nude, and the body having been turned face down after death, Fox feels the bruises found on the actress's arms and legs at the time of her death are definite proof of foul play."

Any bruises on the extremities would indicate some forceful pressure being exerted, Dr. Fox says, "either to hold her down while they gave an injection or to abuse her. These bruises are an important factor, because they would not be present in suicide at all."

John Miner believes the disappearance of the organ samples immediately after the autopsy is another strong indication that homicide is a possibility. As John Miner points out: "They seem to have disappeared. They are not to be found. It could be . . . an indication of something gone wrong. I've never known it to happen before."

Marilyn's friend, Terry Moore, doesn't feel the star took her life, and doesn't know what to believe about the murder theory. "Evidently there's a lot of proof that people have that it could have been. I'm one of these people that say, I don't know."

At the very least, the controversy among medical experts over the reason for Marilyn's death casts strong doubt on the possibilities of suicide and accident.

Is there any way that we can determine conclusively whether it was, indeed, murder?

I think so. The evidence is convincing.

The "official story" claims that Marilyn died of an overdose of sleeping capsules. But what if here, as in so many other areas of the case, the official story is wrong?

Might we not, in uncovering the truth about how Marilyn Monroe died, discover the final answer to the why of her death as well?

Is it possible that in re-examining the evidence about the cause of her death, we might learn the reason . . . and be able once and for all to determine that Marilyn Monroe was murdered?

FILE #21

The Body of the Victim Speaks

The very first question raised by those who are convinced that Marilyn Monroe's death was murder is: if she didn't voluntarily take her own life, then how did that massive overdose of barbiturates get into her body? It defies common sense to imagine that someone forced her to swallow the forty-seven capsules of barbiturates the autopsy report says killed her.

Or could a lethal overdose have been administered by some other means? Is it possible that in this matter, as in so many others, the autopsy results were mistaken?

According to pathologist Thomas Noguchi's official autopsy report, Marilyn Monroe died of "acute barbiturate poisoning" as the result of an "ingestion of overdose." The star had taken the drugs, Noguchi wrote, in order to commit "suicide."

No one has ever disputed the first claim. Toxicological examination revealed that Marilyn had "thirteen milligrams percent phenobarbital" in her blood and "eight milligrams percent chloral hydrate" in her liver. The percentage of either drug far exceeded what medical experts consider a lethal dose.

But Noguchi's second finding, that Marilyn died as a result of "ingestion" of the drugs, has been hotly disputed for the last three decades. At that time, the newly-formed Los Angeles Suicide Investigation Team accepted Noguchi's evaluation as gospel during their inquiry into the actress's death. "We have been asked to give an opinion regarding the intent of Miss Monroe when she ingested the sedative drugs that caused her death."

Apparently, the Suicide Investigation Team did not investigate how Noguchi reached his conclusion that the fatal drugs had been ingested. In fact, the team supported Noguchi's conclusion by citing that the presence of "the completely empty bottle of Nembutal" and "the locked door" of Marilyn's room "were unusual". Unusual it certainly was: in fact, we now know that the door wasn't locked, and that much of the rest of the story Marilyn's physicians and housekeeper-nurse told about the circumstances of her death was equally untrue.

Those who disagreed with the results of the original autopsy, cited two contradictory facts which Noguchi had uncovered. Although Noguchi had found a massive dose of phenobarbital in Marilyn's bloodstream, he found no trace of any sleeping capsules in her stomach. If Marilyn had actually swallowed forty-seven pills, as the official story claimed, then why was there no residue?

Noguchi noted other discrepancies in his findings, but chose to ignore them as well. Years later, in a series of television interviews and in his own autobiography, Noguchi would offer an explanation for this lapse and call for a new investigation. Noguchi said that he, too, had been misled by the official police report, and its story of Marilyn's body being found in a "locked" room.

However, medical experts asked by the police and the district attorney's office to re-evaluate Marilyn's autopsy, have inevitably upheld the original results. It is not known whether the police or district attorney's office informed those specialists that both Dr. Ralph Greenson and Eunice Murray had recanted the stories they told police about finding the star dead behind a "locked door." It is possible these experts might have concurred with the original verdict anyway: there are significant disagreements among professionals in this field about what factors are - and are not - present in deaths caused by an overdose of sleeping capsules.

The question of how those thirteen milligrams percent phenobarbital got into Marilyn's bloodstream is still a subject of controversy.

According to pathologists, there are only three ways a substance can enter the body: orally, by ingestion; via a needle, by injection; and by soaking into the tissues of the skin or digestive track through infusion.

The complex medical issues involved have often confused the public. But enough serious questions have been raised to justify a full-scale investigation. Short of that, it is possible that by comparing the autopsy report, the condition of the body when it was first examined, and the conflicting opinions of the medical experts themselves, we can, discover where the preponderance of evidence lies.

This suggests an obvious starting point for any investigation of how Marilyn Monroe came to die.

INGESTION

The official verdict claims that Marilyn Monroe took her own life by swallowing forty-seven capsules containing barbiturates and an unknown, but very large number of capsules containing chloral hydrate. Those who take issue with this judgment cite three reasons for rejecting those conclusions: the lack of a glass or any container capable of holding liquid at the scene of Marilyn's death; the fact that no remains of any capsules were found in her stomach during the autopsy; and the lack of any liquid in her stomach.

When Sergeant Jack Clemmons arrived at the scene of Marilyn's death that August morning, one of the first questions he asked was how the actress had died. Dr. Ralph Greenson, Marilyn Monroe's psychiatrist, had pointed to a number of empty pill bottles on the night table next to her bed, focused on one closest to the body and in explanation, replied: "She must have taken all the pills in that bottle."

Clemmons didn't question Greenson's explanation. The veteran LAPD officer knew that many people who commit suicide choose an overdose of sleeping pills. An overdose of sleeping pills is neither painful nor messy, like so many other ways of taking one's own life.

But Clemmons did question the fact that there was neither a drinking glass nor any container capable of holding liquid in Marilyn's room

The 1975 LAPD Organized Crime Intelligence Division report on Marilyn's death disputed Clemmons' claim. It offered as "fact" a photograph taken at the scene of Marilyn's death shortly after Clemmons left.

"The photo clearly shows a drinking glass half-filled with liquid on the floor by the bed," the report states. "Also shown is a ceramic vessel which may have contained a liquid for drinking purposes, as it is covered with an inverted cup."

Others, looking at the same photo, have noted that the "glass" the police refer to is very narrow and more than twice as high as a normal drinking glass. They see what the LAPD thinks is a glass as one of those tall, decorative, glass candle holders. They often come in a colored glass cylinder of almost exactly the same size and shape. They also suggest that the police interpretation of the second object as a "ceramic vessel which may have contained a liquid for drinking purposes . . . covered by an inverted cup" — presumably a flask could easily be interpreted as any of a number of other household items as well.

In the course of a formal investigation into Marilyn Monroe's death, computer enhancement and enlargement might resolve the controversy over what these photographs actually show.

But critics of the original verdict point out that even if it were proved that the tall, cylindrical object was a drinking glass, or the other a flask, neither was present at the time of Sergeant Clemmons visit. According to Clemmon's testimony, he made a thorough search of Marilyn's bedroom and the adjoining bathroom at the time of his visit. He is absolutely prepared to state under oath that there was no glass or other drinking container in either room. If a subsequent police examination later that morning discovered a glass sitting in plain sight next to the bed, Clemmons says, it would have to have been placed there after his departure.

It is also of interest to note that Marilyn's master bathroom did not have running water on the weekend of her death. Marilyn was remodeling her private bathroom. The plumbers who were working in the bathroom had turned off the water in order to complete their work. As the work was not completed by late Friday, the water in Marilyn's private bathroom remained off throughout the weekend. Marilyn therefore had no access to water while locked in her bedroom.

Clemmons' testimony is enough to convince Dr. J. DeWitt Fox that however the drugs got into Marilyn's blood stream, it wasn't through ingestion. "One could never take that many Nembutals without water," Fox explains. "The tablets themselves would choke the patient, and be so dry and sticky in her mouth she couldn't tolerate it. And, without water being present, I don't see how she could have gotten them down, and obviously she didn't get them down, because they were never found in her stomach."

In Dr. Fox's professional judgment, the fact that almost no fluid was found in Marilyn's stomach at the time of her death is another strong indication that the actress could not have taken the fatal overdose by swallowing several hands-full of pills. "That's another very questionable factor," Fox explains. "There was very little in the way of fluid in her stomach, only 20 ccs was noted. Yet she was supposed to have taken forty-seven capsules of Nembutal in a very few seconds. Had she done so, she would have probably choked on them."

However, there appears to be even more telling medical evidence that Marilyn could not have died from an overdose of sleeping capsules: the fact that Noguchi failed to find the remains of any of the capsules the actress was said to have taken. According to Dr. Fox, pathologist Sidney Weinberg, Chief Medical Examiner of Suffolk County, New York, and Dr. E. Forrest Chapman, the Medical Examiner of Belleville, Michigan: If Marilyn had actually consumed several dozen capsules, she would have died long before her stomach could have digested such a massive amount of material.

Dr. Fox. maintains "They would have been present in her stomach. But, at the autopsy not a single capsule was found."

Fox believes the fact that Marilyn was found with nothing in her stomach is "the crux of the whole case." From a medical viewpoint, he says, there are urgent questions that need to be answered about Marilyn Monroe's death.

Those are the discrepancy between the high blood level and the absence of any capsules in the stomach or the intestine. That has never been answered in the whole history of the case. I think the average doctor would question that no matter what, whether it was a famous person or an ordinary person. He would certainly question that discrepancy.

However, a number of equally experienced pathologists, including Dr. Thomas Noguchi, who performed the autopsy; John Miner, who witnessed the autopsy and assisted Dr. Noguchi, and Dr. Edward Griesmer, a toxicologist on the staff of the Los Angeles coroner's office believe Dr. Fox is mistaken. In at least fifty percent of deaths resulting from overdose by sleeping pill, they claim, all residue had dissolved before death had occurred. According to these medical experts, "absorption time decreases when the subject is a frequent user of drugs."

John Miner explains it this way: "Sometimes you do find the traces of the capsule in the stomach or the first segment of the small intestine, the duodenum. But, if the drugs had been taken and absorbed completely, it is possible that you will not see the traces. I've seen many an overdose death, where there is not a trace of the capsule in the stomach."

But curiously, Miner, who was the district attorney's official observer at Marilyn's autopsy, also believes that Noguchi may have been wrong; the fatal dose of barbiturates may not have entered Marilyn's system through ingestion. Instead, based on what he saw at the autopsy and learned later from Marilyn's psychiatrist, Miner believes that the barbiturates in her system may have been introduced by "injection or infusion."

"Infusion," Miner explains, "is when a drug is introduced to the body through an enema or suppository." "A suppository is a drug generally, in some sort of glycerin suspension, which will melt in contact with the body tissues. Generally a suppository cannot and does not go beyond the rectum itself. With an enema, on the other hand, a liquid containing the drug is introduced into the large intestine."

"Although drug overdoses via infusion are rare," Miner notes, "they are not unknown. Many people take herbal and sulfa enemas for health, and physicians often prescribe drugs in the form of suppositories."

Some people have such strong phobias about needles and swallowing pills that they have to take prescription and non-prescription drugs via enema.

Could Marilyn Monroe have taken or been given the massive overdose of drugs that killed her in an enema or suppository? It's not as incredible as it sounds.

INFUSION

Several of Marilyn Monroe's friends confirm that the actress was in the practice of taking enemas to relieve chronic constipation — a practice she appears to have picked up somewhere during childhood. Amy Green, who knew Marilyn during her New York days, remembers the star spoke to he several times about using enemas for this purpose. Jeanne Carmen, another New York friend, recalls her complaining about constant constipation — possibly caused by the stress of her career and personal life.

Conjecture that the massive overdose of drugs that killed Marilyn Monroe might have been introduced into her body via infusion, began when Deputy D. A. John Miner noticed an odd discoloration during the autopsy of Marilyn's digestive tract. "The most unusual factor with respect to that autopsy," Miner recalls, "was a purplish discoloration of a portion of the large intestine, the sigmoid colon." Miner felt that only "the inflammatory response of a drug that was absorbed through the large intestine could account for that discoloration."

Two world-famous pathologists, Dr. Breitneck, the foremost pathologist in Europe, and Milton Halpern, the chief medical examiner of the city of New York, concur with Miner's conclusion.

In their best professional opinions, the discoloration of

the colon indicates the possibility that perhaps some, or all, of the drugs were administered by means of an enema or suppository.

Jack Clemmons also rejects the sleeping pill theory, and agrees with Miner that if ingestion is ruled out: "There are only two ways that she could have been murdered. She either had to be given an injection or she had to be given a suppository."

Although the use of an enema in disputed among medical experts, they are united in the belief that the physical evidence rules out the use of a suppository.

According to John Miner, "In the first place, it wouldn't have gotten far enough to discolor the sigmoid colon. Any discoloration and irritation would be confined to the rectum itself. As a result, it is not only unlikely, it is probably beyond the realm of practicality, that if the drug was introduced into the large intestine it was done by suppository."

Dr. J. DeWitt Fox echoes the conclusions of other pathologists on the subject. "The purple color may be an indication of infusion, but not by means of a suppository. The patient has been thought to have a purple colon and this would perhaps indicate that something had been inserted in the rectum and would account for it. But in my opinion, they found no suppositories, and not all of the suppositories would have been absorbed, and some residual of them would be present to account for that. I've never seen any reference to the fact that suppositories cause a purple colon."

Fox has another reason for ruling out the use of a suppository. He believes it would be impossible to get a large enough dosage of barbiturates into an enema to cause death. "Although she could have taken a suppository and had some Pentobarbital in her bloodstream, I don't think the percentage would have been that high."

Fox doesn't believe the drugs were administered via enema, either. He takes a completely different view of the discolored area John Miner saw on Marilyn's colon.

Enemas and suppositories may cause an irritated or red colon, Fox explains, but not purple. "In my opinion, this purple color is simply due to postmortem lividity. In other words, the position of the patient allowed the blood to, by gravity, settle to a certain point . . . and the rectum being a low point. And this would possibly account for the purple."

Instead, it's Fox's best professional opinion that Marilyn Monroe's death was in all likelihood caused by "an intravenous injection."

INJECTION

If Marilyn Monroe didn't swallow the lethal dose, and if it wasn't admitted into her body via enema or suppository, then John Miner might be right. The only possibility left seems to be injection with hypodermic needle.

According to John Miner, the second most common way of introducing an overdose of drugs into the body is by injection. From junkies to diabetics, many people take drugs via a hypodermic needle. It is easy for members of this group to accidentally, or intentionally, inject a fatal overdose.

Many critics of Noguchi's autopsy believe that he may have overlooked vital evidence pointing toward injection as the cause of Marilyn's death. They are supported by the conclusions of Dr. J. DeWitt Fox and other pathologist experts have reached in re-evaluating the original autopsy report. They believe the autopsy results conclusively rule out the introduction of the lethal drugs through any other means.

However, defenders of the original autopsy, point out that the physical evidence does not seem to support the injection theory. Because of the lack of residue in the stomach, Dr. Noguchi later told police investigators, he and Deputy D. A.

Miner both made a careful examination of Marilyn's body for the puncture marks and bruises caused by the use of a syringe. John Miner confirms this story. "We examined the body with magnifying glasses, both of us did, for needle marks, and that was to complete the examination. There were no needle marks on the body."

Considering that Marilyn had been given injections by her doctor only two days before her death, critics of the autopsy have wondered how it is possible that Noguchi found no needle marks anywhere on her body. Some have cried conspiracy and cover-up, others labeled it incompetence or haste.

But there is room for disagreement here, too. The needles on those hypodermics were so small, they say, that the puncture and the bruise it causes would have healed completely within forty-eight hours. As John Miner explains: "If I am correct, what was administered was something like B-12, a vitamin. B-12 would ordinarily be injected into the muscle in the "upper-outer quadrant of the buttock with a very small-gauge needle. That doesn't take a very long needle. A three-inch needle will do. So its a relatively short needle, of very small gauge and does not make a large puncture. And, if you're giving the shot properly, you massage the area with the sterile alcohol cloth spreading the injected substance around, so it isn't in a hard bunch that can cause soreness, and that tends to dissipate the needle mark to a great extent. Forty-eight hours later, it would be difficult to say that needle mark would still be apparent."

"On the other hand", Miner points out, "the amount of drugs found in Marilyn's body was so large that had it been administered by injection, the star would have died almost immediately. The body would have only had minutes in which to begin absorbing all those drugs and a large, visible swelling containing the unabsorbed drugs would remain just beneath the surface of the skin."

Those who feel Marilyn's overdose may have been injected, rather than ingested, have pointed out that a number of conditions occur after death which can disguise needle marks. One of these is the bruise-like discolorations of post-mortem lividity.

According to Dr. Fox: "The blue post-mortem lividity occurred over the front part of the body. This might have masked or covered up any injection which she might have had in her chest."

Those who believe that Marilyn Monroe's death was not a suicide — but murder — think that the bruise-like discoloration caused by postmortem lividity was deliberately used to conceal the fact that the drugs had been injected by hypodermic. Marilyn did not know how to use a hypodermic, they claim, and that fact alone would have forced the coroner's office to convene an official inquest. Therefore, postmortem lividity and the sleeping capsule story were used to cover-up the real means of death.

Sergeant Jack Clemmons is one of many who believe this scenario. "It was obvious to me, apparent to me, I should say, that Marilyn had been placed in that position. I felt at the time that the position of the body had to do with post-mortem lividity. When a person dies, their heart stops beating; the gravity will pull the blood to the lowest part of the body. Marilyn being face down, all the blood came forward. As a matter of fact, the coroners report particularly noted lividity, reddishness around the face and the chest area. I felt at the time that she was placed in that position to disguise needle marks."

Dr. Fox noticed another bruised area on the body which might also have disguised a puncture wound. "She had a bruise on her hip which was possibly from an injection given either the day before by her physician or from the intravenous injection of pentobarbital. So, if she had been given the injection, in the haste of performing the autopsy, it might be easily overlooked."

No needle marks were found on Marilyn Monroe's body, and empty pill bottles were found by the actress's bedside. Yet, if these experts are right, the case for death by injection seems stronger than the case for her having died of an overdose of sleeping capsules.

THE FOURTH ALTERNATIVE

There are only three ways drugs could have entered Marilyn Monroe's body. But experts have proposed a fourth explanation for her death — one that would be conclusive proof of murder. Marilyn, they say, might have been killed by a combination of two of these methods.

"If some of these drugs were taken orally and rendered the patient unconscious," John Miner explains, "an enema could be administered to her without her knowledge that would put enough of the drugs in her to kill her. That she would do it that way to kill herself is highly unlikely."

Dr. J. DeWitt Fox shares Jack Clemmons view that Marilyn was killed by a combination of two different drugs, but believes they were administered in a different way. "The scenario I postulate is that she had either an injection of choral hydrate or drank a Mickey Finn with some chloral hydrate in it to make her unconscious. Following that, she was given an intravenous injection of a tremendously high, lethal dose of Nembutal. Either one alone would be sufficient to kill her, and the combination of the two is just astronomical, probably 100 times the necessary amount.

Clearly, if either of these hypotheses is true, critics of the original coroners verdict are correct. Marilyn Monroe could not have taken her own life . . . her death could have been an accident.

Ironically, it seems that no matter how the drugs got into her body, the evidence always seems to point away from Marilyn having administered them to herself, and toward them having been administered by others . . . away from suicide and toward murder.

Here we come to the final question: if Marilyn Monroe was murdered, then who was her murderer? Is there any reason to believe that behind a conspiracy of lies, silence, and vanishing evidence, we can discover evidence, that, even after the passage of thirty years, will allow us to unmask the murderer.

There is reason to think so.

New evidence, combined with the results of thirty years of personal research, may be able to give us the answer.

FILE #22

The Final Suspects

In 1962, an official coroner's inquest might have resolved all the mysteries around Marilyn Monroe's death. Calling witnesses to testify under penalty of perjury might have brought to light many of the contradictions in the witnesses' stories. Many of them, like Eunice Murray, might have resolved to tell the truth a quarter century earlier.

The story of the "locked" room and the depressed star, upon which the official verdict was based, might have been exposed immediately.

An investigation of the real circumstances of Marilyn's death could have been commenced when the evidence was fresh, and all those who might have had important information to add were available to tell it.

Further, if critics of the official verdict were wrong, and Marilyn's death was the result of a suicide, or even an accident, either possibility could have been either substantiated or very easily disproved.

If, as an ever-increasing mountain of evidence seems to suggest, Marilyn's death was caused by a "hand other than her own," it should not have been difficult to determine whose hand it was. Three decades passed before the cover-up designed to conceal that killer's identity would begin to crumble, allowing us to piece together a scenario of her final minutes . . . to draw aside the curtain of her room and peer inside to see the face — or faces — responsible for her death.

How can we do this after thirty years?

Curiously, no fingerprints were found in Marilyn's house — not even her own, or those of Eunice Murray, Dr. Ralph Greenson or Pat Newcomb! The identity of the killer (or killers) was certainly protected by professionals.

At this late date, we are not going to find tell-tale bloodstains or a betraying peroxide blond hair on the murderer's lapel. But it is possible that, through the process of elimination, the list of suspects may be narrowed down so that some piece of evidence may point to the killer — or definitively rule out all other suspects. In short, to determine who killed Marilyn Monroe, we first need to determine who didn't kill her.

EUNICE MURRAY

Marilyn's then sixty-year-old "housekeeper." The story of her being hired by Marilyn is interesting.

First, Dr. Ralph Greenson suggested that Marilyn purchase her own home. The psychiatrist felt this would help her establish the roots she never had, and increase her much-needed sense of security.

Greenson then suggested Marilyn might be lonely, living by herself in a big house for the first time. He suggested she might want to hire a housekeeper and companion, and recommended Eunice Murray.

Only years later, she revealed that she was a trained psychiatric nurse. Murray, who worked for Greenson for more than fifteen years, was often called upon to take live-in positions with suicidal patients. Marilyn had reportedly already made one suicide attempt that year, and was supposedly despondent ever since she was fired from the movie *Something's Got to Give*.

Mrs. Murray's real assignment seemed to be keeping Dr. Greenson informed of the star's emotional condition and to watching over her for any indication of suicidal behavior. Marilyn apparently sensed this. The actress told friends: "There's a spy in my house."

Something about Murray also rang a warning bell with Marilyn's long-time friend, Jeanne Carmen. "She was rather sneaky," Carmen remembers. "I just didn't like her. And Marilyn was getting very suspicious of her."

Eunice Murray seems an unlikely murderer. Murray could have had no personal motive for killing Marilyn. She was not named in the actress's will and had only known her a few months.

But Murray's strong ties to Dr. Greenson and the presence of her name and personal data in FBI files, made her a likely participant in a cover-up. And, in 1985, Murray finally admitted that she, Dr. Greenson and Pat Newcomb, Marilyn's publicist, had lied about the events of Saturday, August 4, to conceal Bobby Kennedy's presence.

Journalists have even suggested two scenarios in which Murray might have been directly responsible for Marilyn's death. In the first, Murray is thought to have administered the deadly overdose to Marilyn by accident; perhaps when giving her a sedative shot or enema in Dr. Greenson's absence. If so, Dr. Greenson might well have felt responsible enough, or that he owed Murray enough, to help her cover-up the facts afterward.

But if Murray had unwittingly been the cause of Marilyn's death, it is hardly likely the LAPD and other government agencies would have assisted them in such a conspiracy. It is also unlikely that, almost thirty years later Murray or her supporters, would have the power to shut down a grand jury investigation and quell an investigative report on a major national television network.

In a second scenario, it is suggested that Eunice Murray murdered Marilyn under someone else's direction. The psychiatric nurse is said to have intentionally and knowingly administered the massive fatal overdose. But the guilt would also include the person — or persons — who gave Murray those orders.

Some people believe that if Murray did kill Marilyn at someone else's behest — that person could only be Dr. Ralph Greenson. Murray and Dr. Greenson were very close. Greenson constantly did favors and found work for Murray and members of her family. He bought the house Eunice Murray's husband built. They shared similar beliefs about politics and the world. Murray was extremely loyal to Dr. Greenson and guarded his secrets until very late in her life.

Other than the Greenson theory, there is another theory about who might have given Murray the deadly order to kill Marilyn. In this version, the reluctant Murray is believed to have been blackmailed into carrying out the murder by someone who was aware that FBI files name her as a card-carrying member of the Communist Party. Supposedly, Murray was forced to cooperate under threat of exposure — and a possible jail term.

One drawback to this theory is that the McCarthy era — named for the legendary right-wing witch hunter, Joseph McCarthy — was long over by the time of Marilyn's death. In fact, the Kennedy election ushered in a decade-long cycle of increasing liberalism. Even high government officials would have had a hard time justifying any kind of trial of the inoffensive Murray for what the public would have perceived as little more than misguided political enthusiasm.

Dr. Ralph Greenson

He was Marilyn's psychoanalyst and a leader in his profession. Dr. Greenson's ultra-secret patient list constituted a who's who of Los Angeles' business, political and entertainment figures. One colleague described him as "the backbone of psychoanalysis in the western United States."

Professionally, Dr. Greenson seems above suspicion. Yet almost everything the psychiatrist told police about Marilyn's death, and the events leading up to it, was a lie.

Why would someone of such eminence deliberately cover up the truth about a patient's death? The obvious answer is that Dr. Greenson was protecting himself — that he was somehow involved in Marilyn's death. At least one journalist has suggested that Dr. Ralph Greenson might be Marilyn's murderer — who deliberately gave the star a deadly overdose.

If this theory is true, Marilyn may have supplied a vital clue to Dr. Greenson's motivation shortly before her death. The sex goddess told several friends she thought he was falling in love with her.

Almost any man who saw Marilyn could have fallen in love with her. Could Ralph Greenson have been completely immune to Marilyn's incandescent sensuality? It wouldn't be the first time a psychiatrist had fallen for a patient. . . . Nor a patient for their doctor. It could be that Marilyn was imagining Greenson's interest. Patients often fall in love with their doctors, and then imagine those feelings reciprocated. Marilyn, they say, would have been especially susceptible. She was always drawn to intelligent, older men. Dr. Greenson fit both criteria.

Marilyn's analysis seems more believable. Certainly Greenson's involvement with the actress went far beyond the traditional limits of a doctor-patient relationship. He took Marilyn into his home and made her part of his family circle. His wife and children considered her a friend. She often had her sessions there. Greenson also treated Marilyn at her home, often spending many hours a day with her, helping the star work through her emotional problems.

Maybe Greenson, smitten by Marilyn, encouraged her to become more dependent on him rather than help her to become stronger and more self-reliant — the goals of psycho-therapy. In fact, within just a few months after beginning serious treatment with Dr. Greenson, Marilyn was unable to work or cope without his presence. The psychiatrist's guar-antee to movie studio heads that he would ensure Marilyn's ability to work, provided he was granted on-set involvement with his patient, was seen by many of his peers as a violation of professional ethics.

Marilyn told friends that Dr. Greenson often demanded she share her sex fantasies with him during these sessions. When pressed hard enough, Marilyn said, she just fabricated what-ever came to mind. If Marilyn's comments to friends are true, he would have had a motive for murder. Men as eminent as Dr. Greenson have killed for love or jealousy before.

Perhaps Dr. Greenson declared his love only to have Marilyn reject him. Or perhaps he kept quiet but was slowly driven crazy by having to listen to his patient's accounts of affairs with JFK, Bobby Kennedy, José Bolanos and others.

In yet another scenario, Dr. Greenson may have been accidentally responsible for Marilyn's death by unintentionally administering a massive overdose. He and Murray, possibly with the help of Dr. Hyman Engelberg, the star's physician, then covered up Greenson's fatal error.

There are numerous drawbacks to this theory. For one thing, Greenson's actions afterward are more those of a con-science-stricken analyst unable to save his patient than those of a murderer. It is unlikely that Greenson would have spent three hours convincing Deputy District Attorney John Miner that Marilyn did not commit "suicide," — the thesis of his position seventy-two hours earlier — if had he been guilty of her death.

Although Greenson was respected and influential in his profession, it is highly unlikely he would have possesed the power to orchestrate a local, state, and federal government cover-up as extensive and all-encompassing as the one involving Marilyn Monroe's death.

A more compelling reason to believe that Dr. Ralph Greenson did not murder Marilyn and then conceal his complicity in her death is his role in the cover-up. Eunice Murray and others have admitted that Greenson was, in fact, trying to conceal that Bobby Kennedy was at Marilyn's home that fateful evening. To assume he might have killed the star shortly after Bobby left and that two different cover-ups were going on simultaneously — one to protect Bobby Kennedy, the other Ralph Greenson — seems to be stretching coincidence too far.

It is equally improbable that Dr. Greenson killed Marilyn at the orders of someone who was blackmailing or physically threatening him — or his loved ones. The exposure of Greenson's Communist Party affiliations would not have, in all probability, cost him a single client in the wealthy, liberal enclave of Beverly Hills.

As unlikely a suspect as Dr. Greenson seems, the only person ever to come forward claiming to be an eye–witness to Marilyn's death, told reporters that the psychiatrist was directly responsible for her demise. Former Schaefer Ambulance driver, James Hall, describes a dramatic post-midnight visit to the home of the dying actress. According to Hall, he saw Greenson commit deliberate, premeditated murder by plunging a needle directly into Marilyn's heart.

"I absolutely believe that Dr. Ralph Greenson murdered Marilyn Monroe," Hall says.

Hall's story — though convincing — has been disputed on the basis of timing factors. But even if true, Dr. Ralph Greenson would have only been an unwilling instrument.

PATRICIA NEWCOMB

Marilyn and her publicist, Pat Newcomb, maintained a stormy relationship for years. After their fights, however, they always managed to forgive each other and resume their friendship.

Mutual jealousy seems to have been an important element in their relationship: Marilyn was jealous of Newcomb's sophistication, independence and education; Newcomb of her friend's beauty and sexuality.

By the summer of 1962, this jealousy may have been exacerbated by the termination of Marilyn's affair with RFK. Just as Bobby was breaking off his relationshi p with Marilyn, Newcomb is said to have told associates she was having an affair with RFK. Undoubtedly, Marilyn was aware of the gossip. Jeasousy has led to murder before, but if anyone had a reason to be jealous, it was Marilyn, not Newcomb.

A number of new scenarios — some plausible, some not so plausible — seem to suggest that Pat Newcomb was a woman with many possible motives for murdering Marilyn Monroe.

In one possible scenario of the night's events, Marilyn's jealousy was the cause of her own death. Shortly after RFK left Marilyn's home, Newcomb paid a visit to Marilyn. Marilyn accused Newcomb of stealing Bobby from her. The fight became violent, threats were made and the angry Newcomb secretly returned later that evening to kill Marilyn in order to protect herself and her new-found lover from any vindictive retaliation.

A violent, passionate fight between Newcomb and Monroe is plausible in the context of their argumentative relationship and would help to explain the bruises on Monroe's body documented in the autopsy report.

A far different version of the jealousy motive in the Monroe-Newcomb-Kennedy love triangle is the rumored bi-sexual rapport between Marilyn and Pat Newcomb. In this perverse and chilling scenario, Newcomb murdered Marilyn, not because she was in love with Bobby Kennedy and jealous of Marilyn — but because she was in love with Marilyn and jealous of Bobby!

In a third, and even less plausible version of the night's events, Bobby and Marilyn are supposed to have made up after their quarrel. Pat Newcomb, discovering that once again she had lost a man to Marilyn's irresistible sex appeal, carefully plotted and carried out the star's murder.

In a more plausible and equally chilling scenario, Newcomb is said to have been one of the friends Marilyn told about the press conference at which she planned to expose Bobby. Hoping to prevent the exposure of her lover, who had just won the Father of the Year Award, Newcomb is thought to have visited Marilyn that Saturday evening with the intent of dissuading the star from holding the proposed conference. Unable to convince Marilyn to abandon her plans, Newcomb murdered her to protect Bobby Kennedy's reputation.

This version of Newcomb-as-killer makes sense in terms of the subsequent cover-up. Bobby Kennedy might have been so grateful to have Marilyn silenced at last, he exercised all the powers of the attorney general's office and the Kennedy millions to protect Pat Newcomb from exposure. Or Newcomb, realizing the gravity of her crime too late, might even have blackmailed Bobby into shielding her.

Any murder scenario involving Newcomb must explain the administration of the overdose. Since we know from testimony that it was unlikely the fatal overdose was administered in pill form, we must assume that whoever administered the drugs had easy access and was knowledgeable of barbiturates and their administration—knowledgeable enough to administer a shot so well-concelaed that neither Dr. Thomas Noguchi nor Deputy D.A. John Miner could find a trace of it.

Unless Marilyn was already knocked out before Newcomb

arrived,   Newcomb would also have had to restrain her before giving her the fatal shot or suppository. In fact, if Dr. J. DeWitt Fox and other pathologists are correct, the bruises on Marilyn's arm may indicate she was tightly restrained not long before she died; this might suggest that the struggling star was held still while the fatal overdose of barbiturates was injected into her body.

Pat Newcomb would not have been strong enough to subdue and kill Marilyn without the assistance of a third party. Under such circumstances, Newcomb would more likely be an accomplice than the agent of murder.

No, as with Murray and Greenson, Newcomb is not a convincing candidate for murderer. But like them, she was a likely participant in a cover-up.

We now know, thanks to Eunice Murray's 1985 confession, that Pat Newcomb joined them and others in a conspiracy to prevent the public and media from discovering that Bobby Kennedy had visited Marilyn on the evening of August 4. We also know that after a long European vacation, Newcomb returned to a full-time job in Washington — only two doors from Bobby Kennedy's office — and that she has remained loyal to Bobby Kennedy's memory for three decades.

Pat Newcomb may not have been involved in Marilyn's murder; but she was deeply involved in its cover-up.

TWENTIETH CENTURY-FOX

Several journalists have speculated that Marilyn might have been killed or driven to suicide by her studio, then teetering on the edge of bankruptcy and collapse. According to this scenario, one or more executives conspired to cause the star's death and cash in on two multi-million dollar insurance policies: one on Marilyn's life, the other payable if production on *Something's Got to Give* was shut down due to the death of any of the film's stars.

Conspirators were supposedly angered by Marilyn's constant failures to appear for filming. Her absences had forced them to cancel production half-way through shooting at a purported loss of two million dollars. Convinced Marilyn was too emotionally unstable to ever work again, and desperate for cash-flow to keep the studio operating, Fox management saw a way to take advantage their film production insurance policy in order to recoup all the losses the star had cost them — and more.

The contract which insured Fox for millions of dollars against the death of its stars during producition of a film now looked like a potential windfall for a desperate studio. This, combined with the studio insurance on Marilyn's life, left Fox much to gain by her death.

Because the studio had suspended production on *Something's Got to Give*, it could not collect anything on the film's insurance policy. The studio could only recoup the million or so it had invested if Marilyn died while the film was in production.

After terminating Marilyn's contract, the studio suddenly decided to reinstate Marilyn on the picture and reschedule production. The star's death a short week later would have technically entitled Fox to collect on both policies.

Then a hitch developed. Marilyn's death — which was supposed to be taken as an accident — was about to be ruled a suicide. Since life insurance policies don't usually pay off on suicides, studio management sucessfully pressured the coroner's office to alter the verdict to "probable suicide" — allowing the studio to collect.

As unlikely as this scenario seems, there is some support for it. Sergeant Jack Clemmons confirms the large insurance pay-off Marilyn's studio received after her death — and the importance of the "probable suicide" verdict in that pay-off.

"We did know at the time that the studio collected a million dollar policy. Obviously, the studio could not have collected the policy if it had been judged a suicide."

There is other support as well. Lionel Grandison, the coroner's aide who handled Marilyn's case files, remembers "studio people" being in and out of the department during the investigation into her death. Grandison is also one of several witnesses who recall having seen three different versions of the death certificate — the final one reading "probable suicide." Previous versions were "suicide" and "possible suicide."

More compelling evidence of studio complicity in Marilyn's death revolves around the eerie proximity of studio publicity executives to the scene of her death. On the night of August 4, two members of the Fox publicity department, Johnny Campbell and Frank Neill were at Marilyn's house shortly after her death. Their presence was never mentioned to police.

A variation on this theory, that the studio might have deliberately driven Marilyn to suicide, also isn't so farfetched. We have to ask, however, did their actions show a logical momentum toward this end. How were they planning to drive her to suicide? Reinstating Marilyn on *Something's Got to Give* was hardly likely to make her feel suicidal. Nor was tripling her salary! Although, if the studio had followed through with plans to "smear" Marilyn's name at the time of her termination, it is quite conceivable that she would have experienced a setback in both her confidence and her psychological stability — after the difficulties she encountered on set with Cukor.

Could the studio have induced Ralph Greenson, Eunice Murray, Dr. Hyman Engelberg or any of Marilyn's other close associates to help drive the actress to take her own life? Conceivably. But, again, this reads more like bad movie melodrama than real-life murder.

Or could this murder scenario be true? Might a studio head have hired someone to kill Marilyn and make it look like an accidental overdose? Possibly. But, again, it seems unlikely.

There is one serious drawback with this scenario — one that rules out so many other suspects in Marilyn's death as well. Could a powerful, prestigious motion picture studio — especially one on the edge of financial collapse — have engineered the cover-up that followed?

Granted, the studios — which contribute billions a year in taxes and jobs to the local economy — have enormous influence with Los Angeles city and county government. Local officials have always helped to cover up scandals that would have embarrassed the studios and ruined careers. But is it likely they could command the cooperation of the FBI, the Secret Service and the CIA as well?

Or might studio heads have threatened the Kennedys with the exposure of their affair with Marilyn unless they agreed to help them cover up their complicity in her death?

Perhaps. But more likely the studio itself was pressured by the Kennedys into at least helping cover-up Bobby's presence at Marilyn's that day — as the presence of Arthur Jacobs and Fox public relations pros indicates.

There is a final, and perhaps more insurmountable drawback to the studio-as-killer scenario: Hollywood can't keep a secret for thirty minutes — let alone thirty years! Surely by now someone would have confessed to a lover, or a friend at a bar, at least part of the plot — as Peter Lawford and Eunice Murray did later.

THE MAFIA

One of the most compelling of the recent theories about Marilyn's death suggests that the star might have been killed by Mafia hitmen.

According to this scenario, the Mob had two motivations for murdering the ill-fated Marilyn. The first involved Mafia secrets Bobby Kennedy shared with Marilyn over the course of their affair. The second suggests Marilyn was killed as part of an elaborate plot to frame Bobby and destroy his career. As improbable as either of these scenarios might have seemed thirty years ago, today they seem all too-chillingly plausible.

The Mafia had Marilyn under surveillance due to her affair with Bobby Kennedy. That is a fact. We have testimony from the wire-tappers themselves, Bernard Spindel and Fred Otash, among others. We have acknowledgments from high-ranking Mafia members and associates that Sam Giancana and Jimmy Hoffa hired Spindel and Otash to bug Marilyn's house and phone lines. We have recently declassified FBI and Justice Department documents indicating that members of the federal government had been aware of Marilyn's surveillance by organized crime figures.

The object of this wiretapping was definitely Bobby Kennedy. As attorney general, RFK had led a high-profile vendetta against the Mafia, raking their top leaders over the coals in a series of publicly televised hearings. Both Giancana, godfather of the powerful Chicago branch of the Mob, and Jimmy Hoffa, head of the Mob-influenced Teamsters Union, hoped to use evidence of the amour to force Bobby to drop his investigations.

The Mafia is a ruthless organization, unafraid to kill anyone who gets in their way—no matter how important or well-known that person might be. They have hit powerful government officials, world-famous journalists and even major celebrities who have gotten in their way. There is no reason to think that if the Mob wanted Marilyn dead, they would have hesitated to order her execution.

According to the "Mob secrets" version of Marilyn's death, RFK and Marilyn had shared one too many insider stories unearthed by Bobby during his relentless investigation of organized crime. Marilyn's friends concede that Bobby told her many such secrets, and that Marilyn recorded many of them in her little red diary. Aware from their wire-taps that Marilyn had learned these secrets, the Mob is said to have had the actress murdered and her red diary destroyed.

Private investigator Milo Speriglio also claims that his own research into Marilyn's death has convinced him that: "Marilyn Monroe was killed by the Mafia . . . to protect certain people, certain governments."

The Mob, however, had more than one plausible motive for killing Marilyn. Her death might well have been orchestrated to incriminate Bobby Kennedy with the intent of disgracing him from public office — or to provide blackmail material that would force him to abandon his anti-Mob crusade.

Wild as this scenario may sound, two members of Sam Giancana's family — his brother, Chuck, and his cousin, Sammy — swear that it's true. According to the two cousins, Sam Giancana learned that Bobby Kennedy planned to fly down to Los Angeles and see Marilyn on August 4. Fearful that an attempt to blackmail the Kennedys would only lead to exposure of his own secrets and a possible immediate indictment as a member of organized crime, Giancana decided to frame Bobby for Marilyn's murder.

If the Giancana cousins can be believed, Mafia hitmen eavesdropped on Bobby's visit to Marilyn. After listening to a lengthy argument between the enraged Monroe and the attorney general, assassins supposedly heard Bobby tell someone with him, apparently a doctor, to give the star a shot to "calm her down." That was when the killers saw their chance.

As soon as Bobby left, the reputed hitmen — said to be Needles Gianola, Mugsy Tortorella, and two other professional killers — entered Marilyn's home. The already-sedated star struggled at first, but "with all the efficiency of a team of surgeons, they taped her mouth shut and proceeded to insert a specially 'doctored' Nembutal suppository into her anus."

The plot went wrong, Sam and Chuck say, because Giancana underestimated the swiftness with which various branches of the federal government would step in to protect Bobby and erase all evidence of murder. The mobsters found themselves listening to their wiretaps in frustration over the next few hours "as a series of phone calls alerted Bobby Kennedy to Marilyn's death and ultimately mobilized a team of FBI agents to avert the impending disaster. . . ." Soon all evidence of Bobby's affair with Marilyn and of his presence at her house earlier that evening had been erased.

Not long after Chuck and Sammy Giancana broke the above story on national television, however, Giancana's daughter, Antoinette, disputed their entire account of Mob complicity in Marilyn's death. She also disputed Chuck Giancana's claims to have been a member of Mafia inner councils. Instead, she said, her father never trusted Chuck, who had held only a minor position within the organized crime hierarchy. If her father had been involved in Marilyn's death she implied, Chuck would have been one of the last to know about it.

Her father considered Marilyn far more valuable to the Mob alive, Antoinette claims. Alive, she constituted a continuing threat that could be used against Bobby Kennedy. In fact, Marilyn's planned press conference gave Sam Giancana more reason to want her alive.

If Marilyn had lived to carry through with the conference, Bobby would have been publicly disgraced and driven from office without Giancana or the Mob having to involve themselves at all.

Colorful as these scenarios are, however, Antoinette Giancana may be right. There are persuasive reasons for believing that the Mafia did not kill Marilyn Monroe. According to all versions of this scenario, Marilyn was murdered with a drug-laden suppository.

But former Deputy District Attorney John Miner, says it

would have been impossible to load a suppository with enough Nembutal to have caused Marilyn's death. While Dr. J. DeWitt Fox and pathologist Dr. Sidney Weinberg both agree that if Marilyn had been administered a drug-laden suppository, it would have created an observable irritation of the rectum that neither Thomas Noguchi or John Miner could have missed during the autopsy.

If Sam Giancana — or some other member of the Mafia — killed Marilyn Monroe thirty years ago, certainly they might have been able to bribe, influence or blackmail high local and federal officials — possibly even the Kennedy brothers — into covering up for them.

But, would the Mob still have any vested interest in concealing that crime today? The old dons are dead. Most of the new Mafia dons aren't even closely related to the godfathers of Giancana's day.

What motive could current Mob leaders possibly have for the expense and effort of maintaining that cover-up some three decades later?

Whoever killed Marilyn, it was somebody or some organization still powerful and active today — one with a serious interest in keeping its image untarnished.

THE FOUR FACES OF MURDER

In narrowing down the likely suspects in the murder of Marilyn Monroe, a number of criteria have emerged that help to pinpoint and identify the person or persons who were responsible for her death. There are four determinants that can help us to eliminate the remaining suspects and finally glimpse the face of Marilyn's killer.

1) Whoever killed Marilyn was someone (or some organization) powerful enough to engineer a cover-up that included government officials and law enforcement agencies at

every level of local, state and national government.

2) Whoever killed Marilyn still retains an interest in maintaining that cover-up today.

3) Whoever killed Marilyn — or someone acting upon their orders — had the technical know-how to commit cold-blooded murder and make it look like suicide.

4) Whoever killed Marilyn knew that her celebrity would bring the circumstances of her death under intense public scrutiny . . . necessitating a powerful and compelling motivation to take such a risk.

These criteria would seem to rule out most individuals and even powerful criminal organizations like the Mafia — whose misdeeds are so well-known that they would have no reason to cover-up their involvement thirty years after the fact.

Of all those enmeshed in Marilyn's life during her final days, the only suspicious parties who seem to fit these measures are the Kennedys — particularly RFK — or the government agencies — particularly the CIA.

THE CIA

A number of scenarios have implicated various agencies of the federal government in either the cover-up or the murder of Marilyn Monroe.

In one scenario, Marilyn's death was accidental. A government agent unintentionally administered an overdose while trying to sedate Marilyn — possibly at Bobby Kennedy's orders. The agent hoped to keep the actress unconscious and incommunicado until she missed her planned press conference . . . where she had intended to expose her affair with Bobby.

There are several reasons to doubt this possibility. The first, and most important, is that those who were said to have plotted Marilyn's death would have no assurance that the star wouldn't have awakened just as angry, or more so, and rescheduled her conference another time. Whenever she held it, if Marilyn Monroe called a press conference, the press would come.

No. If any government agency was responsible for the death of Marilyn Monroe, they hadn't caused it by accident. And if any government agency was culpable of her murder — which one was it? The Justice Department? The Secret Service? The FBI? The CIA? All four have been accused of such involvements at one time or another.

Any one of these four agencies would have been willing to help the president or the attorney general conceal evidence of their romances with Marilyn. Over the years, all four have been known to have cooperated in covering up the indiscretions of high-level government officials.

All four agencies fit the first two criteria for Marilyn's murder. Arguably several might fit the third. But only one seems to fit the third criteria very neatly.

The only organizations that seem large enough and powerful enough to have successfully enforced a cover-up of their own complicity in Marilyn's death — especially when it involved several branches of the federal government — would seem to be the various branches and agencies of the federal government. In that sense, the FBI, the Secret Service, the Justice Department, and the CIA all have the clout necessary to institute and maintain such a conspiracy.

Certainly, all of these organizations have important public images to maintain. Any one of them would continue to have a vital interest in concealing their involvement in the death of an innocent American citizen, especially a celebrated film star. Bringing appropriate pressure to bear on a district attorney or a chief of police would be easy.

All of these agencies have an excellent working knowledge of the methodology of murder. But in the case of the Justice Department, the Secret Service and the FBI this knowledge is mostly theoretical. They are often involved in the arrest of murderers and, after-the-fact, prepare elaborate reconstructions of how that murder was carried out for training purposes.

But none of these three agencies has any practical experience with murder. Their operatives may shoot an occasional suspect in self-defense. But they do not — as far as we know — carry out cold-blooded killings . . . especially elaborate "terminations" designed to look like suicides or accidents.

The only U.S. organization whose known activities fit this pattern is the CIA.

The CIA was formed to carry out clandestine operations — including assassinations. Field agents are specially trained in a variety of techniques for making murder look like a natural cause, accident or suicide.

But what about the fourth criteria? What about motive? Did the CIA have a compelling reason for arranging Marilyn's death?

Two terrifying lines of logic suggest the CIA might have had more than sufficient motive.

First, Marilyn was killed to prevent her from exposing Jack or Bobby Kennedy — either at the Kennedys' behest, or on the CIA's own initiative. Elements of the CIA were said to have feared social unrest, and an unprecedented political crisis, if the highly-popular JFK became the first American president to be forced from office in public disgrace.

Second, the CIA killed Marilyn because Bobby Kennedy had made her privy to many of the agency's most vital secrets. Marilyn's diary contained references to such then ultra-classified items as the Bay of Pigs invasion; CIA-Mafia plots to assassinate foreign heads of state; and other items about Jimmy Hoffa and the Teamsters; Hoover and various FBI operations; Sinatra and the Mafia; Hollywood-Las Vegas connections; business and political gossip; and the Kennedy family. And Marilyn didn't put everything she knew in her diary.

CIA involvement in the assassination of foreign heads of

state was a violation of international law. If it became public knowledge, the U. S. might have well been brought before the U. N. To have prevented such an embarrassment, the CIA would have considered eliminating Marilyn Monroe.

In this scenario, however, the Kennedys are innocent of Marilyn's murder. Instead, it was plotted and carried out secretly by a small faction within the CIA — without the knowledge of their superiors, JFK or RFK.

But there is strong support for this scenario — from the CIA's arch rivals, the Secret Police of the Soviet Union, the KGB. According to KGB files, recently released by the new Russian government, the Soviet spy organization had agents within the CIA at the time of Marilyn's death. Those informants told KGB spy-masters they had learned that "Marilyn was killed by the CIA because she planned to expose a U. S. plot to murder Cuban dictator Fidel Castro."

Are there substantial reasons to believe that Marilyn was the victim of one of the CIA's "clandestine" activities? That the woman who knew too much was terminated with extreme prejudice? Apparently so.

Are there any strong arguments against it? Almost none.

An interesting question: would CIA agents have dared conduct a hit on a girl-friend of JFK or RFK without being absolutely sure that the affair was completely over?

Would CIA operatives — who are sworn not to conduct operations within the United States — have agreed to assassinate one of the nation's most beloved citizens even if they had been ordered to do so?

Many people believe they would.

The CIA are suspects we can't eliminate. They are the first of all the suspects in Marilyn's death against whom strong arguments can not be marshalled.

But the fact that the CIA had the motive, the method and the will doesn't necessarily make them guilty of Marilyn's murder.

A good detective never thinks he has the puzzle solved the minute he finds a likely-looking suspect. An experienced detective never rests until he has examined *all* the possible perpetrators.

But there is still one important suspect we haven't looked at yet. A suspect numerous witnesses place at Marilyn's residence shortly before her death.

A suspect many people say had a strong motive to murder Marilyn Monroe.

A suspect who had both the power and the will to cover up his crime if he committed it.

Robert F. Kennedy, attorney general of the United States.

BOBBY OR JACK?

Bobby Kennedy has always been suspect number one in the murder of Marilyn Monroe. In *The Strange Death of Marilyn Monroe,* by investigative reporter Frank Capell, published only two years after the star's death, RFK first emerges as the most-likely candidate for Marilyn's murderer. Recently, authors Peter Harry Brown and Patte B. Barham in researching their new book, *Marilyn: The Last Take* — and following up every new lead that has developed since Marilyn's death — independently concluded that all the evidence still suggests Capell was right.

When it comes to Marilyn Monroe's murder Bobby Kennedy has it all: the motive, the power, the will and the opportunity — and, if Bobby did kill her, the ultra-elite, ultra-respectable Kennedy family has a vital interest in keeping his involvement a secret. Business and politics as usual.

Furthermore, there were *two* Kennedy brothers who stood to face public disgrace if Marilyn carried out her threat to expose them in a press conference. Both fit most of the criteria for Marilyn's murderer.

Of the two, JFK — riding the crest of immense popularity with guaranteed re-election ahead — had the most to lose. He was the president of the United States — the most prestigious position in the world. If JFK's relationship with Marilyn were exposed, his political career and marriage would both have been ended. It would have been one of the greatest political disgraces in American history.

Former LAPD Sergeant Jack Clemmons agrees: "Had Marilyn gone public, John F. Kennedy would have had to resign the presidency and the Kennedys would have had to come back to Hyannis. The American public simply would not have permitted them to remain in office any longer. At that time, it would have been worse, much worse, for them than it was for Nixon when he had to leave."

If Marilyn was a liability to anybody, she was a liability to the president.

As President of the United States and as a member of the wealthy Kennedy clan, JFK certainly had the power and resources to institute a cover-up of his or anyone else's complicity in Marilyn's death.

Marilyn's foster-sister, Bebe Goddard, who remembers the Kennedy years vividly, also believes they had the power to orchestrate the cover-up of the star's death. "The reason people participated in the cover-up is because the Kennedy tentacles are so vast and influence people in so many ways. People seem to think that they had a lot to gain by doing these great favors for the Kennedys. I think the LAPD was influenced by the Kennedys. I have learned that people will do almost anything for the Kennedys — in the destruction of records and sending witnesses away. I think it's a very corrupt procedure, but it's a fact of life."

And as with Bobby, the Kennedy clan still maintains

a strange interest in protecting JFK's memory and reputation today.

If JFK were responsible for Marilyn's murder he couldn't have killed her himself. He was in Washington, D. C. that weekend.

According to unimpeachable witnesses, the president was already up working at his desk that Sunday morning.

If JFK was behind Marilyn's death, someone else would have had to commit the murder for him. Most likely such a professional would have been recruited from the ranks of the CIA.

This M.O. however, seems out of character. JFK was cool-headed, amiable and a shrewd manipulator of people and events. If JFK felt Marilyn was about to become a nuisance, he would have thought of a far more subtle way of handling the problem than having her murdered.

Bobby, on the other hand, was hot-headed, impulsive and famed for an ungovernable Irish temper that had gotten him into more than one scrape . . . in college, in congress and as attorney general. Bobby habitually leaped before he looked — as when he tangled with Sam Giancana, forgetting that the Chicago don could blow the whistle on the CIA's unsavory involvement in the plot to kill Castro. Giancana came out the winner.

The Justice Department blinked in court and took the position that they did not really have the jurisdiction to try him at the time.

If either of the Kennedy brothers was involved in Marilyn's death — it was Bobby.

In some ways, Bobby Kennedy has always been the ideal candidate for Marilyn's murderer.

Bobby met all the profile characteristics of her murderer.

Bobby is known to have been at the scene of Marilyn's death shortly before that death occurred.

According to my research and that of Brown and Barham: "Eyewitnesses have placed Bobby Kennedy at Monroe's house at least once — and probably twice — on the evening of her death."

It is on that fatal second visit that Marilyn's death is supposed to have occurred.

More significantly, Bobby had the temperament to have committed the murder and was reported to have been engaged in a violent argument with Marilyn not long before her death. If Bobby were any other ex-lover caught in similar circumstances, the police would have arrested him instantly as a prime suspect.

Bobby also had the motive. Men have killed cast-off mistresses before, when those ladies threatened exposure.

Cause-of-death expert Dr. J. DeWitt Fox has no trouble believing this scenario. "I understand that she had threatened to have a press conference on Monday," Fox told me in an exclusive interview. "She had threatened to expose Bobby Kennedy and his amorous designs and that he told her that he would divorce his wife, leave his kids and marry her. To me that is reason enough itself for somebody to want to put her out of the way."

But all this is theory — not hard evidence. Is there any stronger reason for believing Bobby Kennedy killed Marilyn than there is for believing that JFK or the CIA was responsible? The answer is — yes.

THE TELL-TALE TAPES

Nearly a dozen reputable witnesses claim to have heard tape recordings made the night of Marilyn's death for Mob surveillance expert Bernard Spindel — recordings that directly implicate Bobby Kennedy in Marilyn Monroe's death. Among those who have admitted having heard these tapes or heard

Spindel talk about them are: former Spindel employees, Bill Holt, Michael Morrissey and Earl Jaycox; former Faberge executive Richard Butterfield and his wife, close friends of the Spindels; Dr. Henry Kamin, Spindel's family doctor; free-lance surveillance expert and detective, Fred Otash, who recorded many of the tapes for Spindel; and me.

The most complete description of the contents of these tapes comes from a part-time government consultant vouched for by Mark Monsky, a former vice-president of the NBC Television News Division. According to British journalist Anthony Summers who interviewed the consultant in 1972, "the man said Spindel's tape confirmed what many had long suspected: that Bobby Kennedy had indeed paid two visits to Marilyn's house that fateful Saturday."

In the recordings of the first visit, the RFK/Marilyn conversation started out reasonably. However, they soon began to argue. As the argument continued, their voices grew louder and louder. In the background, the anonymous tipster told Summers, he heard Peter Lawford's voice.

Soon Bobby Kennedy could be heard stomping around the house, searching for something. According to Summer's source, RFK was yelling: "Where is it. Where the fuck is it?"

Some journalists have speculated that Bobby Kennedy was looking for an electronic bug he felt was placed somewhere in Marilyn's house. But if what Summer's source told him Bobby said next is true, then a more likely explanation is that he was looking for Marilyn's red diary.

According to the anonymous government consultant, Bobby was saying: "It's important to the family. We can make any arrangements you want. But we must find it."

There are several reasons for believing Bobby Kennedy was referring to Marilyn's diary and not a suspected electronic eavesdropping device.

The first is his remark to the star about making "any arrangements you want." It doesn't seem likely he would have had to make any arrangements with her about a bug if he found one. But he might have wanted to make some arrangements to compensate her for the surrender of her diary, if he took it from her.

The second reason for believing RFK was looking for Marilyn's diary is his mention of the object's being "important to the family." Considering that Marilyn's main threat had been to expose the brothers' love-them-and-leave-them attitude, not state secrets, it seems far more likely that Bobby was worried about the diary's threat to his marriage and the Kennedy family name.

Bobby had already seen the diary and thrown a fit over it one afternoon when Jeanne Carmen was visiting Marilyn. Aware of Marilyn's threats to expose him and his brother, the brainy attorney general would have known that the actress's diary was almost the only real piece of incriminating evidence she had to support her claims. If he could destroy that diary, he and JFK could safely deny all of Marilyn's accusations — it would be the word of the president of the United States, the U.S. attorney general, and the sworn word of their oh-so respectable political supporters against the word of a woman rumored to be highly unstable, who had spent time in a psychiatric hospital and who suffered from a family history of mental illness.

No wonder Bobby was frantically searching for Marilyn's diary. What the attorney general apparently didn't know was that the diary was locked in a filing cabinet in the guest bedroom on the far side of the house, a room that could only be entered from the outside.

Later on in the tape, after a pause that seemed to indicate it had been edited to condense the passage of time, Summer's source heard a further argument between Marilyn and Bobby. Apparently, Marilyn was raving hysterically at the unrepentant attorney general. Then the source heard the sounds of thumping and of something being lowered onto a bed.

Others who claim to have heard portions of this tape add a further detail. During that last, and possibly fatal argument, Bobby is supposed to have instructed someone to either calm the hysterical star down or to give her "something" to calm her down . . . followed by the thumping sounds and the sound like something being lowered onto the bed.

According to the anonymous government consultant, Lawford and Kennedy then discussed how they could conceal his involvement in the night's events and his presence in L. A. Then RFK gave Lawford detailed instructions on how to begin the cover-up — probably including suggestions of who to call on for help. The tape closed with Bobby telling Lawford he was going to fly back to San Francisco and phone Lawford from there to check on the progress of the cover-up.

I heard this section of the tapes. It was apparently made on the day of Marilyn's death. On the tape, a call is heard coming in from San Francisco. In those days, there was no direct dial fom an operator, and the operator said the call was coming in from the Bay area. On the tape, I heard Bobby Kennedy's voice on the other end of the line saying "Is she dead?".

There is further substantiation for the story of Spindel's tapes. They were confiscated in 1966. Spindel died in 1971.

Any conversations Spindel could have had with others about those tapes would have taken place before 1971. Yet no one outside the cover-up knew that Bobby Kennedy had been at Marilyn's that night or that Marilyn and he had quarreled — until Eunice Murray's and Deborah Gould Lawford's admissions in 1985! If Spindel's tapes didn't exist — where did he get his knowledge.

Or, put it another way: if Spindel was bugging Marilyn's house — and if Bobby Kennedy was there that night, as we now know him to have been — then Spindel would have had tapes of all the evening's events. If others and I have at least heard part of these tapes, then it seems beyond dispute that Bobby Kennedy was in some way culpable in Marilyn Monroe's death

Obviously Spindel's tapes would be the smoking-gun tying Bobby Kennedy directly to Marilyn's death.

So why haven't those charged with conducting the official investigation into Marilyn's death — such as District Attorney Ira Reiner and former D. A. John Van de Kamp — subpoenaed Spindel's tapes? They could prove once and for all whether RFK was guilty of complicity in Marilyn's death?

The damning answer is that those tapes were probably destroyed by New York County District Attorney Frank S. Hogan! Yet another of those actions that provide continuing evidence of a high-level cover-up by government officials in the death of Marilyn Monroe.

The facts are these: At dawn on a cold December day in 1966 — only four years after Marilyn's death — just as Bobby Kennedy was beginning to lay the groundwork for his own bid for the presidency, an unusually large contingent of local police and D. A. investigators raided Bernard Spindel's upstate New York home. They confiscated many of his tapes and much of his equipment. Among the tapes New York officials confiscated were all those containing evidence of JFK's and RFK's affairs with Marilyn — and of Bobby's purported complicity in her death.

Spindel instantly filed suits against the government demanding the return of all his tapes and equipment. An affidavit filed by Spindel cites the specific items New York law enforcement officers seized. Among them was "a confidential file containing tapes and evidence concerning circumstances surrounding the causes of death of Marilyn Monroe."

Then for the first time in a court of law, the affidavit entered into the record a statement suggesting that the original verdict on Marilyn's death was wrong. The confiscated tape, the affidavit reads, "strongly suggests that the official reported circumstances of her death are erroneous."

Spindel died of a heart-attack before his suit reached the courts. But his wife continued the suit after his death.

But her efforts to substantiate her husband's claims by recovering the tapes and turning them over to the public were ultimately to prove in vain. For, while the matter was still before the courts, all Spindel's tapes and files were "routinely" destroyed.

If Bernard Spindel had indeed possessed the smoking gun that would prove Bobby Kennedy's direct responsibility for Marilyn's death, the attorney general no longer had any need for concern — thanks to the efforts of New York D. A. Hogan, a friend of the Kennedy family.

But even if Spindel's tapes did link Bobby with Marilyn's death, they would still leave a number of critical questions unanswered.

Was Robert F. Kennedy, the Attorney General of the United States, actually responsible for the cold-blooded murder of Marilyn Monroe — as so many have suggested? And if he was, did Bobby kill her himself or have someone else do it?

Or might Bobby have caused Marilyn's death unintentionally while trying to calm her down — as others have suggested? Could he — or more likely someone following his orders — have accidentally given Marilyn a lethal overdose . . . when they only intended to sedate her for the night?

The toxicology report suggests that if someone did give Marilyn an overdose that night — it wasn't by accident. The amount of drugs found in her blood and kidneys has been estimated at being one hundred times the size of the normal, sedative dose. Anyone who even knew how to give such a shot might conceivably overestimate the dosage three or four times — but not one hundred times!

However, there is one set of facts that would seem to support the accident theory — the ambulance Abe Landau saw outside Marilyn's house that evening — the ambulance in which the dying star reportedly took a midnight round-trip to the nearest hospital. It hardly seems likely that if Bobby Kennedy had deliberately had Marilyn killed that an ambulance would have been called to save her life.

Sergeant Jack Clemmons believes Bobby or one of his confederates might have called an ambulance as part of their cover-up. "I assume that Bobby Kennedy went there with the idea in mind of talking Marilyn out of going public. And apparently Marilyn was going to go ahead and do it anyway. So Bobby had to switch to 'Plan B.' Marilyn was a little afraid of Bobby and was popping pills trying to keep calm and in control of the situation. I think at a certain point someone handed her a glass of water laced with chloral hydrate. Chloral hydrate is odorless, colorless, tasteless. If someone handed you a glass of water with chloral hydrate in it, you'd drink it and never know anything while drinking it. But in a short time you would just pass out."

At that point, Clemmons believes, they had "the perfect crime." But, according to Clemmons, Bobby and his cohorts grew overconfident. "They decided that Marilyn was beyond recovery. So they made a good show of it. They called an ambulance, when the ambulance failed, it would be too bad. 'Poor Marilyn! We tried to save her but we couldn't.'"

Clemmons believes that Marilyn died before reaching the hospital . . . and someone in the ambulance with her — possibly Peter Lawford — panicked and decided to return to the house with the body for further instructions. "Now if I'm correct," Clemmons says, "and if they had waited another hour and just gone their own way, the next morning sometime someone would discover Marilyn. No one would have been able to prove a thing. No one could have *ever* proved a thing. But, instead, they left a lot of evidence that this was a murder."

Another question still unanswered about that night is: who gave Marilyn the fatal overdose?

Neither Bobby Kennedy nor Peter Lawford had the expertise.

Whether by suppository, hypodermic or a deadly glass of chloral hydrate — someone else actually administered the drug.

Was it a CIA operative or a Justice Department agent?

Sergeant Jack Clemmons' own investigations have convinced him it was neither. Instead, Clemmons believes Bobby Kennedy brought along a doctor — perhaps with the original intent of merely sedating the hysterical Marilyn.

Others postulate a more frightening scenario. They contend that if Bobby Kennedy actually brought a doctor . . . then he already intended to commit murder. In this version of the night's events, Bobby would have blackmailed or bribed — more likely blackmailed — the doctor into cooperating.

Sergeant Jack Clemmons agrees. He, too, feels that the identity of the third man may be the key to our understanding of the nights' events. "We never have been able to find out who those two men were who walked into that house with Bobby Kennedy. Since he was an attorney general, and his brother was president, we originally assumed that they were either Secret Service or FBI men. But some people have speculated that they were the two doctors, Dr. Greenson and Dr. Engelberg. But we don't know that for sure."

Perhaps if we knew the identity of that third man we could finally be certain whether Bobby planned Marilyn's murder with full premeditation beforehand — or if her death was the accidental result of a bungled attempt to sedate her.

Bobby Kennedy and Peter Lawford are dead now. If the

identity of the third man can still be determined at this late date — it would take a grand jury with full subpoena power to uncover it.

Regardless of the explanation for the presence of the ambulance, or ambulances, at Marilyn's home that night — or of who gave the star the overdose that killed her — or even whether that overdose was a sign of murder or accident — one thing is certain: Bobby Kennedy *was* at Marilyn Monroe's home the night of August 4, 1962. There is significant reason to believe that he may have been directly or indirectly responsible for her death.

Two actions later that morning seem to confirm the RFK-as-killer scenario.

The first is that within hours of Marilyn's death, FBI agents visited the phone company and confiscated all the records of Marilyn's long-distance phone calls to Bobby Kennedy. For the next quarter of a century, the FBI and Kennedy loyalists would deny that Marilyn had made any calls to Bobby in the days immediately preceding her death. This is an error that former LAPD head Daryl Gates repeats in his autobiography, *Chief: My Life in the LAPD*.

But photo copies of those records, recently released under the Freedom of Information Act, clearly show that during that time Marilyn actually placed nearly a dozen calls to Washington in a futile attempt to reach Bobby Kennedy.

The second incident that tends to confirm the involvement of the president's younger brother in Marilyn's death is a twenty-minute phone call Peter Lawford placed to JFK at the White House at 6:05 A. M. that fatal Sunday morning — theoretically some minutes earlier than he could have learned of Marilyn's death from even the fastest breaking radio news. According to Brown and Barham: "Some reporters noted that the records of the telephone call might finally be the 'smoking gun' — the tie between Monroe's death and the administration of a sitting president. It also fingers Lawford as the architect of the cover-up."

Anthony Summers reached similar conclusions in his own book, *Goddess*: "The link between President Kennedy and Lawford was significant, coming as it did only two hours after Marilyn's death was reported. The conversation . . . could have been about nothing other than the death of Marilyn Monroe."

There is one final but very telling bit of support for the Bobby-as-killer scenario. The testimony of those involved in the conspiracy to cover-up Bobby's involvement. At some point during the course of their lives when asked what had really happened on the night of Marilyn's death — Eunice Murray, Dr. Ralph Greenson, Dr. Hyman Engelberg and Pat Newcomb—all replied: "Ask Bobby Kennedy."

It almost appears as if each — perhaps driven by guilt or the crushing weight of the cover-up — felt compelled to point the finger at the man they knew could provide journalists with the full story of what really happened to Marilyn Monroe on the night of her death — the man they knew played a central role in the events of that night — Robert F. Kennedy, attorney general of the United States.

In an alternate, less credible version of this scenario, RFK himself was not involved in Marilyn's death. Instead, all he did was have Marilyn sedated by a doctor who administered the normal dosage of Nembutal. It was later, while Marilyn lay in a drugged stupor, that agents of the Mafia or the CIA slipped into the star's house and administered — by injection or suppository — her last overdose.

Clearly, whatever actually happened that night . . . after the morning of August 5, 1962, the Kennedy brothers no longer had anything to fear from their relationship with Marilyn Monroe.

FILE #23

Closing the Case

For over thirty years I have been investigating the death of Marilyn Monroe. I began alone. But I was soon joined by what proved to be an ever-increasing body of journalists, private investigators and retired law enforcement officials. Many others came to scoff — convinced that claims of murder and cover-up were either fanciful delusions or cynical fabrications designed to line the pockets of exploitative journalists. But, remarkably, almost all stayed to add their efforts to the rest — convinced by an objective examination of the evidence that there was more to Marilyn's death than the official story told. As Brown and Barham write of their own investigation in *Marilyn: The Final Take*: "As we followed the tangled story . . . we expected to uncover an accidental death and instead found a murder."

The more hands joined the ranks, the more evidence was amassed. As one new discovery led to the next, incontrovertible proof began to emerge of an incredible array of lies, deceptions and contradictions — along with what appeared to be a systematic pattern of actions on the part of the public officials charged with investigating the case. It was nothing less than an official cover-up of the truth about Marilyn's death.

By now it must be obvious that I believe Bobby Kennedy was instrumental in causing Marilyn Monroe's death — either intentionally or by accident. It must be equally obvious that a percentage of those who have investigated Marilyn's death also with me. We believe that the evidence of BobbyKennedy's guilt is overwhelming and persuasive. But we are also willing to concede that we might be wrong. Honest men differ in their judgments and in their interpretations of events and evidence.

Perhaps those who claim Marilyn was murdered by the Mafia are correct. Perhaps those who feel she was hounded to death by the studio, or some who who believe that agents of the CIA took her life, or those who believe her death was neither homicide nor suicide — but accidental — are correct.

What all those who hold these divergent viewpoints have in common is the belief that only a full and unbiased investigation into the circumstances of Marilyn's death can ever reveal which — if any — of these theories is correct. The only thing we can be certain of now is that the circumstances of her death were not those described to police and the public. We also believe that a number of recent developments more than justify reopening the official inquiry into Marilyn's death. Most important among these developments are:

* The dramatic recanting of the original version of the events leading up to the discovery of the body as told by Marilyn's psychiatrist, Dr. Ralph Greenson, and her house-keeper-nurse, Eunice Murray.

* The equally dramatic disclosures about the presence of public relations specialists, and others — led by Arthur Jacobs and Peter Lawford — who worked throughout the night to erase all traces of Bobby Kennedy's involvement in Marilyn's life.

* Newly discovered eyewitness testimony, backed up by

high-ranking police officials, placing RFK at Marilyn's house not long before her death.

* Dramatic disclosures about a violent argument between Marilyn and Bobby late that evening.

* Continuing controversy over the results of the original autopsy report — climaxed by Thomas Noguchi's own repudiation of those conclusions — and a call for a new investigation.

As recently as 1985, LA District Attorney Ira Reiner, in declining to commit the resources of his department to reopening the investigation into Marilyn's death, described that death as merely of "historical interest." But, Reiner also admitted that murder has no statute of limitations. When the police or the district attorney's office suspects that a murder has been committed, they never close the files or the investigation.

Those who have conducted the unofficial investigation believe that the above set of facts ought to arouse more than a reasonable doubt as to the validity of the original verdict in Marilyn's death. Even the possibility that someone might have been murdered should make that death more than important "historical interest." And certainly that possibility exists in the case of Marilyn's death. It always exists when someone has been the target of systematic surveillance by the heads of organized crime in America. It exists when the victim had possibly had a violent quarrel with her married boyfriend only minutes before her death!

CALL FOR AN INDEPENDENT GRAND JURY

Over the years, many reputable citizens have urged the LA District Attorney's office to reopen the official investigation into Marilyn Monroe's death. Among them James Hudson, former head of the United Press International news syndicate;

George Carpozi Jr., crime reporter, author and a former editor of *The New York Post*; Milo Speriglio, CEO of the Nick Harris Detective Agency; Jack Clemmons, former LAPD Sergeant; Sam Yorty, former mayor of Los Angeles; Michael Antonovich and the entire LA County Board of Supervisors; Thad Brown, former LA chief of detectives; Anthony Summers, the investigative journalist who broke the story of Eunice Murray's dramatic change of testimony; John Miner, former deputy district attorney; Terry Moore, Marilyn's friend and fellow actress; Bebe Goddard, Marilyn's foster sister; James Hall, the ambulance driver who says he witnessed Marilyn's death; Dr. Thomas Noguchi, the pathologist who performed the original autopsy.

Yet the officials who actually have the authority to reopen the case have steadfastly ignored all the dramatic turnabouts of testimony and new revelations . . . They have instead ruled that "no new evidence" has been discovered that would justify a further investigation.

The current LA district attorney's active hostility to any new investigation into Marilyn's death — as well as the uninspiring performances of the department's past investigations — have seemed like part of an official cover-up to many. There's good reason to doubt they would make their best efforts if charged with the responsibility for a new inquiry.

This, plus mounting evidence that high-ranking government officials and departments participated in covering up the actual circumstances of Marilyn's death — has led to a growing call for the appointment of an independent prosecutor through one with the full power of subpoena and charged with sifting all the new evidence . . . to make an objective evaluation of whether the official verdict of "probable suicide" is still valid in Marilyn's case.

This prosecutor should have the power to subpoena witnesses and compel their testimony. Several people who could almost certainly tell us exactly what went on that night — and how Marilyn died — particularly Pat Newcomb, Dr. Hyman Engelberg and Mickey Rudin, refuse to discuss the case.

Dr. J. DeWitt Fox, who has studied the transcripts of the case, also believes the testimony of these witnesses is crucial for resolving the controversies surrounding Marilyn's death. "If I were involved in the investigation of this case, I would want the principal doctors to come forward with as much information as we could obtain, namely Dr. Engelberg who was the attending internist. I think he would have the most information of any of the principals who were involved at the time."

Sergeant Jack Clemmons, the first officer to turn in an official report from the scene of Marilyn's death, agrees: "Dr. Engelberg could tell us. He was involved in it."

In addition to investigating Marilyn's death, an independent prosecutor ought to look into allegations of a high-level cover-up by federal and local officials that continues today. Participation in such a cover-up by an elected official is a felony. According to Jack Clemmons: "Authorities, in concealing this crime, have committed malfeasance of office — and other crimes as well."

As conspiracy to conceal evidence regarding cause-of-death or murder is a felony, many of those whose testimony we need might refuse to testify because of self-incrimination.

Jack Clemmons believes the solution might be to offer selected witnesses immunity from prosecution. "You're going to need to take one of those people, either Dr. Engelberg or Pat Newcomb, and give 'em immunity to get them to spill their guts."

SOME STARTING POINTS

An independent prosecutor, trying to decide where to start in the bewildering mass of old and new evidence surrounding the death of Marilyn Monroe, might well be advised to begin by considering the following list. It contains the main questions that have puzzled journalists and other unofficial investigators over the years. The answers to these questions would resolve *all* the major unsolved mysteries surrounding Marilyn's death.

* How could Marilyn have taken forty-seven Nembutals — when no pills were found in her stomach . . . and no water glass was found by her bed?

* How valid were the original autopsy results?

* Why does Marilyn's death certificate give the time of her death as 3:50 A. M., when the condition of her body suggests that she died many hours earlier?

* Why were no needle marks found during the autopsy, not even those of shots Marilyn's doctor had given her less than three days before?

* What happened to the organ samples that could have conclusively proved the cause of death?

* Why was John Miner's memorandum omitted from the official coroner's report, and why did all the copies vanish from the official files?

* Why did both Dr. Ralph Greenson and Eunice Murray lie about the circumstances of Marilyn's death?

* What went on between Marilyn and RFK during their final moments together?

* Why were ambulances parked in her driveway hours before her death was reported to the police?

* What happened to Marilyn's personal diary?

* Have local and federal officials cooperated in covering up vital information about Marilyn's death?

* And if so — who, besides Robert F. Kennedy, would be powerful enough to orchestrate and maintain a cover-up that has held for almost thirty years?

Until the official investigation is reopened, these — and other questions — will remain unanswered.

"It is because of questions like these," says Lionel Grandison, the man who was forced to sign Marilyn's death certificate, "that thirty years later, this topic is still something for us to talk about."

In addition to exploring these questions, an independent prosecutor should also subpoena a number of key witnesses whose sworn testimony can be expected to add immeasurably to our understanding of Marilyn's death.

THE WITNESSES

There are literally hundreds of witnesses with important information to share about the circumstances of Marilyn Monroe's death, who have never been interviewed. An independent prosecutor investigating Marilyn's death might well be advised to ask the following individuals about these areas of inquiry:

Marilyn's attempts to reach Bobby the night of the 3rd:

Pat Kennedy, sister of the president and the attorney general, former Lawford spouse, whom Marilyn tried to contact. Peter Lawford himself told reporters that he gave the actress the number of the Kennedy compound in Hyannis, where Pat was vacationing.

Elizabeth Francher, assistant to crime reporter Florabel Muir. According to Francher, Muir paid a telephone operator at the St. Francis Hotel for information about Marilyn calling the hotel several times that weekend trying to reach RFK.

The former owners or staff of Briggs' delicatessen, who delivered food and liquor to Marilyn's home the night before her death a possible indication of an impending visit from Bobby Kennedy.

Jean Leon, of Beverly Hills' fashionable La Scala restaurant. He claims Marilyn ordered an expensive dinner that night, and hinted to reporters that he had seen "a very famous person" at Marilyn's home when he arrived with her order.

About the timetable for Marilyn's last day:

Jeanne Carmen, who talked to Marilyn several times that day, the first around 6:00 A.M., the last time around 10:00 P.M.

Arthur James, New York friend. Marilyn tried to reach him that morning, but he did not get the message until Monday, August 6.

Ralph Roberts, Marilyn's masseur, with whom she had a tentative dinner date. He spoke with Marilyn twice that morning and with Dr. Ralph Greenson when he called back around 6:30 P. M.

Steffi Skolsky, columnist Sidney Skolsky's daughter. They seem to have been the last call of the morning. Marilyn told her she planned to see Bobby Kennedy that evening.

Eunice Murray, Marilyn's housekeeper-nurse. She arrived around 10:00 A. M., and recalls Marilyn's going to bed around 8:00 P.M and claimed to have found her dead at either midnight or 3:30 A.M. She later recanted her story of the evening's events, and has never said what did happen, however.

Pat Newcomb, Marilyn's publicist. She slept over on Friday night and remained at Marilyn's until late afternoon.

Norman Jeffries III, Eunice Murray's son-in-law. He might be able to substantiate Murray's account of Bobby's final visit to Marilyn's house.

Joe DiMaggio Jr. He called several times during the day, only to be told she was out, finally connecting with her around 7:00 P.M.

Daniel and Joan Greenson, Dr. Ralph Greenson's son and daughter. They can confirm his timetable and whereabouts for large parts of the day.

Henry Rosenfeld, the wealthy dress manufacturer. He spoke to Marilyn from New York before 9:30 P.M.

Sidney Guilaroff, a film colony hairdresser. He spoke to Marilyn shortly after Rosenfeld's call.

José Bolanos, Marilyn's Mexican lover. He phoned her from a near-by restaurant sometime before 10:00 P.M.

Jeanne Carmen, who talked to Marilyn around 10:00 P.M.

Ralph Roberts, whose answering service took a message from Marilyn before 10:30 P.M.

About the timetable for Marilyn's last night:

Dr. Hyman Engelberg, Marilyn's physician. He prescribed the fatal bottle of Nembutal and could tell us what he knows of Dr. Greenson's and Eunice Murray's lies about the events of that night.

Deborah Gould, former Lawford wife. She told television interviewers that Marilyn called sometime during dinner, around 10:30 P.M., sounding drugged and despondent.

The LAPD officers who interviewed Peter Lawford about his involvement in 1972. The timetable Lawford reportedly gave does not match that of the other witnesses to the evening's events.

Milton Ebbins, Lawford's business manager. Lawford supposedly called to seek his advice, shortly after receiving Marilyn's last call.

Mickey Rudin, Marilyn's attorney. Ebbins is said to have called Rudin immediately after receiving Lawford's call. When Rudin phoned Ebbins back around 4:00 A.M. to report Marilyn's death, Rudin told Ebbins he was phoning from the star's home. Rudin's whereabouts during the intervening five hours are not known.

Joe and Dolores Naarr, Lawford's dinner guests that evening. Lawford phoned them shortly after they returned home at 11:00 P.M. to tell them he was worried Marilyn might have taken an overdose.

George "Bullets" Durgom, Hollywood producer who was Lawford's house guest that night.

Erma Lee Riley, Lawford's long-time servant who was present all evening.

The cover-up at Marilyn's house.

Natalie Jacobs, widow of publicity pro, Arthur Jacobs, was with Arthur at Hollywood Bowl the night of August 4 when he received a message "that something was wrong" and left for Marilyn's house.

Juliet Roswell, former Jacobs' employee. Confirms Natalie Jacobs' version of the night's events . . . Jacobs told Roswell he went out to Marilyn's around 11:00 P.M.

Fred Otash, private investigator. He was hired by Hoffa to bug Marilyn's home. Ironically, the unsuspecting Lawford asked Otash to help clean up evidence of Bobby's presence.

Harry Brand, head of Twentieth Century-Fox Publicity. He was placed at the scene by Marilyn's former business manager, Inez Melson, who later confessed to her own part in the cover-up.

Frank Neill, one of Brand's assistants, said by Melson to have accompanied Brand there.

Johnny Campbell, another Brand assistant. Said by Melson to have assisted in the cover-up that night, he later confirmed Melson's story.

Confirm Mafia bugging of Marilyn's home and
Spindel's story of "smoking gun" tapes of
Bobby's last fight with Marilyn:

Fred Otash. He did the actual taping for the New York-based Spindel.

John Danoff, former Otash employee, who heard the tapes.

Bill Holt, former Spindel employee. He says fellow employee Michael Morrissey heard the tape and described its contents in detail.

Michael Morrissey, former Spindel employee. Today an attorney in private practice he now says he only heard "a few minutes" from the tape.

Earl Jaycox, another Spindel employee. He says Spindel told him of the tapes in 1962.

Richard Butterfield, former Faberge executive, Spindel friend, he also says Spindel told him of the tapes.

Dr. Henry Kamin, Spindel's physician, another person who says Spindel described the tapes to him.

Milo Speriglio, private investigator, who also claims to have heard the controversial tapes.

Bobby Kennedy's Saturday visit:

Eunice Murray. She covered up truth for a quarter of a century and finally confessed that Bobby had been there that day and quarreled with Marilyn.

Pat Newcomb. Apparently told police and press she and Marilyn had quarreled to conceal the real reason for Marilyn's anger that day.

Betty Pollard. Her mother was one of a group of Marilyn's neighbors who regularly gathered for bridge games. She saw Bobby Kennedy enter Marilyn's house around 7:30 P. M.

Jack Clemmons, former LAPD Sergeant. He interviewed Pollard's mother and the other members of her bridge group shortly after Marilyn's death.

Ward Wood, Lawford's neighbor, saw Bobby Kennedy drive up to Lawford's home that day.

Milton Greene, Marilyn's former business partner. He claims Lawford told him of Bobby's visit to Marilyn and the argument that ensued.

Deborah Gould, former Lawford wife, who says Lawford also told her about Bobby's visit.

Thad Brown, former LA chief of detectives. He places Kennedy in LA on August 4.

Finis Brown, retired LAPD detective and Thad Brown's brother, who also places Kennedy in LA.

Hugh McDonald, Officer in charge of the LA county Sheriff's Homicide Bureau . . . also reported Bobby Kennedy in LA that day.

John Dickey, former LA county deputy district attorney. Another who has claimed knowledge of Bobby's presence that Saturday.

Sergeant Robert Byron, the LAPD officer in charge of investigating Marilyn's death. In his report, Byron noted that departmental sources told him Bobby had visited Marilyn's house that afternoon.

Daryl Gates, controversial former LA chief of police. He says police sources informed them of Bobby's presence as soon as he arrived at the airport.

Sam Yorty, former LA mayor, who says William Parker, LAPD chief at the time of Marilyn's death, told him that Bobby had been in town that fateful day.

John Bates, wealthy Kennedy supporter. He swears Bobby was with him at his San Francisco ranch until at least 10:00 P.M. that night.

How Bobby Kennedy flew back to San Francisco in time for church on Sunday morning:

Patricia Conners, the daughter of Lawford's helicopter pilot Hal Conners. She says her father was out late on a charter that night but admits he often ferried Bobby Kennedy around on visits to the West Coast.

James Zonlick, vice president of the Los Angeles Air Taxi Service, former Conners employee. He confirms Conners frequently ferried Bobby between San Francisco and LA

Ed Connelly, former Conners pilot. He remembers a night "late in 1962" when Conners landed at Lawford's beachside home without landing lights to pick up "an important passenger."

About the ambulances seen in Marilyn's driveway:

Abe Landau, Marilyn's neighbor, was returning home from dinner with his wife around 1:00 A.M. when he noticed an ambulance parked outside Marilyn's house.

Jack Clemmons, former LAPD officer. He interviewed other neighbors who substantiate Landau's story.

James Hall, former Schaefer Ambulance employee. He claims to have answered a call to Marilyn's around 3:30 A.M He revived the comatose star and saw Dr. Ralph Greenson give her a fatal injection. He told district attorney interviewers that he drove the ambulance seen outside Marilyn's that night. He also remembered being accompanied by Murray Leib.

Murray Leib (aka Leibowitz). This was the Schaefer employee who Jim Hall claims accompanied him on the call Leib admits he was the driver normally selected to handle celebrity cases, but says that he was not one of those at Marilyn's that night with either Hall or Hunter.

Professionals who offer strong dissenting opinions to the original autopsy report:

Dr. Thomas Noguchi, the pathologist who conducted the autopsy, recently questioned his own observations and called for a re-examination of the autopsy results.

John Miner, the deputy D. A. who attended Marilyn's autopsy, believes there is an important indication that Marilyn's overdose might have been administered via enema.

Dr. Sidney Weinberg, chief medical examiner of the county of New York. He examined the original autopsy reports and concluded Noguchi overlooked important indications that Marilyn's death could not have been suicide and might have been murder.

Dr. J. DeWitt Fox, an expert witness in cause-of-death trials, who supported Dr. Weinberg's views after his own examination of the autopsy reports.

About apparent official attempts to cover up the facts about Marilyn's death:

Robert Byron, the LAPD sergeant who conducted the official police investigation into Marilyn's death. Why did he note that Murray's, Greenson's and Engelberg's stories sounded "rehearsed" but never interrogated them about it?

Sergeant Marvin Iannone, the officer Sergeant Jack Clemmons left in charge of the scene of Marilyn's death. What happened to the alterations in the physical evidence that took place while he was in charge?

John Van de Kamp, former LA district attorney. Why did he ignore Eunice Murray's recanting of her original story, and Walt Schaefer's admission that one of his ambulances had been called to Marilyn's house hours before the police were called? He dismissed the testimony of Sergeant Jack

Clemmons and Lionel Grandison, concluding that "there was no compelling reason to reopen the case."

Ira Reiner, LA district attorney. He shut down a grand jury investigation into Marilyn's death and took the unprecedented step of removing the jury's foreman and suspending the investigation.

Sam Cordova, the grand jury foreman Reiner fired. What about the evidence he found that convinced him Marilyn's death deserved an official investigation?

Sam Yorty, former LA Mayor. Why did the LAPD lie to him about the files it kept on Marilyn's death?

Lionel Grandison, former deputy coroner's aide. What happened to the official cover-up he saw going on inside the coroner's office, and why was he reluctant to sign the official death certificate?

Jack Clemmons, the first LAPD officer known to have visited the scene of Marilyn's death. What about the cover-up he saw going on inside the police department?

John Miner, former deputy D. A. Why does he think his memorandum — the only official dissent to the finding of suicide — was ignored, and why did all the copies disappeared from the official files.

Milo Speriglio, Nick Harris Detective Agency head . . . about the evidence he has collected which proves an official cover-up.

Alleged Mafia involvement in Marilyn's last days:

Fred Otash, the surveillance expert sub-contracted by Bernard Spindel to supervise the bugging of Marilyn's home. Who was Otash working for, and what did he believe the information obtained was to be used for?

John Danoff, the Otash employee designated to pick up full

tapes and replace them with blank ones, could corroborate Otash's story.

Chuck Giancana, brother of Chicago godfather, Sam Giancana. Chuck claims personal knowledge that Sam ordered Marilyn's murder and also claims that he knows the identities of the four killers who made the hit.

Sammy Giancana, Chuck and Sam Giancana's cousin, who substantiates Chuck's story of a Mafia-directed hit on Marilyn Monroe.

Milo Speriglio, private detective, who claims first-hand knowledge that Marilyn was murdered by the Mob, and says he knows the names of the men involved in her death.

Annette Giancana, Sam Giancana's daughter. She disputes Chuck's and Sammy's story and says Marilyn was more valuable to her father alive than dead, but admits her father had Marilyn under surveillance.

Those who have died, whose testimony might have made a vital difference if they had been subpoenaed at the time of Marilyn's death and compelled to tell what they knew to an official investigating board . . . and what they might have said:

Dr. Ralph Greenson, Marilyn's psychiatrist. First he told officials Marilyn committed suicide, then he told them she didn't, probably could have told us *exactly* how Marilyn died.

Walter Schaefer, owner of Schaefer Ambulance Co. He admitted in 1985 that one of his ambulances had answered a call to Marilyn's Fifth Helena address the night of her death.

Guy Hockett, owner of Westwood Memorial Cemetery. He picked up Marilyn's body that morning and could have testified to the extent of *rigor mortis* , thus helping establish the time of death.

Dr. Theodore Curphey, LA County Coroner. He could have explained altered reports and why he ignored Miner's memorandum, and why he forced Lionel Grandison to sign the death certificate.

Hal Conners, Peter Lawford and Bobby Kennedy's helicopter pilot, who was said to have flown Bobby back to San Francisco that fateful night.

Peter Lawford, brother-in-law of JFK and RFK. He later confessed to several people that he had taken a private investigator — Fred Otash — to Marilyn's that night to erase evidence of Bobby's involvement with her.

Arthur Jacobs, Marilyn's publicist. He could have explained what occurred at Marilyn's house between 11:00 P.M., when he arrived, and 4:25 A. M., the next morning, when Dr. Greenson called the police.

Bernard Spindel, the master wire-tapper. He could have testified to the contents of "the smoking gun" tape that supposedly linked Bobby Kennedy directly with Marilyn's death.

Inez Melson, Marilyn's former business manager. She could have described the full details of the cover-up that began that night at Marilyn's house.

The "ladies of the club." They played bridge with a neighbor of Marilyn's every week and told numerous friends and investigators that they had seen Bobby Kennedy enter Marilyn's house that evening.

Sam Giancana, one-time head of the Chicago Mafia. What did he know about Marilyn's death?

Johnny Roselli, the Giancana henchman who had once dated Marilyn for a few months. What did he know about Giancana's involvement in Marilyn's death?

Jimmy Hoffa, the corrupt head of the Teamsters Union, who was apparently another buyer of Spindel's "tell-all" tapes.

Bobby Kennedy, Marilyn's lover and attorney general of the United States. What really happened that night at Marilyn's house?

Jack Kennedy, president of the United States. What did he and Peter Lawford talk about at 6:05 A.M. the morning of Marilyn's murder, and what did he know of his brother's complicity in her death?

THE POWER OF PUBLIC OUTRAGE

When I first started investigating Marilyn Monroe's death thirty years ago, most of the American population didn't believe that her death might have been a murder. Today, according to Milo Speriglio: "More than 90% of the nation believes that Marilyn Monroe did not commit suicide; the majority of them agree it was murder."

A spate of television specials and new books about Marilyn's death seem to have turned the tide. Apparently the public is convinced; only the public officials with the authority to reopen the case remain unconvinced — or reluctant — to reopen the case. Until someone in authority, either at the local or state level in California, moves to investigate the case or appoint an independent prosecutor, the official verdict of "probable suicide" will remain on the books — and the cover-up will remain a success.

After thirty years of evidence, what will it take to motivate public officials into reopening the investigation into Marilyn's death?

The power of public opinion. In other words — it will require action by *you*! According to Sergeant Jack Clemmons: "The only thing that will ever bring it to a full investigation is public outrage." If enough citizens let the duly appointed public officials of the city of Los Angeles and the state of California know they will not be satisfied until there is an investigation — there will be an investigation.

Do you believe there is more to Marilyn Monroe's death than the original story told?

Do you believe there is reasonable doubt about the validity of the official verdict?

Do you want to know if officials of your government helped participate in a cover-up — perhaps deliberately concealing evidence of murder by one of the privileged and powerful?

Do you feel Marilyn deserves to have the stain of suicide removed from her name?

In short, if you believe Marilyn deserves justice — and her day in court — then there is something you can do to help. Write a letter expressing your outrage at the last thirty years of inactivity and ask for the appointment of an independent prosecutor. Send your letter to:

The Investigation Team
The Marilyn Files
P.O. Box #93058
Hollywood, CA 90093-0058

Please do this as soon as possible. Feel free to add your comments and suggestions, too. Your ideas are welcome. New evidence, additional clues and tips are always given our immediate attention. We are sure that there must be some people out there who have important information to share, something that just might be valuable to our efforts. We will also keep your identity confidential if you request it.

A few months ago our investigative team, in cooperation with Producers' Video, Inc., of Los Angeles, produced a video called "The Marilyn Files." It was the beginning of our concentrated effort. This book is the second salvo. Coming next is a live, syndicated television special, also called "The

Marilyn Files," again produced in cooperation with Producers' Video, Inc. Each of these efforts is part of our overall plan to finally force the issue.

How do we do this? How can we — without the big bankrolls and political clout — achieve a legal landslide that will wash away the last vestiges of this criminal cover-up? The last page of this book contains a form letter for you to fill out or duplicate, but it is more than a letter, it is a vote for our cause, a petition to re-open this case and conduct a thorough investigation, finally, into the death of Marilyn Monroe.

Make a copy of that letter and send it to:

Hon. Michael D. Antonovich
LA County Board of Supervisors
Hall of Administration Bldg.
500 West Temple Street., Suite 869
Los Angeles, CA 90012

Supervisor Antonovich has long supported the public in their quest for a new investigation of Marilyn's death. Antonovich spearheaded the ill-fated 1985 request for a grand jury inquiry. Antonovich would like to add your letter to his efforts to have the investigation reopened.

If you, and enough others like you, write in, we will have the additional ammunition we need to force the issue on various levels and Supervisor Antonovich will be able to get an independent prosecutor appointed — for a full-scale official investigation into the facts surrounding Marilyn Monroe's death.

Until then the cover-up continues.

And the Marilyn Files remain open.

Epilogue

"If you've noticed in Hollywood, where millions
and billions of dollars have been made, there aren't
really any kind of monuments or museums. . . . nobody
left anything behind, they took it, they grabbed it
and they ran. . . ."

— Marilyn Monroe, 1962

Author's Postscript

As this book goes to press, I believe that we have definitely established that Marilyn Monroe was murdered.

The official verdict of probable suicide is ludicrous, and nothing more than an expedient excuse for the cover-up operation. This book explains in great detail, and with an objective viewpoint, all the circumstances leading up to Marilyn's death. All of the participants are named and described, every possible scenario is outlined and explained. The full array of testimony and evidence is presented, including the documents themselves. As the title indicates, these are *The Marilyn Files*, indeed.

Although this book is as close as one can get to an indictment, I cannot be the judge and jury in this case. But I do have an opinion. And like a tough prosecutor—who also happens to be an author—I am entitled to share that opinion with you. It is my right to do that; and yours to accept it or deny it, or offer a valid argument, the American system of due process.

Due process is but one of the many things Robert F. Kennedy had on his mind when he arrived in Los Angeles to meet with Marilyn Monroe on Saturday, August 4, 1962. These streams of thought totally enveloped RFK and Marilyn in a bizarre pattern. RFK was heavily involved with both the CIA and the Mafia simultaneously: a tricky maneuver at best, but Bobby's forte.

He was masterminding the CIA's Operation Mongoose, the plan to liquidate Fidel Castro by using mobster hitmen (including such notable partners as Sam Giancana and John

Roselli). At the very same time RFK was pushing his Hoffa Squad to get Jimmy Hoffa in jail and accelerate the anti-racketeering program he designed. Bobby had no problem in hiring the enemy to do his dirty tricks while actively planning their destruction.

Bobby was also feuding with J. Edgar Hoover, while utilizing him and the FBI in a variety of ways. Hoover's files and tapes would prove very revealing, and would alert the Kennedy brothers to the efficiency of Hoover's snooping. Marilyn would be labeled a security risk. Her affairs with both JFK and RFK were documented and filed, for reference.

The dualities and intensities of these concerns, along with Bobby's tendency to be a cold and ruthless executive when necessary, did not bode well for Marilyn's health . . . especially when RFK viewed a security risk as a national and personal matter.

On Monday, August 6, in San Francisco, RFK had a private dinner with John McCone, head of the CIA. They had much to discuss. Meanwhile, back in Los Angeles, the coroner's staff and toxicologists were completing their autopsy of Marilyn Monroe . . . and what had been a mag-nificent female creature had become a set of body parts and chemical analyses.

Until we get some last pieces of evidence, and force the testimony of witnesses who have refused to cooperate—and that is one of the primary goals of *The Marilyn Files*—this is what I think happened on the night of August 4, 1962:

If you ask who would gain the most by Marilyn's death— all motives and priorities considered—the answer is the Kennedys—JFK and RFK specifically. Bobby had good reason to be concerned about Marilyn's state of mind on August 4. She knew too much about him, his brother, and some extremely sensitive political issues that were explosive enough to threaten the Kennedy administration and, perhaps, ignite an international incident. What Marilyn knew was enough to destroy two careers, and permanently damage a great political dynasty.

Marilyn was not a woman to be ignored, or punished. Not any more. She had survived a number of romantic failures and marriages; she understood that relationships had to end. But she was not a woman to be spurned, or dumped. Not this time. Not after all the promises. Not without an explanation.

Unreturned phone calls were the last insult. Bobby sensed that Marilyn's threats were very real. A Marilyn Monroe press conference would receive international attention. What she would say could make every front page. It would be a disaster beyond calculation. For the U.S. Government. For the Kennedy family.

Dr. Greenson couldn't calm her down. Peter Lawford wasn't able to handle it. Bobby had to take matters into his own hands. With typical Kennedy bravado, he would see Marilyn himself and somehow stall her or otherwise solve the problem. When he confronted her and was unable to reach any kind of compromise, his options were few. And Bobby was a very controlling personality; a man capable of great anger. He was the attorney general of the United States, after all. How could this woman be holding him hostage? What would the family say?

Whether his relationship with Marilyn was deeply romantic, or a wild and risky dalliance, is difficult to know. Bobby was not known to be the womanizer his brother and father were. What is important, though, is what Marilyn thought. And she believed all the sweet and beautiful promises Bobby told her.

So here we have two of the most important and colorful personalities of that time on a collision course—with anger and passion barely contained. One wrong word or action could trigger an unstoppable series of consequences.

The meeting did take place. Bobby did visit Marilyn at her home that evening of August 4. And their words were not kind, but cruel. A violent argument turned physical. Marilyn had to be stopped. Silenced. Nothing temporary would be acceptable. A postponed press conference was just that, postponed, and then likely to become even more volatile. Too much was at stake to gamble with a Hollywood blonde—even Marilyn Monroe—and what she might say or do.

Bobby had been toughened by his experience in the Justice Department. Only recently he had been dealing with the likes of Hoffa and Castro. He knew the CIA solution to problems. He knew where to get professional help at a moment's notice. He recognized when an escalating situation had to have damage control applied. It was the logical move. It was the politically correct move.

Bobby, however, didn't consider one vital factor—Marilyn's immediate reaction and her resolve. The ignition point was reached. Damage control was not enough. Whatever Bobby expected he was not prepared for an enraged Marilyn who would not be reasonable...who would again threaten him. The point of no return had been reached. Marilyn had to be silenced permanently if necessary.

And it did become necessary—for country, family and self. A tough but purely logical decision by the Attorney General.

The decision was quickly implemented with professional assistance...by men who were trained for such assignments; the dirty tricks of diplomacy.

RFK knew the job was in capable hands. He gave his approval. He had no choice and Jack agreed.

After making sure the deed was done, he raced to the airport for his late flight to San Francisco where he would join his wife and children and attend church in the morning.

Back at the house, there would be a beehive of activity in setting the scene, removing all important papers, sanitizing the area, rehearsing the official story, giving all the cast of characters their scripts and roles.

There was a show to produce. Once again Marilyn was the star. But it was a tragedy and she never saw the reviews.

By the time the police arrived, everything was in order. Every last fingerprint was erased, even Marilyn's. Clothes and linens were washed and dried. Any problematic evidence was flushed.

There were several teams that performed that night. The first team, specialists from the CIA and Secret Service—loyal to their leader—completed their mission regarding Marilyn and then removed all materials they could find that could embarrass or compromise the Kennedys or the government. The next team, doctors and publicists, made sure that all the medical and personal angles were covered in an appropriate way. The scene had to make sense for both the police and the media.

Then the legal and corporate types had their turn at checking everything. It was a very busy house that night. Many people had many ideas on what happened and what to do next. In this barely controlled chaos mistakes could happen—and did.

Bobby Kennedy's team did their job and left swiftly. Professionalism at its best. But those who had to handle things from that point on were working at a disadvantage. They all knew something different. The need to know was part of the cover-up plan. In the confusion and the rush of time not everyone played the game according to plan. Remember, this was a highly-charged event, and many of the players were amateurs. Not everyone knew the same level of information. It became a cover-up of the cover-up.

And then the LAPD arrived, and the clock was ticking. It still is. Jack Clemmons' story still stands as the one untainted testimony. He was the first LAPD officer to arrive. Everything that was done or said before and after his report is colored by the whitewash of successive cover-up stories. Now, thirty years later, the whitewash is peeling, layer by layer. We are finally getting to the raw surface.

Yes, in my opinion, Robert F. Kennedy killed Marilyn Monroe.

No, he didn't apply the final touch...that fatal dose of Nembutal. But like the general he was, he gave the command. Marilyn died.

Impossible, you say? So was the Bay of Pigs. So was the assassination of John F. Kennedy; the assassination of Robert F. Kennedy. So was the disappearance of Jimmy Hoffa; the murder of Sam Giancana; the murder of John Roselli. And there's more, as a study of the unholy alliance of the Mafia and the CIA illustrates. Generals and presidents don't ever have to pull the trigger or push the button. They just make the decision—and live or die with it, as we have seen. That is the picture and the frame. It is almost complete now. We only need a few more pieces to the puzzle and another conspiracy of lies can finally be filed away.

Robert F. Slatzer

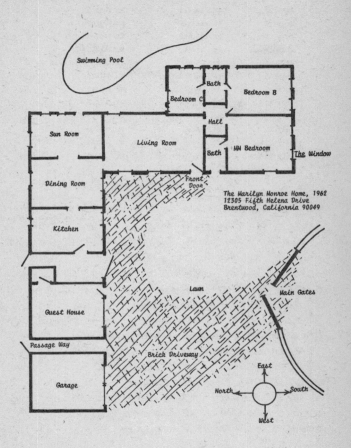

Swimming Pool

Bath

Bedroom C

Bedroom B

Sun Room

Living Room

Hall

Dining Room

Bath

MM Bedroom

The Window

Kitchen

Front Door

The Marilyn Monroe Home, 1962
12305 Fifth Helena Drive
Brentwood, California 90049

Lawn

Guest House

Main Gates

Passage Way

Brick Driveway

Garage

East

North

South

West

June 20	Brooklyn, N.Y.	#75-1367
June 20	Brooklyn, N.Y.	Mrs. Rosten - Collect
June 25	Washington	RE 7-8200
July 2	Washington	RE 7-8200
July 2	Washington	RE 7-8200
July 6	San Diego	GR 6-1890
July 6	San Diego	DiMaggio - Collect
July 9	New York City	EL 5-2288
July 9	New York	MU 3-6522
July 16	Washington	RE 7-8200
July 16	New York City	CR 3-7792
July 17	Fullerton	TR 1-3190
July 17	Washington	RE 7-8200
July 17	Washington	RE 7-8200

LONG DISTANCE

MUNROE PHONE CALLS —
FROM TWO PHONES
4761890   & 472X4830

P O BOX 1647:
6400 Sunset:
Hollywood:

	7/18	NYC	BR 91195	3 "	
	7/23	WASH (D.C)	RE 78200	1 "	
	7/28	NYC	PL 92497	10 "	*Kennedy?*
4830	7/30	N.Y.C.	LA 41000	1 "	
	7/30	WASH (D.C)	RE 78200	8 "	
	7/30	BKLN	TR 51367	13 "	
	7/31	NYC	TR 72212	11 "	
	8/3	BKLN	TR 51367	32 "	
	8/4	ANANE	GR 61890	5 "	

Part of the missing telephone records documenting Marilyn's calls to
RFK at the Justice Department (RE7-8200). . .calls were made from
both of Marilyn's two telephone lines.

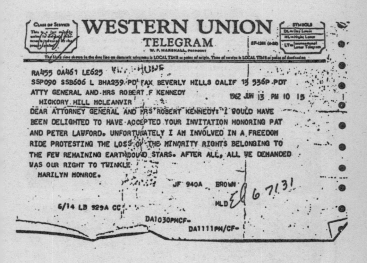

WESTERN UNION

TELEGRAM

W. P. MARSHALL, PRESIDENT

The filing time shown in the date line on domestic telegrams is LOCAL TIME at point of origin. Time of receipt is LOCAL TIME at point of destination

RA455 OA461 LE625

SSP090 SSB606 L BHA259 PD FAX BEVERLY HILLS CALIF 13 536P PDT

ATTY GENERAL AND MRS ROBERT F KENNEDY   1962 JUN 13 PM 10 15

  HICKORY HILL MCLEANVIR

DEAR ATTORNEY GENERAL AND MRS ROBERT KENNEDY: I WOULD HAVE

BEEN DELIGHTED TO HAVE ACCEPTED YOUR INVITATION HONORING PAT

AND PETER LAWFORD. UNFORTUNATELY I AM INVOLVED IN A FREEDOM

RIDE PROTESTING THE LOSS OF THE MINORITY RIGHTS BELONGING TO

THE FEW REMAINING EARTHBOUND STARS. AFTER ALL, ALL WE DEMANDED

WAS OUR RIGHT TO TWINKLE.

  MARILYN MONROE.

                        JF 940A   BROWN

                                   HLD

  6/14 LB 929A CC

              DA1030PMCF

                  DA1111PM/CF

Marilyn's ironic telegram to the Robert F. Kennedys, sent only a
matter of weeks before her death.

NY 100-57673

An article in the July 3, 1956 edition of
the "Daily Worker" reflected that ARTHUR MILLER and
MARILYN MONROE were married in a civil ceremony at
White Plains, New York, on Friday, (June 29, 1956),
and were subsequently remarried at Katonah, New York, on
July 1, 1956, in the Jewish faith.

An article in the June 21, 1956, edition of
the "New York Journal American", a daily newspaper, captioned
"House To Quiz MILLER On Passport Dispute", reflected
that ARTHUR MILLER, Broadway playwright, would interrupt
his romance with Hollywood's MARILYN MONROE, "today" to
appear before the House Committee on Un-American Activities
(HCUA). According to the article, MILLER was scheduled to
testify on his "passport hassle" with the United States
State Department and further that the members were
certain to quiz MILLER on his alleged links with "some
29 organizations cited as Communist fronts by the
House Committee on Un-American Activities or the United
States Attorney General."

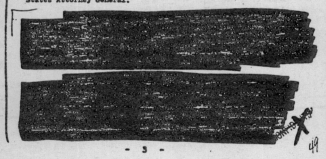

- 3 -

Excerpts from FBI reports indicating surveillance of Arthur Miller
during 1956, and describing concerns regarding Marilyn Monroe's
involvement with known Communists (4 pages).

NY 100-57673

INFORMANTS   ADMINISTRATIVE PAGE

Identity of Source	Date of Activity And/or Description of Information	Date Received	Agent to whom Furnished	File Number where Located

Careful consideration has been given to each source concealed and T symbols were utilized only in those instances where the identity of the sources must be concealed.

ADMINISTRATIVE

_____ received an anonymous telephone call from an unidentified male during which he stated that ARTHUR MILLER had been and still was a member of the CP and was their cultural front man. The anonymous caller said that MILLER's religious marriage ceremony to actress MARILYN MONROE and MILLER's public statements were so much cover up. _____ according to the anonymous caller, MARILYN MONROE had drifted into the Communist orbit and money from MARILYN MONROE Productions was finding its way into the CP. This source stated that MARILYN MONROE Productions was filled with Communists.

Mrs Arthur Asher Miller

This information is being placed in the Administrative portion of this report because it appears to be received by this Bureau second or third hand, and is suitable for general information only.

N.Y.
EٰNGLEC
CALIF

5

OSR

JUDITH KILEEN CAMPBELL
Apartment 201
1200 North Flores
Los Angeles, California
Telephone No. OL 6-0055

b7C

b7C

b7C

     As set out above in this report, on January 11, 1962,
ROSSELLI and   were observed leaving
Romanoff's Restaurant in Beverly Hills with a blonde woman.
This woman and ROSSELLI entered the Ford Thunderbird bearing
California license VPC 488, which is registered to JUDITH E.
CAMPBELL, 1200 South Flores, Los Angeles, California.

92-3267-118

FBI report on blonde woman seen with John Roselli, a top Mafia
figure in Hollywood. Note that the car belonged to Judith Campbell,
better known as Judith Exner, whose affair with JFK was exposed in
1975. Was the blonde MM?

COUNTY OF LOS ANGELES

OFFICE OF CORONER

AUTOPSY CHECK SHEET

Name _Marilyn Monroe_   File # _81128_   Date _8/5/62_   Time ____

EXTERNAL EXAM		**PERITONEUM**		**BRAIN Wt**
Sex		Fluid		Dura _1440_
Race		Adhes		Fluid
Age		**LIVER Wt** _1890_		Ventric
Height		Caps		Vessels
Weight		Lobul		Ears
Hair		Fibros		Nasal Sin
Eyes		G B		**PITUITARY**
Sclera		Calc		
Teeth		Bile ducts		
Mouth _Lips typ_		**SPLEEN Wt** _190_		
Tongue _89.7_		Color		
Nose		Consist		
Chest		Caps		**TOXICOLOGY**
Breasts		Malpig		
Abdomen		**PANCREAS**		
Scar		**ADRENALS**		**SECTIONS**
Genital		**KIDNEYS Wt** _350_		
Edema		Caps		
Skin		Cortex		
Decub		Vessels		
HEART Wt _300_		Pelvis		**GROSS IMPRESSION**
Perfored _62_		Ureter		
Hypert _1.1_		**BLADDER**		
Dilat _1.0_		**GENITALIA**		
Muscle _65_		Prost		
Valves _9.5_		Testes		
Coroner _7_		Uterus		
AORTA		Tubes		
VESSELS		Over		
LUNGS Wt		**OESOPHAGUS**		
R _465_		**STOMACH**		
L _420_		**DUOD & SM INT** _20 cc_		
Adhes		**APPENDIX**		
Fluid		**LARGE INT**		
Atelectasis		**ABDOM NODES**		
Oedema		**SKELETON**		
Congest		Spine		
Consol		Marrow		
Bronchi				
Nodes				
PHARYNX				
TRACHEA				
THYROID				
THYMUS				

Deputy Medical Examiner

COUNTY OF LOS ANGELES
OFFICE OF CORONER
BODY FULL LENGTH ANTERIOR

Name Marilyn Monroe   Date 8/5/62   File # 8 1127

no needle mark.

R

3" long surgical scar

5" long surgical scar

L

M.D.
Deputy Medical Examiner.

76A69 - Gb 3-59

NAME _Marilyn Monroe_ Date _8/5/62_ File # _81128_

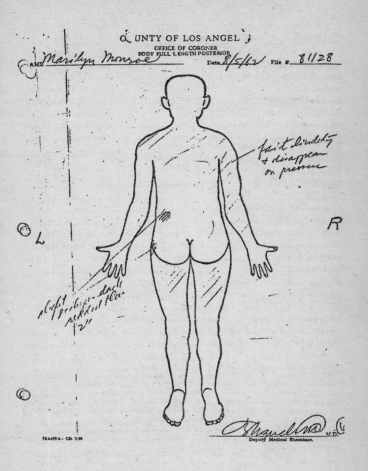

faint lividity
+ disappear
on pressure

L   R

slight post-mort
nakint tear
2"

Deputy Medical Examiner. M.D.

Tape # 292. Start 478 End 496

CORONER
COUNTY OF LOS ANGELES
CASE REPORT

Case No. 81128
Taken by CRONK

Post Mortem at Coroner   Crypt # 33   Request of

NAME MARLYN MONROE   AGE 36   Sex F   Race C   Date and Time of Death 8-5-62 3:30 A.M.

Place of Death 12305 Fifth Helena Dr. - Brentwood   Pronounced Dead by Dr. Eullesee

Reported by Sgt. Clemmons   Address W. L.A.   Phone 876-1890

Date 8-5-62   Time 5:25 P.M. (4:25 A.M. Brush)   Phone at Scene

Police Investigation ☐ Yes ☐ No   Police Agency

Officer _____ Date _____ Time _____ A.M. P.M.   Supplemental Request

REPORTED AS:
☐ Natural
☐ Accident
☐ Suicide ?
☐ Homicide
☐ Undetermined

BARBS - OVERDOSE
Dec. was removed from Bed - Covered with a sheet & Blanket

Residence of Deceased SAME

Occupation Actress   Religion

Employer Movie Studio   Soc. Sec. ? Number: Military No.?   Vet.?

Next of Kin Gladys Baker   Address _____ Phone

Relationship Mother   Notified by _____ at _____ A.M. P.M.

Weight 117   Ins. Height 65½   In. Hair Blonde   Teeth U own L own   Eyes Blue   Mustache None

Tattoo or Deformity None Noted   Condition of Body Discolored

Prints ☒ Yes ☐ No   Sent: FBI _____ CII _____ FBI No. _____ L.A. No.

Personal I.D. By: _____ Address

City _____ Relationship _____ Phone _____ Initials and Date

Brought in by Dambacher - Pace   Date 8-5-62   9:00 A.M. P.M.   On. Mortuary   Door Sealed ☒ Yes ☐ No

Property ☐ Yes ☒ No   P.A. Case ☐ Yes ☒ No   P.A. Notified by _____ Date _____ Invest.

Remains Removed by Chase & Suese   Release Received 8-6-62   Receipt # 677555

Released to Westwood Village   on 8-6-62   By L J M

INQUEST ☐ Yes ☐ No   Held on _____ Inquest Deputy

Verdict 8-7-62 A - Noguchi - 8-5-62

CERTIFICATE ISSUED: Pending 8-7-62 By DKS   FINAL _____ By

REMARKS: obtained the following from Guy Hackett Westwood Village mortuary. Dec. was found at approx. 3:30 by Housekeeper Eunice Murray, who got up to check on Dec. and she found the Bed Rm. Door locked. She called Dr. Engleberg who came over immediately. The Dr. took the peek from the fire place & Broke the Bed room window to gain admittance; Dr. pronounced death at 3:35 pm. The mortuary att. stated all doors & windows were sealed. Dec. Mother is apparently in a San. Body is discolored but no evidence of any trauma.   Chase

See above   Deputy

Name Marilyn Monroe   CORONER   Case No. 81128

Date 8/5/62 Time 10:30 1962   COUNTY OF LOS ANGELES   OUT to 8/6/62   Dr. T. Noguchi

MEDICAL REPORT

☒ INVESTIGATION ☒ AUTOPSY ☒ PENDING ☒ FINAL ON 8/6/62 8-7-62

CAUSE OF DEATH: LABORATORY

acute Barbiturate poisoning

Due to:

ingestion of overdose

Other Conditions:

☐ Micro.
☐ Neuro.
☐ Bact.
☐ Photo By. R✓
☐ Date
☒ Toxicology
  ☒ Alcohol
  ☒ Barbs.
  ☐ C.O.
  ☐ Too Long for Alcohol
  ☐ Other—Explain Below

SPECIMENS SUBMITTED

refer to supplementary 8/23/62

Probable   Liver, Kidney, Stomach & contents, urine & blood

MODE OF DEATH ☐ NATURAL ☐ ACCIDENT ☒ SUICIDE ☐ HOMICIDE ☐ ABORTION ☐ UNDETERMINED

Evidence of Injury ☐ Yes ☒ No Describe:
Injury at work ☐ Yes ☒ No
Place of Injury

MORTUARY RECORD Body removed to Corosin Dept by Gall Date Time 9 P.M.

Embalmed by Maxwell License No. 3673 Blood Sample Taken ☐ No ☒ Yes

Date Time A.M. P.M. By order of Crypt No. 33

Medical Evidence ☒ Yes ☐ No Described Chloral Hydrate Body Temp N/A Taken By

Embalmer's Observations Nembutal Condition of Body Discolored

Clothing ☐ Yes ☒ No

PHYSICAL DESCRIPTION Age 36 Sex Fe Race Cau Complexion Med Wt 117 lbs. Ht 5½ in

Hair Blonde Teeth Good Eyes Blue Pupils Norm. Scars, amputations, beard

Appliances on body None   Tattoo or deformity None Noted

HISTORY Hospitalized ☐ Yes ☒ No Hospital Report ☐ Yes ☒ No Hospital No.

In Bed at Residence   Hospital From Time A.M. P.M. TO Time A.M. P.M.

For Poss. overdose Barbs.

Location of pain   How long

Vomiting   Medication Administered

Unconscious   Convulsions

Supplied By Mrs. Murray Hackett   Address Westwood Village mort   Phone

Physician Engelberg   Address   Phone

Diagnosis or Comment

MEDICAL EXAMINER'S COMMENTS:
Information taken by Gall

See Autopsy report & diagram

A - MRC - 8-5-62

T. Noguchi M.D.

REPORT OF CHEMICAL ANALYSIS
LOS ANGELES COUNTY CORONER
Toxicology Laboratory
Hall of Justice
Los Angeles, California

File No. 81128   I

Name of Deceased   Marilyn Monroe

Date Submitted   August 6, 1962   Time   8 A.M.

Autopsy Surgeon   T. Noguchi, M.D.

Material Submitted:

Blood x	Liver x	Stomach x
Brain	Lung	Lavage
Femur	Spleen	Urine x
Kidney x	Sternum	Gall bladder
Drugs x	Chemicals	Intestines x

Test Desired: Ethanol, Barbiturates

Laboratory Findings:

Blood: Ethanol   Absent

Blood: Barbiturates   4.5 mg. per cent
Phenobarbital is absent

Drugs:
(1) 27 capsules, #19295, 6-7-62, Librium, 5 mgm. #50
(2) 17 capsules, 20201, 7-10-62, Librium, 10 mgm. #100
(3) 26 tablets, #20569, 7-25-62, Sulfathallidine, #36
(4) Empty container, #20858, 8-3-62, Nembutal, 1½gr.#25
(5) 10 green capsules, #20570, 7-31-62, Chloral Hydrate, 0.5 gm. #50 (Refill: 7-25-62 - original)
(6) Empty container, #456099, 11-4-61, Noludar, #50
(7) 32 pink capsules in a container without label
Phenergan, #20857, 8-3-62, 25 mg. #25

Examined By _R.J. Abernethy_ Head Toxicologist. Date   August 6, 1962

REPORT OF CHEMICAL ANALYSIS
LOS ANGELES COUNTY CORONER
Toxicology Laboratory
Hall of Justice
Los Angeles, California

File No. 81128   I

Name of Deceased   Marilyn Monroe   1st Supplement

Date Submitted   August 6, 1962   Time   8 A.M.

Autopsy Surgeon   T. Noguchi, M.D.

Material Submitted:

Blood x	Liver x	Stomach x
Brain	Lung	Lavage
Femur	Spleen	Urine x
Kidney x	Sternum	Gall bladder
Drugs x	Chemicals	Intestines x

Test Desired   Chloral Hydrate, Pentobarbital

Laboratory Findings:

Blood: Chloral Hydrate   8 mg. per cent

Liver: Pentobarbital   13.0 mg. per cent

Drugs: Correction - delete #7 on original report of August 6 and add:

         (7) 32 peach-colored tablets marked MSD in prescription type vial without label.

         (8) 24 white tablets #20857, 8-3-62, Phenergan, 25 mg. #25

(SEE ORIGINAL REPORT)

Examined By *R. J. Abernethy* Head Toxicologist. Date August 13, 1962

One of three different Certificates for Death signed by Lionel Grandison, this one lists cause as Probable Suicide.

I performed an autopsy on the body of   MARILYN MONROE

at the Los Angeles County Coroner's Mortuary, Hall of Justice, Los Angeles,

and from the anatomic findings and pertinent history I ascribe the death to:

ACUTE BARBITURATE POISONING

DUE TO: INGESTION OF OVERDOSE

(final 8/27/62)

ANATOMICAL SUMMARY

EXTERNAL EXAMINATION:

1. Lavidity of face and chest with
   slight ecchymosis of the left side
   of the back and left hip.

2. Surgical scar, right upper quadrant
   of the abdomen.

3. Suprapubic surgical scar.

RESPIRATORY SYSTEM:

1. Pulmonary congestion and minimal
   edema.

LIVER AND BILIARY SYSTEM:

1. Surgical absence of gallbladder.

2. Acute passive congestion of liver.

UROGENITAL SYSTEM:

1. Congestion of kidneys.

DIGESTIVE SYSTEM:

1. Marked congestion of stomach with
   petechial mucosal hemorrhage.

Dr. Noguchi's detailed Coroner's Report (6 pages).

2. Absence of appendix.

3. Congestion and purplish discoloration
   of the colon.

EXTERNAL EXAMINATION:

The unembalmed body is that of a 36-year-old
well-developed, well-nourished Caucasian
female weighing 117 pounds and measuring
65½ inches in length. The scalp is covered
with bleached blond hair. The eyes are
blue. The fixed lividity is noted in the
face, neck, chest, upper portions of arms
and the right side of the abdomen. The
faint lividity which disappears upon pressure
is noted in the back and posterior aspect
of the arms and legs. A slight ecchymotic
area is noted in the left hip and left side
of lower back. The breast shows no significant lesion. There is a horizontal 3-inch
long surgical scar in the right upper
quadrant of the abdomen. A suprapubic
surgical scar measuring 5 inches in length
is noted.

The conjunctivae are markedly congested;
however, no ecchymosis or petechiae are
noted. The nose shows no evidence of
fracture. The external auditory canals
are not remarkable. No evidence of trauma
is noted in the scalp, forehead, cheeks,
lips or chin. The neck shows no evidence
of trauma. Examination of the hands and
nails shows no defects. The lower extremities show no evidence of trauma.

BODY CAVITY:

The usual Y-shaped incision is made to
open the thoracic and abdominal cavities
The pleural and abdominal cavities contain

no excess of fluid or blood. The mediastinum
shows no shifting or widening. The diaphragm
is within normal limits. The lower edge
of the liver is within the costal margin.
The organs are in normal position and
relationship.

CARDIOVASCULAR SYSTEM:

The heart weighs 300 grams. The pericardial
cavity contains no excess of fluid. The
epicardium and pericardium are smooth and
glistening. The left ventricular wall
measures 1.1 cm. and the right 0.2 cm.
The papillary muscles are not hypertrophic.
The chordae tendineae are not thickened or
shortened. The valves have the usual number
of leaflets which are thin and pliable.
The tricuspid valve measures 10 cm., the
pulmonary valve 6.5 cm., mitral valve 9.5
cm. and aortic valve 7 cm. in circumference.
There is no septal defect. The foramen
ovale is closed.

The coronary arteries arise from their usual
location and are distributed in normal
fashion. Multiple sections of the anterior
descending branch of the left coronary artery
with a 5 mm.. interval demonstrate a patent
lumen throughout. The circumflex branch
and the right coronary artery also demonstrate
a patent lumen. The pulmonary artery contains
no thrombus.

The aorta has a bright yellow smooth intima.

RESPIRATORY SYSTEM:

The right lung weighs 465 grams and the left
420 grams. Both lungs are moderately congested
with some edema. The surface is dark red
with mottling. The posterior portion of the
lungs shows severe congestion. The tracheo-
bronchial tree contains no aspirated material
or blood. Multiple sections of the lungs

show congestion and edematous fluid exuding from the cut surface. No consolidation or suppuration is noted. The mucosa of the larynx is grayish white.

LIVER AND BILIARY SYSTEM:

The liver weighs 1890 grams. The surface is dark brown and smooth. There are marked adhesions through the omentum and abdominal wall in the lower portion of the liver as the gallbladder has been removed. The common duct is widely patent. No calculus or obstructive material is found. Multiple sections of the liver show slight accentuation of the lobular pattern; however, no hemorrhage or tumor is found.

HEMIC AND LYMPHATIC SYSTEM:

The spleen weighs 190 grams. The surface is dark red and smooth. Section shows dark red homogeneous firm cut surface. The malpighian bodies are not clearly identified. There is no evidence of lymphadenopathy. The bone marrow is dark red in color.

ENDOCRINE SYSTEM:

The adrenal glands have the usual architectural cortex and medulla. The thyroid glands are of normal size, color and consistency.

URINARY SYSTEM:

The kidneys together weigh 350 grams. Their capsules can be stripped without difficulty. Dissection shows a moderately congested parenchyma. The cortical surface is smooth. The pelves and ureters are not dilated or stenosed. The urinary bladder contains approximately 150 cc. of clear straw-colored fluid. The mucosa is not altered.

Marilyn Monroe
81128
Aug. 5, 1962

5

GENITAL SYSTEM:

The external genitalia shows no gross
abnormality. Distribution of the pubic
hair is of female pattern. The uterus
is of the usual size. Multiple sections
of the uterus show the usual thickness of
the uterine wall without tumor nodules.
The endometrium is grayish yellow, measuring
up to 0.2 cm in thickness. No polyp or
tumor is found. The cervix is clear,
showing no nabothian cysts. The tubes are
intact. The openings of the fimbria are
patent. The right ovary demonstrates
recent corpus luteum hæmorrhagicum. The
left ovary shows corpora lutea and albicantia.
A vaginal smear is taken.

DIGESTIVE SYSTEM:

The esophagus has a longitudinal folding
mucosa. The stomach is almost completely
empty. The contents is brownish mucoid
fluid. The volume is estimated to be no
more than 20 cc. No residue of the pills
is noted. A smear made from the gastric
contents and examined under the polarized
microscope shows no refractile crystals.
The mucosa shows marked congestion and
submucosal petechial hemorrhage diffusely.
The duodenum shows no ulcer. The contents
of the duodenum is also examined under
polarized microscope and shows no refractile
crystals. The remainder of the small
intestine shows no gross abnormality. The
appendix is absent. The colon shows
marked congestion and purplish discoloration.
The fecal contents is light brown and formed.
The mucosa shows no discoloration.

The pancreas has a tan lobular architecture.
Multiple sections shows a patent duct.

6

SKELETOMUSCULAR SYSTEM:

The clavicle, ribs, vertebrae and pelvic
bones show no fracture lines. All bones
of the extremities are examined by palpation
showing no evidence of fracture.

HEAD AND CENTRAL NERVOUS SYSTEM:

The brain weighs 1440 grams. Upon reflection
of the scalp there is no evidence of contusion
or hemorrhage. The temporal muscles are
intact. Upon removal of the dura mater the
cerebrospinal fluid is clear. The superficial vessels are slightly congested. The
convolutions of the brain are not flattened.
The contour of the brain is not distorted.
No blood is found in the epidural, subdural
or subarachnoid spaces. Multiple sections
of the brain show the usual symmetrical
ventricles and basal ganglia. Examination
of the cerebellum and brain stem shows no
gross abnormality. Following removal of
the dura mater from the base of the skull
and calvarium no skull fracture is demonstrated.

Liver temperature taken at 10:30 a. m.
registered 89° F.

SPECIMEN:

Unembalmed blood is taken for alcohol and
barbiturate examination. Liver, kidney,
stomach and contents, urine and intestine
are saved for further toxicological study.
A vaginal smear is made.

T. NOGUCHI, M. D.
DEPUTY MEDICAL EXAMINER

TN:ag:G
8-13-62

STATEMENT BY THEODORE J. CURPHEY, M.D.
CHIEF MEDICAL EXAMINER-CORONER
COUNTY OF LOS ANGELES

Now that the final toxicological report and that of the psychiatric consultants have been received and considered, it is my conclusion that the death of Marilyn Monroe was caused by a self-administered overdose of sedative drugs and that the mode of death is probable suicide.

The final toxicological report reveals that the barbiturate, previously reported as a lethal dose, has been positively identified as nembutal by the toxicologist.

In the course of completing his routine examination, the toxicologist, Mr. Raymond Abernathy, discovered in addition to the nembutal present a large dose of chloral hydrate.

Following is the summary report by the Psychiatric Investigative Team which has assisted me in collecting information in this case. This team was headed by Robert Litman, M.D., Norman Farberow, Ph.D., and Norman Tabachnick, M.D.:

"Marilyn Monroe died on the night of August 4th or the early morning of August 5, 1962. Examination by the toxicology laboratory indicates that death was due to a self-administered overdose of sedative drugs. We have been asked, as consultants, to examine the life situation of the deceased and to give an opinion regarding the intent of Miss Monroe when she ingested the sedative drugs which caused her death. From the data obtained, the following points are the most important and relevant:

"Miss Monroe had suffered from psychiatric disturbance for a long time. She experienced severe fears and frequent depressions. Mood changes were abrupt and unpredictable. Among symptoms of disorganization, sleep disturbance was prominent, for which she had been taking sedative drugs for many years. She was thus familiar with and experienced in the use of sedative drugs and well aware of their dangers.

"Recently, one of the main objectives of her psychiatric treatment had been the reduction of her intake of drugs. This has been partially successful during the last two months. She was reported to be following doctor's orders in her use of the drugs; and the amount of drugs found in her home at the time of her death was not unusual.

"In our investigation, we have learned that Miss Monroe had often expressed wishes to give up, to withdraw, and even to die. On more than one occasion in the past, when disappointed and depressed, she had made a suicide attempt using sedative drugs. On these occasions, she had called for help and had been rescued.

"From the information collected about the events of the evening of August 4th, it is our opinion that the same pattern was repeated except for the rescue. It has been our practice with similar information collected in other cases in the past to recommend a certification for such deaths as probable suicide.

"Additional clues for suicide provided by the physical evidence are: (1) the high level of barbiturates and chloral hydrate in the blood which, with other evidence from the autopsy, indicates the probable ingestion of a large amount of the drugs within a short period of time; (2) the completely empty bottle of nembutal, the prescription for which was filled the day before the ingestion of the drugs; and (3) the locked door which was unusual.

"On the basis of all the information obtained it is our opinion that the case is a probable suicide."

RALPH R. GREENSON M D
436 NORTH ROXBURY DRIVE
BEVERLY HILLS · CALIFORNIA

July 15, 1963

Miss Wolf
Gang, Tyre, Rudin & Brown
6400 Sunset Boulevard
Los Angeles, California

Dear Miss Wolf:

The following is an itemized account explaining
the bill for professional services which I sent to the estate
of Marilyn Monroe for the sum of $1400. I shall list below
the date and place where the psychiatric interview took place:

Sunday, July 1	Patient's Home	
Monday, July 2	Office	
Tuesday, July 3	Office	
Wednesday, July 4	Patient's Home	
Thursday, July 5	Office	
Friday, July 6	Office	
Sunday, July 8	Patient's Home	
Monday, July 9	Office	1962
Tuesday, July 10	Office	
Wednesday, July 11	Office	
Thursday, July 12	Office	
Friday, July 13	Office and Patient's Home	
Monday, July 16	Office	
Tuesday, July 17	Office	
Wednesday, July 18	Office	
Thursday, July 19	Office	
Thursday, July 20	Office	
Monday, July 23	Office and Patient's Home	
Tuesday, July 24	Office	
Wednesday, July 25	Office and Patient's Home	
Thursday, July 26	Office	
Friday, July 27	Office	
Monday, July 30	Office	
Tuesday, July 31	Office	
Wednesday, August 1	Office	
Thursday, August 2	Office and Patient's Home	
Friday, August 3	Office	
Saturday, August 4	Patient's Home.	

Explanation: All office visits lasted a minimum of 1½ hours.
All visits to the home were approximately 2 hours in duration.
On those days on which it was stated that the patient was seen

RALPH R. GREENSON M D
436 NORTH ROXBURY DRIVE
BEVERLY HILLS CALIFORNIA

both at the office and at her home, it means there were two
separate visits on that particular day. I had arranged
with Miss Monroe that her fee would be $50. per hour.
However, since she needed a great deal of extra time and
since I did not want her to think I gave her extra time
or made extra visits for monetary reasons, I decided that
I would charge her $50. for every day that I saw her pro-
fessionally. The sum of $1400. therefore represents the
fact that I saw her professionally on 28 days from July 1
through August 4, 1962.

Very truly yours,

Ralph R. Greenson, M.D.

RRG:as

Dr. Ralph Greenson's Creditor's claim against the Estate of Marilyn
Monroe...note the unusually heavy appointment schedule between
doctor and patient...32 visits in less than a month—up to the day
Marilyn died.

Re Death Report of Marilyn Monroe - L.A. Police Dpt.

Death was pronounced on 8/5/62 at 3:45 A.M., Possible Accidental, having taken place between the times of 8/4 and 8/5/62, 3:35 A.M. at residence located at 12305 Fifth Helena Drive, Brentwood, in Rptg. Dist. 814, Report # 62-509 463.

Marilyn Monroe on August 4, 1962 retired to her bedroom at about eight o'clock in the evening; Mrs. Eunice Murray of 933 Ocean Ave., Santa Monica, Calif., 395-7752, J. 61390, noted a light in Miss Monroe's bedroom. Mrs. Murray was not able to arouse Miss Monroe when she went to the door, and when she tried the door again at 3:30 A.M. when she noted the light still on, she found it to be locked. Thereupon Mrs. Murray observed Miss Monroe through the bedroom window and found her lying on her stomach in the bed and the appearance seemed unnatural. Mrs. Murray then called Miss Monroe's psychiatrist, Dr. Ralph R. Greenson of 436 North Roxbury Drive, Beverly Hills, Calif, Cr 14050. Upon entering after breaking the bedroom window, he found Miss Monroe possibly dead. Then he telephoned Dr. Hyman Engelberg of 9730 Wilshire Boulevard, also of Beverly Hills, CR 54366, who came over and then pronounced Miss Monroe dead at 3:35 A.M. Miss Monroe was seen by Dr. Greenson on August 4, 1962 at 5:15 P.M., at her request, because she was not able to sleep. She was being treated by him for about a year. She was made when Dr. Greenson found her dead with the telephone receiver in one hand and lying on her stomach. The Police Department was called and when they arrived they found Miss Monroe in the condition described above, except for the telephone which was removed by Dr. Greenson. There were found to be 15 bottles of medication on the night table and some were prescription. A bottle marked 1½ grains Nembutal, prescription #20853 and prescribed by Dr. Engelberg, and referring to this particular bottle, Dr. Engelberg made the statement that he prescribed a refill for this about two days ago and he further stated there probably should have been about 50 capsules at the time this was refilled by the pharmacist.

Description of Deceased: Female Caucasian, age 36, height 5.4, weight 115 pounds, blonde hair, blue eyes, and slender, medium build.

Occupation: Actress, Probable cause of death: overdose of nembutal, body discovered 8/5/62 at 3:25 A.M. Taken to County Morgue - from there to Westwood Mortuary. Report made by Sgt. R. E. Byron, #2730, W. L.A. Detective Division. Next of kin: Gladys Baker (Mother).

Coroner's office notified. The body was removed from premises by Westwood Village Mortuary.

(8/5/62 11 AM WLA hf - J. R. Brukles 5d29)

Original LAPD Death Reports, Follow-up Reports and Re-Interview
Reports completed in August of 1962 (5 pages).

TYPE CRIME				ADDITIONAL MAJOR CRIMES COMMITTED—TYPE INCIDENT				
DEATH REPORT								
DATE AND TIME OCCURRED 8-4/5-62 8P/3:35A				DATE AND TIME OF THIS REPORT 8-6-62 4:15P		LOCATION OF OCCURRENCE 12305 Fifth Helena Dr.		DETL. DIST. 824
VICTIM'S NAME (as listed on orig. report) MONROE, Marilyn				LIC OR INVOLVED VEHICLE		CONNECTING PROPERTY REPORTS		
Property Recovery		TOTAL		PARTIAL	NONE	Additional Property	LOSS THIS REPORT $	
Property Disposition		BOOKED		RELEASED BY DEPT			RECOVERY	
Case Status	REPORT UNFOUNDED		CLEARED	RECLASSIFY TO.			MAINTAIN WANTS IN PROPERTY FILE?	YES NO
	COMPLAINT REFUSED	X	INVEST CONT					
PERSON(S) ARRESTED		LA OR J NO		SEX DESC AGE HGT. WGT. HAIR EYES			RTA DATE CHARGE	CRT. DIV.

(1) EXPLAIN INVESTIGATION PROGRESS AND STATUS (2) DESCRIBE ANY CHANGE IN M.O. (3) WHEN VICTIM AND/OR WITNESSES LISTED IN CRIME REPORT HAVE NOT BEEN INTERVIEWED, GIVE REASON. (4) IF ADDITIONAL PROPERTY LOSS INVOLVED, ITEMIZE, DESCRIBE AND SHOW VALUE, LISTING ALL SERIAL NUMBERS. IF PARTIAL RECOVERY, LIST PROPERTY RECOVERED, USING ITEM NUMBER, DESCRIPTION (SERIAL NO., MONOGRAMS, ETC.) AND VALUE AS IT APPEARS ON INITIAL REPORT. EXPLAIN ANY CHARGES FOUND NECESSARY TO PROPERTY DESCRIPTIONS DEVELOPED DURING INVESTIGATION

ITEM NO	PERSON REPORTING OR ADDITIONAL PERSONS INTERVIEWED	RESIDENCE ADDRESS	CITY	RESIDENCE PHONE	BUSINESS PHONE

Upon reinterviewing both Dr. Ralph R. Greenson (Wit #1 and Dr. Hyman Engelberg (Wit #2) they both agree to the following time sequence of their actions.

Dr. Greenson received a phone call from Mrs Murray (reporting person) at 3:30A, 8-5-62 stating that she was unable to get into Miss Monroe's bedroom and the light was on. He told her to pound on the door and look in the window and call him back. At 3:35A, Mrs Murray called back and stated Miss Monroe was laying on the bed with the phone in her hand and looked strange. Dr. Greenson was dressed by this time, left for deceased residence which is about one mile away. He also told Mrs Murray to call Dr. Engelberg.

Dr. Greenson arrived at deceased house at about 3:40A. He broke the window pane and entered through the window and removed the phone from her hand.

Rigor Mortis had set in. At 3:50A, Dr. Engelberg arrived and pronounced Miss Monroe dead. The two doctors talked for a few moments. They both believe that it was about 4A when Dr. Engelberg called the Police Department.

A check with the Complaint Board and DLA Desk, indicates that the call was received at 4:25A. Miss Monroe's phone, GR 61890 has been checked and no toll calls were made during the hours of this occurrence. Phone number 472-4830 is being checked at the present time.

DATE AND TIME TYPED	DIVISION	CLERK	INTERVIEWING OFFICER(S) SI	SER. NO	DIVISION/DET	PERSON REPLACING REGRATION(?)	
			R E BYRON 2730 WLA D			X	

DEATH REPORT

DATE AND TIME REPORTED TO P.D. 8-5-62 3:55	**TYPE** (TRAFFIC, NATURAL, SUICIDE, ACCIDENTAL, HOMICIDE, ETC.) Possible accidental
DR No. 63-509 463	
DATE AND TIME DEATH OCCURRED 8-5-62 3:35A	**LOCATION OF OCCURRENCE** 12305 Fifth Helena Drive	**REPORTING DISTRICT** 814
LOCATION OF ORIGINAL ILLNESS OR INJURY Bedroom	**CITY**	**REPORTING DISTRICT**	**TYPE OF ORIGINAL REPORT**
NAME OF DECEASED MONROE, Marilyn	**RESIDENCE ADDRESS** at	**CITY**	**BUSINESS ADDRESS**	**CITY**

CAPTION DECEASED	SEX Female	DESCENT Cauc	AGE 36	HEIGHT 5-4	WEIGHT 115	HAIR blnd	EYES Blu	BUILD slender	COMPLEXION med

IDENTIFYING MARKS AND CHARACTERISTICS; CLOTHING AND JEWELRY WORN

OCCUPATION OF DECEASED Actress	**PROBABLE CAUSE OF DEATH** Menental	**REASON** (SUICIDE, ILLNESS, PRIVACY, ETC.)
DATE AND TIME DECEASED DISCOVERED 8-5-62 3:25AM	**DISCOVERED BY** (NAME) Eunice Murray	**REMOVED BY** (NAME OF MORTUARY) Westwood Mortuary
RELATIVES NOTIFIED BY Not	**INVESTIGATIVE DIVISIONS OR UNITS NOTIFIED** (DIVISION OF UNIT AND PERSON) Sgt Byron, #2730 West L. A. Detective Division

	RELATIONSHIP	RESIDENCE ADDRESS	CITY	RESIDENCE PHONE	X	BUSINESS PHONE	
NEAREST RELATIVE GLADYS BAKER, (Mother)		Unk					
PERSON REPORTING DEATH TO POLICE DEPARTMENT Mrs. Eunice Murry					X		
PERSON DISCOVERING DECEASED					X		
PERSON IDENTIFYING DECEASED					X		
NAME Ralph R. Greenson Dr. Hyman Engelberg					CR 14060 CR 54366	X	
PERSON IN ATTENDANCE See above		**BUSINESS ADDRESS**	CITY	RESIDENCE PHONE	X	BUSINESS PHONE	X

RECONSTRUCT THE CIRCUMSTANCES SURROUNDING THE DEATH (2) **DESCRIBE PHYSICAL EVIDENCE, LOCATION FOUND, AND GIVE DISPOSITION.**

Deceased retired on 8-4-62, at about 8PM. At approximately 12AM, R/P observed light in bedroom of deceased. She (R/P) went to the door, but was unable to arouse deceased. At about 3:30 a.m., she noticed the light was still on and upon trying the door found it locked. R/P went to the bedroom window and observed deceased lying in bed in what she termed and seemed unnatural. She (R/P) called Mr. #1, who is deceased's psychiatrist. Upon arrival he broke the bedroom window and upon entering found deceased possibly dead. He then called deceased on 8-4-62, 5:15... at her request, because she was unable to sleep. Dr. Greenson had seen it #2, who came and pronounced deceased dead at 3:25AM. Dr. Greenson had been treating her for acute one year when he found deceased she was nude, lying on her stomach, with phone receiver in her hand. The Police Dept. was notified and found deceased in above described condition with the exception of phone which had been moved by Mt #1. On the night stand there were about 15 bottles of medication, some of which were prescription. One bottle with prescription number 20853, marked 1½ grains Menutal, prescribed by Dr Engelberg. Dr. Engelberg stated that he had prescribed a refill about two days ago, that there probably should have been about 50 capsules at time of refill.

Coroner's Office Notified. Deceased Village Mortuary assigned and removed

DATE AND TIME TYPED 8-5-62 11:30 A.M. bf	**DIVISION**	**CLERK**	**INTERVIEWING OFFICERS** Sgt R E Byron 2730 WLA Det	**SERIAL NO.**	**DIVISION**	**RD NO.**	**DATE**	**AGE NO**	**SIDE**
WATCH COMMANDER APPROVED	**SERIAL NO.** 577			27		hc			②

RE-INTERVIEW OF PERSONS KNOWN TO MARILYN MONROE

Date & Time Occurred	Location of Occurrence	Division of Occurrence
August 6, 1962	Various	

Name, Rank, Assignment, Division	Date & Time Reported
H. ARMSTRONG, COMMANDER, WEST L. A. DETECTIVE DIVISION	8-10-62 8:30A

The following is a resume of the interview conducted in an effort to obtain the times of various phone calls received by Miss Monroe on the evening of her death. All of the below times are estimations of the persons interviewed. None were able to state definite times as none checked the time of these calls.

MILTON RUDIN –

Mr. Rudin stated that on the evening of 8-4-62 his exchange received a call at 8:25P and that this call was relayed to him at 8:30P. The call was for him to call Milton Ebbins. At about 8:45P he called Mr. Ebbins who told him that he had received a call from Peter Lawford stating that Mr. Lawford had called Marilyn Monroe at her home and that while Mr. Lawford was talking to her, her voice seemed to "fade-out" and when he attempted to call her back, the line was busy. Mr. Ebbins requested that Mr. Rudin call Miss Monroe and determine if everything was alright, or attempt to reach her doctor. At about 9P, Mr. Rudin called Miss Monroe and the phone was answered by Mrs. Murray. He inquired of her as to the physical well being of Miss Monroe and was assured by Mrs. Murray that Miss Monroe was alright. Believing that Miss Monroe was suffering from one of her despondent moments, Mr. Rudin dismissed the possibility of anything further being wrong.

MRS. EUNICE MURRAY –

Mrs. Murray stated that she had worked for Marilyn Monroe since November, 1961, that on the evening of 8-4-62 Miss Monroe had received a collect call from a Joe DiMaggio, Jr. at about 7:30P. Mrs. Murray said that at the time of this call coming in, Miss Monroe was in bed and possibly had been asleep. She took the call and after talking to Joe DiMaggio, Jr., she then made a call to Dr. Greenson and Mrs. Murray overheard her say, "Joe Jr. is not getting married, I'm so happy about this." Mrs. Murray states that from the tone of Miss Monroe's voice, she believed her to be in very good spirits. At about 9P, Mrs. Murray received a call from Mr. Rudin who inquired about Miss Monroe. Mr. Rudin did not talk to Miss Monroe. Mrs. Murray states that these are the only phone calls that she recalls receiving on this date. Note: It is officers opinion that Mrs. Murray was vague and possibly evasive in answering questions pertaining to the activities of Miss Monroe during this time. It is not known whether this is, or is not intentional. During the interrogation of Joe DiMaggio, Jr., he indicated he had made three phone calls to the Monroe home, only one of which Mrs. Murray mentioned.

JOE DiMAGGIO – Miramar Hotel, Room 1035, Santa Monica

Mr. DiMaggio was informed of the rumor which quoted him as saying that

Date & Time Typed	Divn. Rptg.	Clerk	Employee's Reporting	Ser. No.	Div.
8-10-62 9A	WLA	jg	R. E. BYRON	2730	WL
Supervisor Approving		Serial No. 57	LT. G. H. ARMSTRONG, COMDR	59	WL

he would not invite Mr. Lawford to the funeral services because
he could have saved Marilyn's life and didn't. Mr. DiMaggio
denied this, stating that he had not talked to any member of
the press, nor had he said such a thing to anyone who might
have repeated it to the press. He stated that the decision to
limit the number of people was a mutual agreement, decided upon
in order to keep from hurting the feelings of many of Marilyn's
friends who might be accidentally overlooked.

JOE DiMAGGIO, JR. - Miramar Hotel, Room 1035, Santa Monica

Joe DiMaggio, Jr. was in his father's suite and interviewed
immediately after the above interview. He stated that he had
placed three collect calls to Miss Monroe on 8-4-62 and that the
first call was about 2P. He could overhear the operator talk to
Miss Murray who informed the operator that Miss Monroe was not
in. The second call was placed at approximately 4:30P and again
was answered by Mrs. Murray, and again he was unable to contact
Miss Monroe. The third call was placed at approximately 7P and
on this occasion Mrs. Murray stated that she would see if
Miss Monroe was available and in a few moments Miss Monroe came on
the phone and he held a short conversation with her. During the
conversation, he told Miss Monroe that he was not going to get
married. The time of the last call is estimated to be 7P, as
he states it was during the 6th or 7th innings of the Angels-
Orioles baseball game in Baltimore.

PETER LAWFORD - ███████████   (1)

An attempt was made to contact Mr. Lawford, but officers were
informed by his secretary that Mr. Lawford had taken an airplane
at 1P, 8-8-62. It is unknown at this time the exact destination,
however his secretary stated that she did expect to hear from
him and that she would request that he contact this Department
at his earliest convenience.

R. E. Byron 32730
W.L.A. Detectives

Police Reports on Marilyn Monroe Death

8-5-62	W.L.A.	W.L.A.
Lt. L. Selby, OIC, Homicide Special Sec., R.H.D.		8-27-74

At the request of Commander McCauley, an attempt was made to determine the number and type of police reports taken by this Department in connection with Marilyn Monroe's death which occurred in W.L.A. Div. on Aug. 5, 1962. Commander McCauley also requested we determine if any of these reports were still available at this time.

In this regard, Sgt. Sturgeon, O.I.C., R. & I. Div., was contacted and requested to make a search of R. & I. files in an attempt to locate any reports we may have. He stated he could locate no records pertaining to the 1962 death of Miss Monroe. He further stated that all original crime reports that are controled by R. & I. Div. are destroyed after a 10-year retention period. All reports, file cards, and DR blotters are included in the destruction.

Note: Attached is a copy of correspondence dated Sept. 4, 1973, to Assistant Chief D. F. Gates from Assistant Chief D. H. Speck pertaining to the "retention and destruction of crime reports."

The files at R.H.D. were checked for any records of the death of Miss Monroe. This division has no such records.

Investigators contacted W.L.A. Div. and were informed that they had no crime reports in their files pertaining to Miss Monroe's death. It was further determined from present W.L.A. investigators that the original W.L.A. detective who handled that case was Sgt. R. E. Byron, now retired.

Mr. Byron was contacted ▬▬▬▬▬▬▬▬▬▬▬▬▬▬▬▬▬▬▬▬▬▬▬▬① He stated he was called to the scene of Miss Monroe's death. Lieuts. Gregoire and Armstrong also responded. Byron stated he completed a death report and believes that he classified it as "accidental." Byron believes that he subsequently made a follow-up report to the original death report but is not sure how that was classified.

Byron does not have copies of any of these reports nor does he know of any existing copies.

-28-74 1010 RHD	rc		①
	L. A. Murray	6692	RHD

LAPD report on retention and destruction of crime reports...stating that there were no reports in LAPD files on the death of Marilyn Monroe...as of August 27, 1974.

LOS ANGELES POLICE DEPARTMENT

DARYL F. GATES
Chief of Police

TOM BRADLEY
Mayor

P. O. Box 30158
Los Angeles, Calif. 90030
Telephone:
(213) 485-4391
Ref#: 1.4.2

August 24, 1983

Mr. Robert F. Slatzer
1680 Vine Street, Suite 1000
Hollywood, CA 90028

Dear Mr. Slatzer:

We have processed your request of August 23, 1983, for all files or records under your name, pursuant to the Freedom of Information Ordinance of 1983 (FOIO).

The Los Angeles Police Department maintains intelligence and investigative files and records which relate only to criminal acts and terrorist activity. A search has revealed that, under the provisions of the FOIO, there are no files or records pertaining to you which the Department is able to release.

Very truly yours,

DARYL F. GATES
Chief of Police

John H. Cleghorn

JOHN H. CLEGHORN, Captain
Commanding Officer
Anti-Terrorist Division

AN EQUAL EMPLOYMENT OPPORTUNITY—AFFIRMATIVE ACTION EMPLOYER

LOS ANGELES POLICE DEPARTMENT

BOARD OF
POLICE COMMISSIONERS

STEPHEN D. YSLAS
President
MAXWELL E. GREENBERG
Vice President
STEPHEN D. GAVIN
REVA B. TOOLEY
SAMUEL L. WILLIAMS

WILLIAM G. COWDIN
Secretary

TOM BRADLEY
Mayor

EXECUTIVE OFFICE
SUITE 144-150, PARKER CENTER
150 N. LOS ANGELES STREET
LOS ANGELES, CA 90012

MAILING ADDRESS
BOX 30158
LOS ANGELES, CA 90030

485-3531

February 15, 1984

Mr. Robert F. Slatzer
7171 Pacific View Drive
Hollywood, CA 90028

Dear Mr. Slatzer:

The Board of Police Commissioners is unable to find
any records under your name pursuant to the Freedom
of Information Ordinance (FOIO) of 1983.

The Freedom of Information Act of 1983 applies only
to records of the Public Disorder Intelligence
Division (PDID) and Anti-Terrorist Division (ATD).

Very truly yours,

BOARD OF POLICE COMMISSIONERS

WILLIAM G. COWDIN
Secretary

PUBLIC ANNOUNCEMENT
MARILYN MONROE FILES

MARILYN MONROE DIED ON AUGUST 4, 1962. THE LOS ANGELES POLICE
DEPARTMENT AND THE LOS ANGELES COUNTY CORONER'S OFFICE CLASSIFIED
THE DEATH AS A "PROBABLE SUICIDE", BASED UPON EVIDENCE AT THE DEATH
SCENE, INTERVIEWS OF ACQUAINTANCES, AND THE FINDINGS OF THE AUTOPSY.

THE OFFICIAL INVESTIGATIVE REPORTS WERE RETAINED IN LAPD FILES FOR
10 YEARS. IN ACCORDANCE WITH RECORD RETENTION POLICY AND LAW,
(LOS ANGELES CITY ADMINISTRATIVE CODE 12.1 et seq) THE OFFICIAL FILES
WERE DESTROYED IN 1973.

IN OCT. 1975 OUI MAGAZINE PUBLISHED AN ARTICLE THAT QUESTIONED THE
CLASSIFICATION OF MISS MONROE'S DEATH AS A PROBABLE SUICIDE. SEVERAL
ISSUES RAISED IN THE ARTICLE PROMPTED THE LOS ANGELES POLICE DEPART-
MENT TO REVIEW THE CASE AND PREPARE AN INTERNAL REPORT ADDRESSING
EACH OF THOSE ISSUES.

IN THAT REVIEW PROCESS IT WAS LEARNED THAT THE OFFICIAL FILES HAD
BEEN DESTROYED. HOWEVER, COPIES OF MOST, PERHAPS ALL, OF THE
RELEVANT LAPD REPORTS WERE FOUND IN THE PRIVATE ARCHIVES OF DECEASED
DEPUTY CHIEF OF THE DETECTIVE BUREAU, THAD BROWN. THOSE COPIES WERE
INCLUDED AS ADDENDA TO THE CONFIDENTIAL INTERNAL INVESTIGATIVE
MANAGEMENT REPORT.

CHIEF DARYL F. GATES, UPON CONSIDERING THE NUMEROUS PUBLIC REQUESTS
FOR ACCESS TO ANY REPORTS RELATED TO THE DEATH OF MISS MONROE AND
THE PASSAGE OF 23 YEARS SINCE HER DEATH, HAS DECIDED TO MAKE THE
INTERNAL INVESTIGATIVE REPORT ACCESSIBLE TO THE PUBLIC. THOSE
PORTIONS THAT THE LAW REQUIRES TO BE KEPT CONFIDENTIAL HAVE BEEN
REDACTED. THIS ACTION HAS BEEN TAKEN WITH THE CONCURRENCE AND
ASSISTANCE OF MR. LOU UNGER, ASSISTANT CITY ATTORNEY.

OFFICE OF THE DISTRICT ATTORNEY
COUNTY OF LOS ANGELES
18000 CRIMINAL COURTS BUILDING
210 WEST TEMPLE STREET
LOS ANGELES, CALIFORNIA 90012
(213) 974-2501

IRA REINER
DISTRICT ATTORNEY

TO: EACH SUPERVISOR

FROM: IRA REINER
           District Attorney

SUBJECT: BOARD OF SUPERVISORS MOTION OF OCTOBER 8, 1985,
           REGARDING THE DEATH OF MARILYN MONROE

DATE: NOVEMBER 7, 1985

In response to your motion of October 8, 1985, we have reviewed
a letter dated September 23, 1985, from a Mr. Robert F. Slatzer
to Supervisor Michael Antonovich relating to the death of Marilyn
Monroe.

For this office to approach the Criminal Justice Committee of the
Grand Jury with a request for an investigation into the death of
Ms. Monroe, we would first need to have sufficient cause to
believe that a crime has been committed and that the crime
occurred within the time frame permitted by the California Statute
of Limitations. Murder, of course, is not barred by any statute
of limitations; however, no evidence, new or old, has been brought
to our attention which would support a reasonable belief or even
a bare suspicion that Ms. Monroe was murdered.

As public prosecutors we cannot support a Grand Jury investigation
concerning matters of historical interest by artificially cloaking
them in the guise of a criminal inquiry.

kms

c: Executive Officer, Board of Supervisors
    Chief Administrative Officer
    Foreman, Los Angeles County Grand Jury

The astounding Ira Reiner letter of November 7, 1985, wherein he
dismisses any reason for a reinvestigation of the death of Marilyn
Monroe.

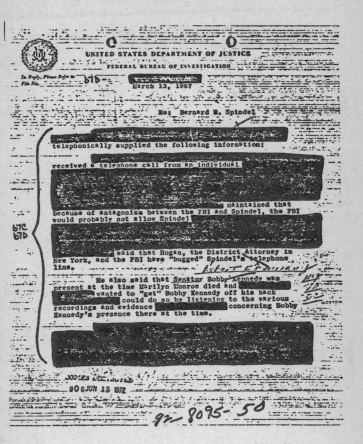

UNITED STATES DEPARTMENT OF JUSTICE

FEDERAL BUREAU OF INVESTIGATION

March 13, 1967

Re: Bernard B. Spindel

telephonically supplied the following information:

received a telephone call from an individual

maintained that because of antagonism between the FBI and Spindel, the FBI would probably not allow Spindel

said that Hogan, the District Attorney in New York, and the FBI have "bugged" Spindel's telephone line.

He also said that Senator Bobby Kennedy was present at the time Marilyn Monroe died and wanted to "get" Bobby Kennedy off his back could do so by listening to the various recordings and evidence concerning Bobby Kennedy's presence there at the time.

90 6 JUN 15 1972

92-8095-50

An FBI document reporting on the Spindel tapes and their incrimination of RFK at Marilyn Monroe's home when she died.

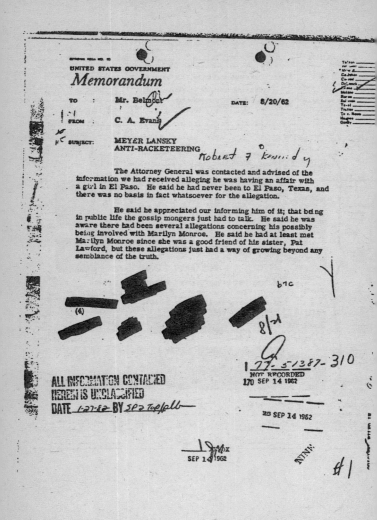

An FBI memorandum linking RFK to Marilyn Monroe . . . probably
one of many collected at the request of J. Edgar Hoover.

UNITED STATES DEPARTMENT OF JUSTICE
FEDERAL BUREAU OF INVESTIGATION

67C

It was reported that ███████████████ age

NK 65-5712

40, has considerable information concerning sex parties
which took place at the Hotel Carlyle in NYC, and in
which a number of persons participated at different
times. Among those mentioned were the following individuals:

ROBERT F. KENNEDY
JOHN F. KENNEDY

PETER LAWFORD

MARILYN MONROE

67C

ALL INFORMATION CONTAINED
HEREIN IS UNCLASSIFIED
DATE _____ BY _____

162-100760

NOT RECORDED
141 JUL 22 1965

Spindel Sues to Get Back Seized RFK Tape on Hoffa

By JOSEPH J. COHEN
World Journal Tribune Staff

Wiretap expert Bernard B. Spindel today filed a motion to get back confiscated material about Marilyn Monroe's death and a tape of a conversation with "Robert F. Kennedy concerning James Hoffa."

Spindel, in the motion before Supreme Court Justice Owen McGivern, said the material was taken during a raid on his Holmes, N. Y., home last Thursday by State Police. Spindel's home was raided again yesterday.

The motion, to be heard tomorrow, lists 76 items that Spindel claims were taken illegally during the Thursday raid. Among the items mentioned in the motion were:

"My confidential file containing tapes and evidence concerning circumstances surrounding and the causes of the death of Marilyn Monroe, which material strongly suggests that the officially-reported circumstances of her demise are erroneous.

"An original tape recording," the motion continued, "of a conversation, taken in a car owned and operated by me, between Robert F. Kennedy, James Kelly, and me concerning James Hoffa."

None of the persons named were identified further in the legal paper.

HOME SEARCHED

State police, accompanied by representatives of the New York Telephone Co., yesterday searched Spindel's Kent Township home and laboratory, seizing part of his collection of electronic devices and hauling them off in a small truck.

Spindel's wife, Barbara, 43, suffered a heart attack during the raid and was taken to Putnam County Community Hospital in Brewster, N. Y. She is

BERNARD SPINDEL

reported in satisfactory condition.

Spindel was arrested for possession of stolen property after his wife was rushed to the hospital. He was later released in $1,000 bail.

"My wife never had any trouble with her heart before," the 43-year-old electronic expert said. "It was this raid coming after Thursday's raid that so upset her."

The Thursday raid was conducted by men from Manhattan District Attorney Frank Hogan's office and State Police. Spindel claimed he recorded the entire nine-hour raid electronically.

Spindel would not say if he recorded yesterday's raid. "Let's say I have a good legal reason for withholding the information," he told a reporter.

But he said all of his telephone equipment had been bought from either surplus houses or the Graybar Electric Co., a Western Electric distributor. "I have the receipts and canceled checks to prove it," he added.

DENIES TAKING PART

A spokesman for the New York Telephone Company denied that any of their employees actually took part in the raid. "We were asked along by the state police to identify our equipment. I understand that our men did identify some of the equipment as belonging to us."

Spindel said that one of the phone company men had signed the search warrant. The state police at Brewster said the warrant was not available.

Spindel was one of 28 eavesdropping experts indicted Friday in Manhattan.

Yesterday's arrest, he said, brings the total number of times he was arrested to 208. He has been brought to trial six times but has never been convicted.

Several years ago he was cleared of wiretapping charges with James Hoffa, the Teamster's president.

An account of the NY District Attorney's raid on the home of wiretap expert Bernard Spindel. The raid was on December 15, 1966. What the story doesn't report is the extent of Spindel's collection of tapes . . . more than 10 hours on Monroe and the Kennedys, plus other show business and Mafia personalities. Duplicates of these tapes reportedly still exist despite governmental efforts to destroy all such evidence.

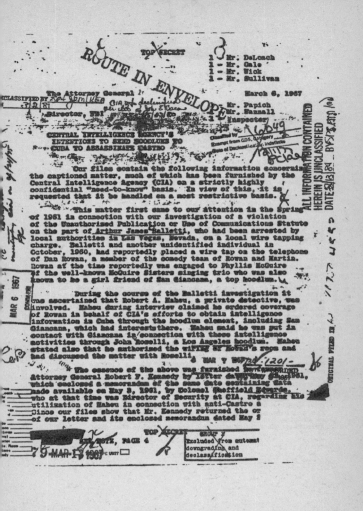

TOP SECRET

ROUTE IN ENVELOPE

1 - Mr. DeLoach
1 - Mr. Gale
1 - Mr. Wick
1 - Mr. Sullivan

The Attorney General   March 6, 1967

                                                         Mr. Papich
Director, FBI   Mr. Wannall
                                                         1 Inspector

CENTRAL INTELLIGENCE AGENCY'S
INTENTION TO SEND HOODLUMS TO
CUBA TO ASSASSINATE CASTRO

          Our files contain the following information concerning
the captioned matter, much of which has been furnished by the
Central Intelligence Agency (CIA) on a strictly highly
confidential "need-to-know" basis. In view of this, it is
requested that it be handled on a most restrictive basis.

          This matter first came to our attention in the spring
of 1961 in connection with our investigation of a violation
of the Unauthorized Publication or Use of Communications Statute
on the part of Arthur James Balletti, who had been arrested by
local authorities in Las Vegas, Nevada, on a local wire tapping
charge. Balletti and another unidentified individual in
October, 1960, had reportedly placed a wire tap on the telephone
of Dan Rowan, a member of the comedy team of Rowan and Martin.
Rowan at the time reportedly was engaged to Phyllis McGuire
of the well-known McGuire Sisters singing trio who was also
known to be a girl friend of Sam Giancana, a top hoodlum.

          During the course of the Balletti investigation it
was ascertained that Robert A. Maheu, a private detective, was
involved. Maheu during interview claimed he ordered coverage
of Rowan in behalf of CIA's efforts to obtain intelligence
information in Cuba through the hoodlum element, including Sam
Giancana, which had interests there. Maheu said he was put in
contact with Giancana in connection with these intelligence
activities through John Roselli, a Los Angeles hoodlum. Maheu
stated also that he authorized the wiring of Rowan's room and
had discussed the matter with Roselli.

          The essence of the above was furnished to
Attorney General Robert F. Kennedy by letter dated May 22, 1961,
which enclosed a memorandum of the same date containing data
made available on May 3, 1961, by Colonel Sheffield Edwards,
who at that time was Director of Security at CIA, regarding his
utilization of Maheu in connection with anti-Castro a
Since our files show that Mr. Kennedy returned the or
of our letter and its enclosed memorandum dated May 2

TOP SECRET

SEE NOTE, PAGE 4

GROUP 1
Excluded from automatic
downgrading and
declassification

The Attorney General

to us for filing purposes, a copy of the May 22, 1961, memorandum is attached hereto for your information.

You will note that Colonel Edwards advised he personally contacted Robert Maheu during the Fall of 1960 for the purpose of using Maheu as a "cutout" in contacts with Sam Giancana in connection with CIA's clandestine efforts against Castro. Colonel Edwards stated that Giancana's activities were completely "backstopped" by Maheu, who would frequently report Giancana's actions and information to Edwards. No details or methods used by Maheu or Giancana in accomplishing their missions were reported to him, according to Edwards, as such involved "dirty business," of which Colonel Edwards could not afford to have knowledge. Accordingly, he said he had no prior knowledge of the above-mentioned wire tapping by Balletti.

Further with respect to this matter, I was informed of the following on a highly confidential basis by former Attorney General Kennedy during a conference in my office on May 9, 1962:

He indicated that a few days prior thereto he had been advised by CIA that Robert A. Maheu had been hired by CIA to approach Sam Giancana with a proposition of paying $150,000 to hire some gunmen to go into Cuba and kill Castro. He further stated CIA admitted having assisted Maheu in making the "bugging" installation in Las Vegas (referred to above) which uncovered this clandestine operation and for this reason CIA could not afford to have any action taken against Giancana or Maheu. Mr. Kennedy stated that upon learning CIA had not cleared its action in hiring Maheu and Giancana with the Department of Justice he issued orders that CIA should never again take such steps without first checking with the Department of Justice.

Mr. Kennedy further advised that because of this matter it would be very difficult to initiate any prosecution against Giancana, as Giancana could immediately bring out the fact the United States Government had approached him to arrange for the assassination of Castro. He stated the same was true concerning any action we might take against Maheu for any violation in which he might become involved.

On June 20, 1963, Mr. William Harvey, an official of CIA, advised that he had held a meeting with John Rose (referred to above as Maheu's link with Giancana) for of closing out the entire matter with which Roselli is involved. In this connection, Harvey stated that CIA

- 2 -

The Attorney General

established contact with Roselli in "early 1961" with respect to
a sensitive operation against Castro. Harvey said that for all
intents and purposes the operation was discontinued and canceled
after the ill-fated Bay of Pigs invasion in April, 1961, but
Roselli had not been completely cut off, as he periodically
indicated he was in a position to be of assistance.

It appears Roselli has since that time, nevertheless,
used his prior connections with CIA to his best advantage. For
example, in May, 1966, when contacted by Agents of this Bureau
in connection with our current investigation of his activities
he refused to talk and immediately flew to Washington, D. C.,
and consulted with Colonel Sheffield Edwards, who is now retired
from CIA. Colonel Edwards in turn advised CIA, which told us.
Mr. Howard J. Osborn, the present Director of Security, CIA,
freely has admitted to us that Roselli has CIA in an unusually
vulnerable position and that he would have no qualms about
embarrassing CIA if it served his own interests. In furnishing
this information, Mr. Osborn asked that it be held within this
Bureau on a strictly need-to-know basis.

In light of the above information furnished us by CIA
and former Attorney General Kennedy, it appears that data which
came to our attention in October, 1960, possibly pertains to the
captioned matter. At that time a source close to Giancana
advised that during a conversation with several friends Giancana
stated that Fidel Castro was "to be done away with very shortly."
Giancana reportedly assured those present that Castro's
assassination would occur in November, 1960, and that he had
already met with the assassin-to-be on three occasions, the last
meeting having taken place on a boat docked at the Fontainebleau
Hotel, Miami Beach, Florida. Reportedly, Giancana claimed that
everything had been perfected for the killing and the "assassin"
had arranged with a girl, not further described, to drop a "pill"
in Castro's drink or food.

Also of possible interest is a news article carried in
the August 18, 1963, issue of the "Chicago Sun Times." This
article carried the headline, "CIA Sought Giancana's Help For
Cuba Spying," and it was reported therein that CIA agents had
contacted Giancana in an effort to obtain Cuban intelligence
after Castro came into power.

Enclosure

1 - The Deputy Attorney General (Enclosure)

- 3 -

Index

– PETITION –

To Whom It May Concern:

I am a concerned citizen of these United States. I believe in justice and due process for everyone.

This letter of petition is my personal and urgent request for a complete and final investigation into the death of Marilyn Monroe—an unsolved crime that has remained clouded by doubt and tainted by suspicion since August 4, 1962.

On the basis of substantial new evidence and corroborating testimony, it is now clear that there has been an obvious pattern of long-term cover-up, contradiction, secrecy, propaganda and suppression—along with individual and official malfeasance—in this celebrated case.

There is still more information to be discovered, evidence to be analyzed. . .and witnesses who must be subpoenaed to testify under oath. It is time to find the truth.

I believe it is now necessary to appoint an independent prosecutor and grand jury to investigate this case with dignity and diligence. . .and to reach a just and legal conclusion.

The ever-growing legend of Marilyn Monroe demands no less than this. But, more important, the life story of every human being deserves an honest ending.

_____

Signature   Date

Name _____

Address _____

City _____ State_____ Zip_____

Telephone _____

(please feel free to make reproductions of this petition for others. . .see last pages of File #23 for mailing addresses and instructions)